Last Impressions

Last Impressions

Jane Austen's Endings

Theresa M. Kenney

UNIVERSITY OF TORONTO PRESS
Toronto Buffalo London

Toronto Buffalo London
utppublishing.com

Printed in the USA

ISBN 978-1-4875-5986-1 (cloth)
ISBN 978-1-4875-5987-8 (paper)
ISBN 978-1-4875-5989-2 (EPUB)
ISBN 978-1-4875-5988-5 (PDF)

Library and Archives Canada Cataloguing in Publication

Title: Last impressions : Jane Austen's endings / Theresa M. Kenney.
Other titles: Jane Austen's endings
Names: Kenney, Theresa M., author
Description: Includes bibliographical references and index.
Identifiers: Canadiana (print) 2025012453X | Canadiana (ebook) 20250124564 | ISBN 9781487559861 (cloth) | ISBN 9781487559878 (paper) | ISBN 9781487559892 (EPUB) | ISBN 9781487559885 (PDF)
Subjects: LCSH: Austen, Jane, 1775–1817 – Criticism and interpretation. | LCSH: Closure (Rhetoric) | LCSH: Fiction – Technique. | LCGFT: Literary criticism.
Classification: LCC PR4037 .K46 2025 | DDC 823/.7 – dc23

Cover design: Liz Harasymczuk
Cover image: The Picture Art Collection / Alamy Stock Photo

We wish to acknowledge the land on which the University of Toronto Press operates. This land is the traditional territory of the Wendat, the Anishnaabeg, the Haudenosaunee, the Métis, and the Mississaugas of the Credit First Nation.

This book has been published with the assistance of the University of Dallas.

University of Toronto Press acknowledges the financial support of the Government of Canada, the Canada Council for the Arts, and the Ontario Arts Council, an agency of the Government of Ontario, for its publishing activities.

Canada Council for the Arts
Conseil des Arts du Canada

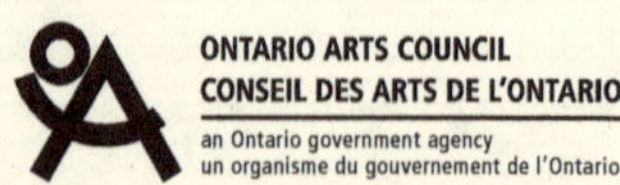

Funded by the Government of Canada
Financé par le gouvernement du Canada

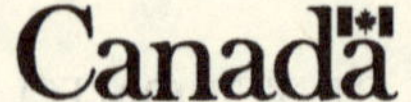

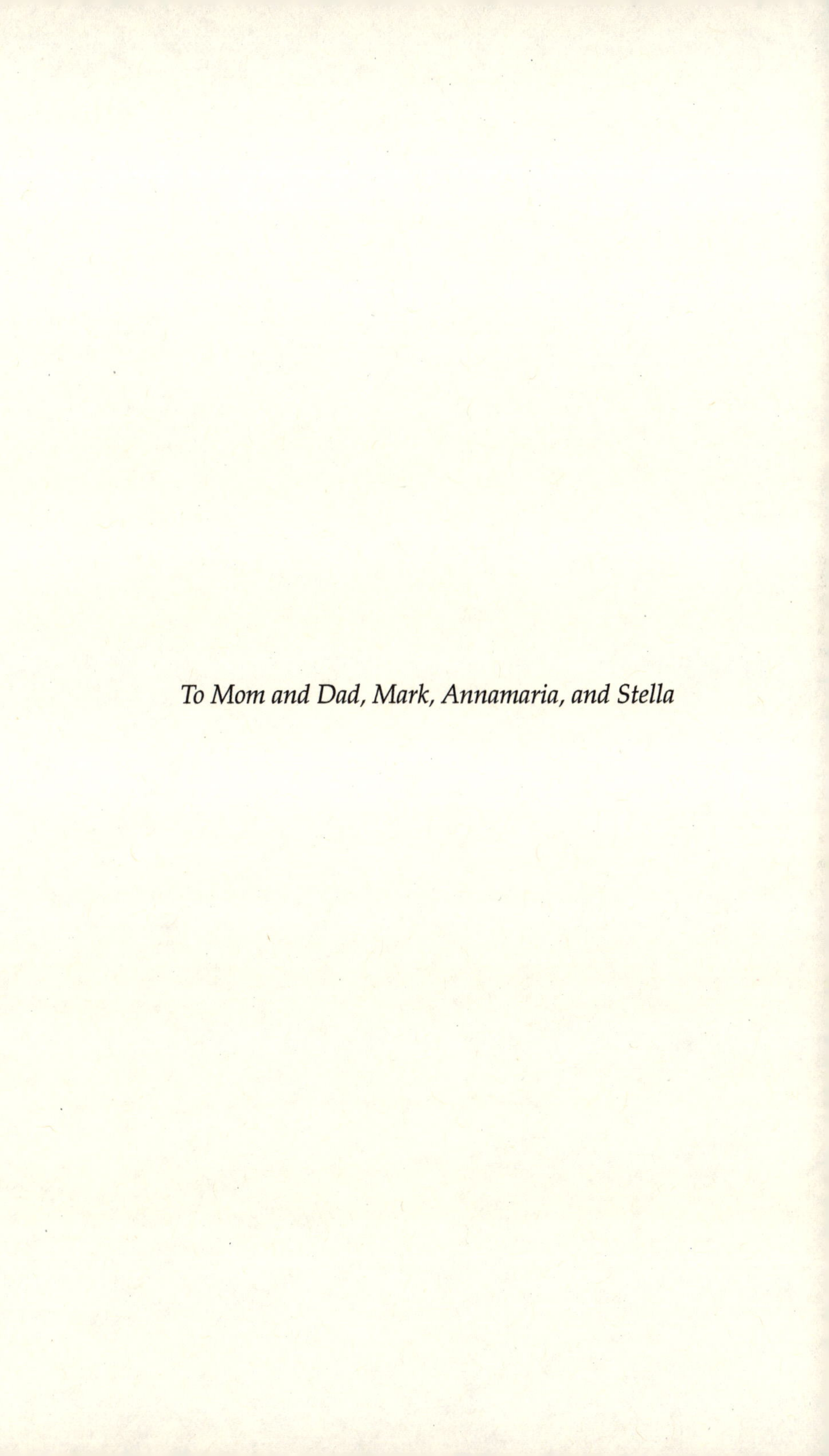

To Mom and Dad, Mark, Annamaria, and Stella

Contents

Acknowledgments

I have so many obligations, I will never be done thanking people if I make an account of them all. This book could never have been if it were not for the kind assistance of treasured family members and friends.

First, thanks are due my home institution, the University of Dallas, which granted me the sabbatical I needed to finish the first draft of this book, and funded my presentations at many Austen conferences. I would like to thank Susan Allen Ford and the editorial staff at the journal of the Jane Austen Society of North America, *Persuasions*, for the kind permission to use in several chapters of this book edited portions of my articles originally published there.

Thanks to friends and critics who gave advice, chief among whom are Diane Capitani, who has been such a helpful reader of portions of this book, and Dr. Cheryl Kinney, M.D., who has read and commented on *all* of it. Cheryl epitomizes Mr. Knightley's ideal of faithful friendship in telling the truth rather than what one wishes to hear. Diane's help to me during her illness and Cheryl's amidst her myriad cares and obligations as a surgeon are true gifts of friendship. My gratitude goes out also to Susan Jelen, Beni Mayer, Chris Peirson, and Joyce Tarpley, for their unfailing encouragement and advice. With their usual willingness and alacrity, my sister Maria Kenney Burchill and my friend Alissa Mann helped me find some references and track down facsimiles of Rev. Thomas Jefferson's sermons; it's great to have librarians in the family circle! I'm very grateful.

Next, I need to thank the two people who have discussed these chapters with me the most, and have seen the book through from its inception to its conclusion: my sister Anne Kenney and my husband, Mark Doody. Jane Austen had no truer friend in her sister, Cassandra, than I have in mine, and many an insight contained here has arisen at her prompting. Her advice is always sound. Mark is as funny as Henry Tilney, as perceptive as Mr. Darcy, as fond of truth as Mr. Knightley, and as domestic as Edmund. As in the case of Captain Wentworth and Anne Elliot, it took quite a few years after our initial parting for our reunion to occur, resulting in the letter that changed everything, and then the proposal, which, like Edward Ferrars's, was readily accepted: "he did not, on the whole, expect a very cruel reception. It was his business, however, to say that he *did*, and he said it very prettily" (*SS*, III.13.415). Like our two daughters, Annamaria and Stella, he has had to endure months of my being too busy writing to pay much attention to the "best blessings of [my] existence." Talking with him and Anne, both perceptive readers of Austen themselves, has provided most of the joy of this project.

Abbreviations

E — *Emma*, edited by Richard Cronin and Dorothy McMillan (1815; Cambridge: Cambridge University Press, 2005)

LS — *Lady Susan*, in *Later Manuscripts*, edited by Janet Todd and Linda Bree (1793–4; Cambridge: Cambridge University Press, 2008)

MP — *Mansfield Park*, edited by Edited by John Wiltshire (1814; Cambridge: Cambridge University Press, 2013)

NA — *Northanger Abbey*, edited by Barbara M. Benedict (1817; Cambridge: Cambridge University Press, 2006)

P — *Persuasion*, edited by Janet Todd (1817; Cambridge: Cambridge University Press, 2006)

PP *Pride and Prejudice*, edited by Pat Rogers (1813; Cambridge: Cambridge University Press, 2013)

SS *Sense and Sensibility*, edited by Edward Copeland (1811; Cambridge: Cambridge University Press, 2006)

Last Impressions

CHAPTER ONE

Austen's Telos: Speeding Truth into the World

"It is a truth universally acknowledged, that a single man in possession of a good fortune must be in want of a wife." This opening sentence is one of the most famous in English literature – justly so – but what of the closing sentences of Austen's novels? Do they convey anything besides a general bustling to get her characters married and off stage as quickly as possible, once she has nothing else witty to say about any of them – or for them to say? Critics have found fault with all of Austen's endings, even such an ebullient one as *Pride and Prejudice*'s: Judith Newton claims that "most readers of *Pride and Prejudice* find the end less satisfactory than the beginning," with Elizabeth dwindling "by degrees into a wife,"[1] and Marvin Mudrick laments the dissipation of ironic language into moral seriousness, claiming that Darcy's complexity is "ironed out"' to "flatness" as Austen conceals herself "behind a fogbank of bourgeois morality."[2]

Mary Poovey considers its ending "politically irresponsible,"[3] though Claudia Johnson sees the "mutually improving debates" of the protagonists as a "step towards, rather than 'escape' from, constructive political commentary."[4]

How does one judge the endings of the novels when Austen's idea of happiness might be different from our own, might even be an affront to modern concepts of political responsibility and gender relations? Adam Potkay argues, in regard to the contrast between the fictional characters' happiness and our evaluation of their lives, that "the word 'happiness' does not refer only to a feeling or subjective state, but designates as well an evaluation of a life or the narrative of a life. Accordingly, in representing the lives of fictional characters, novelists invite their readers to assess both what happy or flourishing lives might be, and the narrative routes, variously composed of circumstances and choices, by which such lives might be attained."[5]

Thus, if we look back at the cited critics' assessments, we need to understand the premises behind them, their definition of a flourishing life. Mudrick's use of the word "dwindling" implies that he finds Austen's view of a flourishing existence disappointing, and Johnson's use of the word "escape" implies that there is something bad about a novel that does not provide "constructive political commentary." What "political irresponsibility" might consist of in Austen's day is something the reader might well find perplexing. Whether approving or disapproving, the critics' world views form the basis of all their judgments of what Austen does or does not do. This chapter proposes an openly stated, probable world view for Austen and the majority of her contemporary readers that I take as the philosophical foundation for my statements about narrative techniques Austen uses in her conclusions.

Although she is not writing political tracts, or proposing utopian ways of life, Austen does pose problems to her readers in her final chapters. The modern reader's disbelief in the happy ending of marriage is perhaps the biggest obstacle her current admirers have to face; however, it is not a narrative problem she was completely unaware of, as if she lived in a time when all marriages were happy and stable or as if she always represented marriage as a satisfactory conclusion, at least to the interwoven stories of the secondary cast. The closing down of the potentialities that were presented in the beginnings of the novels in a ratified pairing of heroine and chosen spouse, the ending of anticipation and surprise, is a challenge Austen knew she was facing in narrating the novels' ends, as we see by her careful use of surprise even in what might appear to be conventional epilogues. Austen proposes a road to happiness for her female protagonists that necessarily includes marriage, but not all the marriages are the same, and not all of them content readers equally well.

The heroine's happiness, nonetheless, appears to be the telos of every Austen novel. Not to speak about her telos is not to look at the novel as a whole work of art but only to read it piecemeal. As David Kaufman says about endings in general, "we have not yet moved closer to why we have such a 'deep need for intelligible Ends,' nor why, despite Kermode's reference to the Apocalypse or Ricoeur's use of Augustine, critical discomfort with narrative's teleological essence seems so deeply rooted."[6] In this book, I propose that Austen understands that her narratives have a telos.

I accept the arguments of Ruderman, Emsley, and others that Austen is writing comedies, and that a happy ending for her means happiness, not just marriage, for her heroines.[7] The issue of happiness that looms so large in the Western philosophical tradition is on Austen's mind throughout her oeuvre. Early in her career, she has Edward Ferrars say to Elinor and Marianne, "I believe I wish as well as every body else to be perfectly happy; but, like every body else it must be in my own way. Greatness will not make me so" (*SS*, I.17.105). "My own way": is this an individualistic credo, and does it justify all paths to happiness? Edward's later behaviour shows he does not believe his personal happiness should trump all other claims on him. And, when taken in context, the reader finds that Elinor immediately corrects Edward's statement, or adds nuance to it, by admitting the necessity of a respectable income for happiness. One upshot of this entire conversation is to allow the reader to understand that happiness is not merely an internal disposition, and it cannot be found completely in the traditional stoic indifference to outside circumstances. Like the early assertions of other characters in Austen's oeuvre, Edward's statement may need some modification as events unfold. The fact that it has become an aphorism independent of the novel in which it is spoken does not prove Austen intends for it to be taken as a general truth, or a proof of the wisdom of the speaker, any more than the line uttered by Caroline Bingley that appears on the English ten-pound note – "I declare after all there is no enjoyment like reading" – reflects the actual views of the speaker. However, Edward acknowledges that his family assumes incorrectly what makes for happiness, an observation every reader looking at the complacent Ferrars family, who are undisturbed in their own narcissistic self-satisfaction, probably shares. Austen presumes we understand that complacency is not happiness. The path to happiness taken by Mrs. Ferrars, Fanny Dashwood, and Robert Ferrars is one no reader wishes to take. Although one could say that characters as diverse as Lucy Steele, Lydia Bennet, and William Elliot have all gotten what they most wanted, no reader seriously desires the kind of happiness available to such characters. We have learned to see that they are content with what is shameful, or with what is too little. As Karen Valihora notes in reference to *Emma*, "morally inadequate characters have limited terms of reference; their ability to reflect on larger orders and arrangements stops at Maple Grove."[8]

We might call what Austen distinguishes as the happiness proper to her heroines and their spouses "joy," to differentiate it from the contentment a Mrs. Elton or a Lydia Bennet might experience. Adam Potkay, who has written extensively on the issue of happiness in the classical tradition, through Spenser and Donne to the novel, uses Austen's *Sense and Sensibility* as his proof text for separating happiness and joy from each other. In distinguishing these two emotions, he asserts:

> Joy is an episodic or dispositional element in an individual's emotional life, and as such not subject to public evaluation in quite the same way as happiness is. That is to say, while

> it is possible or even common to know someone who thinks he's happy but to claim to know better – one need only the proper intonation to render ironic the phrase "Mr Blifil thinks he's happy" – the person who experiences joy does so, by contrast, regardless of your assessment or approval. And yet joy, which is arguably with desire and sorrow one of the three fundamental emotions of narrative, can nonetheless be subjected to ethical discipline: the novelist can, and often does, prompt her reader to feel joy and grief at the right thing.[9]

Austen's heroines might indeed differ in what they require for happiness but, in every case in the six completed novels, living a life of virtue is one requirement for the greatest possible happiness, or joy, which is allotted only to the heroine. Unlike Potkay, Austen does not distinguish between the two words, even though she clearly believes that there is a distinction. She uses the word "happiness" in an elastic way: it can connote the lower register of happiness for the less virtuous characters but also her heroine's superior type of happiness. She is like Dante, who uses the word "amor" in many ways – it can mean hedonism, as it does in *Inferno* 5, but it is also his word for divine love in *Paradiso* 31, for instance. Neither Austen nor Dante differentiates the polyvalent term in any way but by connotation in context. The reader might rebel at Austen's training, but she is prompting us "to feel joy and grief at the right thing." Every heroine in her own way has a strong sense of self, which she does not allow outside influences to destabilize, and that self-definition includes a set of unbreakable moral standards. Moreover, each woman's happiness in her chosen marriage depends on her chosen partner's sharing of those unequivocal goals. Thus Austen falls into the broader Western philosophical tradition that from classical times onward considered an examined life, in which the human being devotes himself or herself to the highest ideals and exerts self-control to achieve them, the best, if not in fact the only, path to true happiness. Alexander Pope says in *An Essay on Man* "That virtue only makes our bliss below; / And all our Knowledge is, ourselves to know," and "Know, then, this truth (enough for man to know) / 'Virtue alone is happiness below.'"[10] Pope may not represent the opinion of all late eighteenth-century Englishmen and -women, but his summation of the philosophical tradition in these lines would have been familiar to Austen. Even David Hume, with whom she would have had little in common, believed there was no happiness without virtue. E.M. Dadlez and Karen Valihora would like to moor Austen's understanding of morality and human society in philosophers of her century; however, those very philosophers are quite firmly planted in a biblical and classical world view without which their understandings of the passions or of aesthetics do not function at all.[11] To start from the human being's emotional or artistic reactions, the passionate and the aesthetic, à la Hume or Shaftesbury, is to start the wrong way around with Austen, as if she thought the ideal of a pure conscience or of the good of the human community could spring up from a morass of amoral data.

Although I will be discussing Austen's view of human nature and its end, as well as her view of truth and its communicability, the ensuing chapters focus on issues of narrative technique and thematic concerns in the finales of the novels rather than simply pursuing an argument about virtues and happiness, which is territory already explored by others. Austen's attention to form, content, and tone in all the novels shows that she is presenting us with a scale of happiness that we can recognize and that reveals her philosophical or even religious foundations. Although, with respect to *Emma*, Valihora argues that "the concluding passages of the novel, in which all, finally, find their proper place, suggest a kind of quietism, even as the narrative moves toward the completion of perfection, the closing of a perfect circle," Austen's idea of a closure that endorses virtuous living as the road to happiness does not seal circles neatly.[12] It is only in examining closely what she does as an artist that we can see her subtlety even within a traditional ending, including a trajectory forward towards maturation rather than circling back to the initial state.

Through their seeming sameness – that trajectory towards happiness through marriage to the right man – the endings of Austen's novels might offer the reader an additional formal challenge apart from their reflection on social mores. I would argue that Austen is also aware of this pitfall. In days gone by, some literary critics were content to dismiss all six completed novels' closures as a type: in *Closure in the Novel*, Marianna Torgovnick labelled them "epilogues" and had little more to say about them.[13] But as Torgovnick herself recognized, when the endings of such novels as *Crime and Punishment* fall into the same category, we may well wonder what kind of diversity may persist under a dismissive heading. The endings of *Don Quixote, Bleak House, Jane Eyre,* and *Cousin Silas* are all epilogues, as are countless others. Even if all of Austen's novelistic endings may fall into this group, such a classification does little to help the reader understand what Austen intends her final chapters to do. As Anne Toner has pointed out recently, Austen from her youth made conciseness and exclusion of anything extraneous part of her artistic credo.[14] This characteristic strategy applies to the closures of her novels as well. Readers respond to the six endings very differently, and the reason for this lies within the pages themselves, in Austen's purposeful narrative choices, in her language, in what she conceals, and in what she reveals. Reading the endings merely as epilogues, I would suggest, might have the effect of writing off Austen's continued work as an artist in the final pages, as if she were simply cutting off threads, like a novelistic Lachesis.

Of the three classical Fates, Austen is more like a Clotho, the spinner of the thread, than the dreaded wielder of the shears. Her imagination is creative rather than destructive. My aim in this book is to show that her conclusions are deliberate creations, not afterthoughts or accidents hastily conceived, and not careless dismissals. Even in the end, perhaps especially there, Austen is teaching the reader how to spin the thread while she herself must bring the string of words to a halt. The conclusions of her novels are not sealed off narratively or catechetically, even though she is capable of producing closure that is satisfying to the reader. Austen shows that it is possible to create an ending that does not destroy or subvert but fulfils. Tragedy teaches through destruction, comedy through creation. Austen writes no tragedies. If the witty and complex aphorism of *Pride and Prejudice*'s beginning, or the fractured fairy tale of three differently fated sisters in the opening of *Mansfield Park*, seems more impressive than those novels' endings, it is only because we have not attended sufficiently to Austen's strategies for her conclusions, which, after all, come from the same pen.

As a narrative craftswoman, Austen seems to have in mind both her knowledge of what readers desire and a purpose she has wanted to accomplish in the course of each particular novel, as Lorrie Clark has discussed.[15] That purpose is partly moral, partly tonal. Although one cannot hope to convince any reader to accept Austen's own particular definition of the happiness that her heroines attain through marriage and social stability at the end of the novels, one can hope to demonstrate that she is a purposeful artist with an end in view, and that she pays particular attention to the closures she provides to her readers. Austen's medium is words, but she is an artist, not a propagandist, a cultural historian, or an influencer. To divorce the study of her books from her chosen medium is like studying Michelangelo while ignoring marble or paint. Nor are Austen's endings mere cultural objects; in fact, they are often severe critiques of her own culture. Looking at large narrative structures merely for themes, political or otherwise, results in poor reading of Austen, whose famous claim to be working on a small bit of ivory should, rather, lead us to treat her prose as a lapidary construction, and to close read carefully, just as one does with lyric poetry.[16] Just as the lyric is a neglected genre in our day, however, so is prose as an art, as a craft. The minute a reader begins to analyse the actual details of Austen's narrative strategies, many critical summations of her endings seem oafish or at least tone deaf, because they ignore the carefully chosen words on the page.

To attend to Austen's conclusions means recognizing that each includes a mix of straightforward assertion and satire. She provides both playful, witty observations and serious assurances. Although Austen often allows wit a great deal of play in her conclusions, they do not strike the reader as equally satiric or potentially self-deconstructive. That is partly because in each novel there is also a positive good, or several positive goods, gained, which she celebrates. Yet, not avoiding acid commentary, Austen's version of realism does not permit her a simple "and they lived happily ever after," although her heroines do for the most part depart from us into a life of happiness. But she always has more to say than just that. The reader must respond to the combination of the sweet and the acid, the commendatory and the pejorative, that Austen confects in each separate close.

Jane Austen left behind few recommendations about how to construct a story, and most of these exist in her advice to her niece Anna Austen, when her young relation was trying her hand at novel writing. For the most part, this advice had to do with organizing and beginning the work. She said almost nothing about closure, her strategy for ending, but what she did say is most telling. In 1808, she wrote to her sister, Cassandra, about something Cassandra's friend, English cricketer William Deedes, had written. Here are her standards for judgment, according to which she praises his work: "He has certainly great merit, as a Writer; he does ample justice to his subject, & without being diffuse, is clear & correct … He certainly has a very pleasing way of winding up a whole, & speeding Truth into the World."[17] The phrase "winding up a whole" indicates Austen, in the tradition of Aristotle's *Poetics*, values a unifying closure that addresses all narrative threads, while "speeding Truth into the World" supports not only her sense of the didactic value of an author's work, but something more. According to her, Deedes does more than send or transmit, he *speeds* truth into the world. Writers need to aim and shoot swiftly to accomplish their goal. Austen is so swift readers needs to slow her down to look carefully at what she is doing or they will miss it. And she permits herself a word only the most daring pronounce today: truth.

What Does Austen Mean by "Truth"?

If Austen believes that a conclusion must speed truth into the world, she also believes that there is such a thing as truth and also that the writer's work is to disseminate it. The postmodern reader will be brought up short by both presumptions. Austen does not pause to explain her words to Cassandra because she need not in her day and age, or in her family circle. What we might challenge her to prove, she takes for granted. Why is her assertion uncomplicated for her, when her portrayals of human nature are in fact complex? To answer that question, we need to look more closely at both elements of what she considers the end of her artistic work.

For a Christian of any stripe in Austen's day, truth has a solid basis in a being whose actual nature is the truth and who cannot lie. The *Spectator*, which is cited in *Elegant Extracts*, a book Austen owned, designates God as the source of truth as one proof of the immortality of the soul: the writer considers that this immortality is guaranteed by "the nature of the Supreme Being, whose justice, goodness, wisdom, and veracity, are all concerned in this point."[18] Even more significantly, Austen subscribed to the publication of two sermons by the Anglican clergyman Thomas Jefferson in 1808. In the first, Jefferson articulated the common Christian belief that God is truth and is incapable of deceit, stating, "from the Testimony of Him, who, we know, is incapable of deceiving us, we have perfect Assurance of 'an Inheritance eternal in the Heavens,' which awaits the Righteous."[19]

Austen's upbringing as the daughter of an Anglican clergyman also steeped her in the biblical understanding of truth. As St. John says in his second epistle,

> 18 Little children, it is the last time: and as ye have heard that antichrist shall come, even now are there many antichrists; whereby we know that it is the last time.
>
> 19 They went out from us, but they were not of us; for if they had been of us, they would no doubt have continued with us: but they went out, that they might be made manifest that they were not all of us.
>
> 20 But ye have an unction from the Holy One, and ye know all things.
>
> 21 I have not written unto you because ye know not the truth, but because ye know it, and that no lie is of the truth. (2 Jn:18–21)

Jesus's words on which this understanding of truth is founded were well known to all: "And ye shall know the truth, and the truth shall make you free" (Jn 8:32). To this quotation must be added his words from the farewell discourse at the Last Supper, also in the Gospel according to John:

> 16 And I will pray the Father, and he shall give you another Comforter,
> that he may abide with you for ever;
> 17 Even the Spirit of truth; whom the world cannot receive, because it
> seeth him not, neither knoweth him: but
> ye know him; for he dwelleth with you, and shall be in you.
> 18 I will not leave you comfortless: I will come to you. (Jn 14:16–18)

Truth emanates from God, who is truth and who shares truth with his followers, a truth that is going to be unseen and unknown by "the world." One would not have to be particularly pious to begin with this premise in the late eighteenth and early nineteenth century. Even Shaftesbury, who was later to be credited (falsely) with the idea that the ability to withstand ridicule is the test of truth, claimed in a letter to Whig jurist Lord Sommers, "Truth is the most powerful thing in the World, since even Fiction it-self must be govern'd by it, and can only please by its resemblance, The Appearance of Reality is necessary to make any Passion agreeably represented."[20]

Not only do eighteenth-century aesthetics make such an appeal to truth, but the idea that lack of truthfulness is displeasing is also generally accepted. In Francis Bacon's well-known words,

> "What is truth?" said jesting Pilate, and would not stay for an answer. Certainly there be that delight in giddiness, and

> count it a bondage to fix a belief; affecting free-will in thinking, as well as in acting … There remain certain discoursing wits which are of the same veins, though there be not so much blood in them as was in those of the ancients. But it is not only the difficulty and labor which men take in finding out of truth, nor again that when it is found it imposeth upon men's thoughts, that doth bring lies in favor; but a natural though corrupt love of the lie itself.[21]

Austen might or might not have read this particular essay by Bacon, but she shows herself conversant with both kinds of avoidance of truth in her novels – the desire to remain free from bondage to something conclusive, and the desire not to be compelled to a certain action by knowledge of what is true. Almost all her characters show themselves to be liable in one way or another to both the delight and the difficulty Bacon describes. Corrupt lovers of lies are scarcer on the ground, though one thinks of John Thorpe. She is concerned with her characters' relations to the truth about themselves and others, certainly, but she also imagines art as having the expression of truth as its goal.

Austen's world does not in general see truth as allied to power, but it does see a fallen world as embracing untruth for the sake of power, as Vicesimus Knox says in *On the Spirit of Despotism*:

> Ignorance of the grossest kind, ignorance of man's nature and rights, ignorance of all that tends to make and keep us happy, disgraces and renders wretched more than half the

> earth, at this moment, in consequence of its subjugation to despotic power. Ignorance, robed in imperial purple, with pride and cruelty by her side, sways an iron scepter over more than one hemisphere. In the finest and largest regions of this planet which we inhabit, there are no liberal pursuits and professions, no contemplative delights, nothing of that pure, intellectual employment which raises man from the mire of sensuality and sordid care, to a degree of excellence and dignity, which we conceive to be angelical and celestial. Without knowledge or the means of obtaining it, without exercise or excitements, the mind falls into a state of infantile imbecility and dotage; or acquires a low cunning, intent only on selfish and mean pursuits, such as is visible in the more ignoble of the irrational creatures, in foxes, apes, and monkies. Among nations so corrupted, the utmost effort of genius is a court intrigue or a ministerial cabal.[22]

With such an idea of the dignity and excellence that human beings are capable of attaining, Austen will of course ally the misuse of the intellect with those characters focused on material and social success. Therefore, it is her Lucy Steeles, Isabella Thorpes, Aunt Norrises, and William Elliots who rely on "low cunning, intent only on selfish and mean pursuits."

Moreover, it would be hard to maintain that Austen is simply, or even primarily, affected by the Scottish Enlightenment and the Romantic poets when it comes to her understanding of the word "truth," although she understands the way the early Romantics such as Crabbe and Cowper are thinking of the relationship between fact and subjectivity, as we see in Mr. Knightley's meditation on his own potential for error in *Emma*:

> But while so many were devoting him [Frank Churchill] to Emma, and Emma herself making him over to Harriet, Mr. Knightley began to suspect him of some inclination to trifle with Jane Fairfax. He could not understand it; but there were symptoms of intelligence between them – he thought so at least – symptoms of admiration on his side, which, having once observed, he could not persuade himself to think entirely void of meaning, however he might wish to escape any of Emma's errors of imagination. *She* was not present when the suspicion first arose. He was dining with the Randalls family, and Jane, at the Eltons'; and he had seen a look, more than a single look, at Miss Fairfax, which, from the admirer of Miss Woodhouse, seemed somewhat out of place. When he was again in their company, he could not help remembering what he had seen; nor could he avoid observations which, unless it were like Cowper and his fire at twilight,
>
> "Myself creating what I saw," brought him yet stronger suspicion of there being a something of private liking, of private understanding even, between Frank Churchill and Jane. (III.5.372–3)

Austen depicts Mr. Knightley doubting his own observation, or rather his own suspicions arising from his interpretation of what he has observed, but, while quoting Cowper attesting to Romantic subjectivity, she is also dismissing Cowper in this particular case. Mr. Knightley doubts himself, although his observations are actually correct. He is not creating what he sees but actually seeing it for what it truly is. The only thing he does not know is that Jane is as complicit as Frank in this flirtation, and that it is more than a flirtation: the two have made the commitment to marry each other at some future date. In a novel that treats so much of the potential for misinterpretation of things observed, Austen confirms that there is a truth to be known, and that Mr. Knightley knows it, however much he might question his own deduction. This is Austen's way of providing stability in what might have been a scene confirming that observation is unreliable because of subjective predispositions. In fact, she is saying the opposite.

Truth is not what the subject wants it to be. To leap forward a few decades to Friedrich Nietzsche, one of the greatest influences on the modern conception of truth as purely relative, the philosopher says in "On Truth and Lies in the Nonmoral Sense" that, "in so far as the word 'knowledge' has any meaning, the world is … interpretable, otherwise it has no meaning behind it, but countless meanings – 'Perspectivism.'" Nietzsche is not endorsing perspectivism here, but he understands its power. Such an endless variety of possible interpretations Austen would no doubt consider nonsensical. However, before Nietzsche, she is indeed investigating the following possibilities he outlines:

> It is our needs that interpret the world; our drives … Every drive is a kind of lust to rule; each one has its perspective that it would like to compel all the other drives to accept as a norm.

> Deception, flattering, lying and cheating, talking behind the back, posing, living in borrowed splendor, being masked, the disguise of convention, acting a role before others and before oneself – in short, the constant fluttering around the single flame of vanity is so much the rule and the law that almost nothing is more incomprehensible than how an honest and pure urge for truth could have arisen among men. They are deeply immersed in illusions and dream images; their eye only glides only over the surface of things … their feeling nowhere leads into truth, but contents itself with the reception of stimuli, playing, as it were, a game of blind man's bluff.[23]

Nietzsche convicts the whole world of "fluttering around the single flame of vanity" and their eyes of gliding "only over the surface of things." Without a truth to be known beneath the surface, without a connection between humility and truth, however, Nietzsche's accusations are as pathetically moral as the morality he calls purely subjective. His condemnation of the world means nothing if there is no truth.

Thus, when Austen portrays the same fluttering, immersion, and gliding, it is not to show that each character has his or her own truth that is really just a reflection of the vain self, but that the best characters can emerge from this endless round of self-satisfaction into a clearer grasp of reality, imperfect though it may be. For Austen, a heroine confronted by facts previously unknown will make deductions that lead to greater knowledge of the truth. She will know the truth about others and about herself, and that is the aim of her trajectory in the story. This truth may be partial, but it is adequate to her ability to choose the right course for herself and judge others justly. Austen is deeply interested in the notion that human vision is always partial but can be adequate. In *Emma*, she invites the reader to confront the idea of the incommunicability of the wholeness of truth:

> While he [Mr. Knightley] spoke, Emma's mind was most busy, and, with all the wonderful velocity of thought, had been able – and yet without losing a word – to catch and comprehend the exact truth of the whole; to see that Harriet's hopes had been entirely groundless, a mistake, a delusion, as complete a delusion as any of her own – that Harriet was nothing; that she was every thing herself; that what she had been saying relative to Harriet had been all taken as the language of her own feelings; and that her agitation, her doubts, her reluctance, her discouragement, had been all received as discouragement from herself. And not only was there time for these convictions, with all their glow of attendant happiness; there was time also to rejoice that Harriet's secret had not escaped her, and to resolve that it need not and should not.
>
> Seldom, very seldom, does complete truth belong to any human disclosure; seldom can it happen that something is not a little disguised, or a little mistaken; but where, as in this case, though the conduct is mistaken, the feelings are not, it may not be very material. Mr. Knightley could not impute to Emma a more relenting heart than she possessed, or a heart more disposed to accept of his. (III.13.469–70)

The chapter closes with perhaps the tersest and most comical expose of Mr. Knightley's own subjectivity, as we see Frank Churchill rise from villain to very good sort of fellow in a single sentence in direct accord with Mr. Knightley's knowledge of the degree of Emma's involvement with him. However, Austen clearly shows that there is a truth to be conveyed and, more importantly, a truth to be known, even when those involved cannot speak it fully. There is something in her characters' world that is beyond words. I believe this is why Ian Watt called her a "moral realist," though he never defined the term.[24] Austen as a moral realist accepts that the world of ethics and moral conduct contains just those kinds of "facts" Nietzsche denies exist. Her portrayal of the society of her time contains many subtleties, and she remarks on many inequities and hypocrisies, but there cannot be inequity or hypocrisy if there is no bar of justice and sincerity that her characters fail to attain.

The challenge of expressing truth in a way that will speed it to the world requires of the author a balancing act. Austen uses an impressive variety of strategies to close off her narratives. However, the reader who is forging forward through the plot to find out what will happen may not recognize or know how to categorize the elements that make up the conclusion. In this book, I will be looking at only a few of these strategies, and, for the sake of clarity and unity, I will focus mostly on one aspect of the ending of each novel. Readers will quickly see that most of these strategies – Socratic irony; metalepsis; challenging and affirming parent-child bonds; retrospection; dislocation in space and time; *desengaño* or conversion; apophasis and ellipsis to guide the reader to deductions; and oracular pronouncements – appear in all the books, often arising from the secondary characters rather than the narrator. They are among the most important strategies Austen uses to aim her narratives towards their ends.

For Jane Austen, What Is "Happiness"?

Austen aims her heroines towards happiness. A comic ending means nothing more or less than this. But what does Austen consider happiness? In agreement with MacIntyre, Ryle, Ruderman, Emsley, Kubic, Gallop, and many others, I understand her view to be essentially Aristotelian and, more importantly, Christian.[25] Although Johnson notes that "Austen's care to establish the standards of her characters' happiness provides us with an index to their moral imaginations, tempers, and resources that enables us to engage in judicious moral evaluation," she quickly elides "the liberal tradition of moral philosophy" with the more modern sense of happiness with oneself, self-approbation, and does not actually define happiness.[26] The *Stanford Encyclopedia of Philosophy* draws the sharp distinction between the two world views – classical/Christian and modern – at the outset of its definition of happiness:

> There are roughly two philosophical literatures on "happiness," each corresponding to a different sense of the term. One uses "happiness" as a value term, roughly synonymous with well-being or flourishing. The other body of work uses

> the word as a purely descriptive psychological term, akin to "depression" or "tranquility." An important project in the philosophy of happiness is simply getting clear on what various writers are talking about: what are the important meanings of the term and how do they connect? While the "well-being" sense of happiness receives significant attention in the contemporary literature on well-being, the psychological notion is undergoing a revival as a major focus of philosophical inquiry … The main accounts of happiness in this sense are hedonism, the life satisfaction theory, and the emotional state theory.[27]

Most readers would agree that it is Lydia and not Elizabeth Bennet whose definition of happiness might approximate hedonism, whereas the *eudaimonia* of the philosophers is the real telos Austen's heroines seek. Her heroines in the juvenilia all seek the happiness of hedonism, and their self-satisfaction in it is exactly what makes the reader laugh. As "The Beautifull Cassandra" closes, the felonious heroine "Cassandra smiled and whispered to herself 'This is a day well spent.'"[28] The heroine of "Henry and Eliza" returns to her parental home, Harcourt Hall, after blowing up the prison in which she was held by a Duchess, and thus "gained the Blessings of thousands, & the Applause of her own Heart."[29] These are not young ladies seeking philosophic happiness, and readers' awareness of that is why we find them funny.

That does not mean that Austen sacrifices her heroines as characters to a system in her later works. Although happiness is a chief end towards which she directs her heroines, each of the six novels possesses a unique tonal quality that the closure strives to maintain, even in granting a happy ending to the protagonist. The end of a novel reveals, as René Girard argued in *Deceit, Desire, and the Novel*, the shape and conviction of the whole.[30] The conclusions do not cheat and destroy the shape of the plots that precede them. They rather seem to confirm the tonal qualities and revisit so as to resolve in part the moral or social problems the story has considered. As opposed to a later novelist such as, for example, George Eliot, Austen does not wish for her heroines to sacrifice their desires to progress towards a new Comtian or Feuerbachian morality. She does not seem sure a better world is to be had. She does not erase desire as if it were an inhibition to a fine and admirable life, as Eliot and Henry James will later, or as something to be punished mercilessly, as Thomas Hardy will. She thinks that as an author she should fulfil the desires of the good characters she has created, and that this artistic choice will result in an image of flourishing and satisfaction, though because the telos is marriage and the creation of a new family and not the beatific vision, Austen also includes unharmonious elements to remind the reader that this is earth, not heaven.[31]

What Does Austen Mean by "Human Nature"?

What did Austen's generation believe about human nature? Beliefs were in flux in the Age of Revolution, and the Scottish Enlightenment – as well as its European cousins – was attempting to define the human in a way different from the conventional Christian view.

Later in the nineteenth century, fully embracing the idea spread by the Romantic poets of Austen's day, as I have said above, Friedrich Nietzsche would proclaim that all truth is subjective and that the claim for truth arises from the will to power.[32] One could not only say that modern theoreticians accept without question Nietzsche's formulation, but also that one could read Austen's claim for truth as just one more assertion of power by a hubristic *auteur*. As a materialist, Nietzsche claims that all morality belongs to the realm of the "unreal": "There are no such things as moral facts. Moral judgment has this in common with the religious one, that it believes in realities which are not real. Morality is only an interpretation of certain phenomena: or, more strictly speaking, a misinterpretation of them … Moral judgment must never be taken quite literally: as such is sheer nonsense. As a sign code, however, it is invaluable: to him at least who knows, it reveals the most valuable facts concerning cultures."[33]

Philip Rieff argues in *My Life among the Deathworks: Illustrations of the Aesthetics of Authority* that the educated western world is dwelling in a universe whose language has changed substantially from that of Judeo-Christian culture. His point, that the modern or third world, as he calls it, promotes the cutting off of vertical sources of authority, makes even clearer than Alasdair MacIntyre's claims for Jane Austen as the last writer of the Christian West that her language about truth, happiness, and human nature must be understood as other than that of modern academic culture.[34]

Since we tend to read Austen's works as cultural objects rather than as deliberately created works of art, we might be tempted to attribute to Austen a modern, post-Nietzschean attitude, in particular if we wish to mark her as before her time, or to claim a kind of sophistication for her which would make her our fellow. To create a monument to her culture, however, seems not to be Austen's end: she announces the telos of the novel herself, in *Northanger Abbey*, in oft-quoted words. In this famous passage, the reader can see that the concept of subjective truths is alien to Austen as a citizen of late-eighteenth and early nineteenth-century England. There, the narrator tells us that the novel's role is to convey "the most thorough knowledge of human nature, the happiest delineation of its varieties, the liveliest effusions of wit and humor ... to the world in the best chosen language" (I.5.23). While one might note that Austen does not say what the aim of revealing the knowledge of human nature might be, she does imply that novels reference a touchstone of excellence and mimetic verifiability. There is no "most" if there is not a lesser knowledge, a less happy delineation, a less lively effusion, and less well-chosen language. Austen is aiming for this superlative accomplishment, which requires knowledge of the human being as well as artistic craft. The words "human nature" stand at the centre of her recognizably Anglican, Christian artistic world. While the modern reader might wonder if there is such a thing as human nature, something about being human that can be universalized, that is unequivocal, Austen does not. She recognizes diversity in the varieties of that nature, but it is still human nature wherever she encounters it and tries to portray it for her reader.

As Michelle Albert Vachris and Cecil E. Bohanon argue in "Human Nature and Civil Society in Jane Austen,"[35] a "feedback mechanism," such as Adam Smith describes in the *Theory of Moral Sentiments*, operates in Austen's characters who receive reactions to their behaviour from others and are themselves observers of human nature: Smith proposes that humans develop morally by observing the reactions of others and developing an "impartial spectator," or "the man within the breast."[36] I would argue that, given the didactic nature of Austen's art,[37] she imagines the novel as just such a feedback mechanism, and her goal is to nurture or reinvigorate the "impartial spectator" in her reader. But to do so always requires keeping the basis of human nature in mind, what we might call a varying invariable. As Sir Thomas remarks in *Mansfield Park*, "human nature needs more lessons than a weekly sermon can convey" (II.7.288). His own conversion demonstrates the dramatic irony of his earlier speech but does not detract from its truth. Austen would not be so successful a satirist if she did not know what norms her audience would recognize through infractions thereof.

Human nature as the basis for artistic imitation would be far from new to Austen, since we read of it first in Aristotle and perhaps see it first in Homer. She would have been familiar as we all are with Hamlet's famous declaration about "the purpose of playing, whose end, both at the first and now, was and is, to hold as 'twere the mirror up to nature: to show virtue her feature, scorn her own image, and the very age and body of the time his form and pressure" (*Hamlet*, III.ii.20–1). Austen uses the term "human nature" quite often, especially in her works of fiction.[38] There is no doubt that she is making reliable and verisimilar delineation of human nature a prime end of her art, "in which the most thorough knowledge of *human nature*, the happiest delineation of its varieties, the liveliest effusions of wit and humour, are conveyed" (*NA*, I.5.31). And she writes in the same novel of Ann Radcliffe's followers and the sensational Gothic novel: "as were the works of all her imitators, it was not in them perhaps that *human nature*, at least in the Midland counties of England, was to be looked for" (*NA*, II.10.205).

Austen also uses the term for comic effect in *Northanger Abbey*: "That little boys and girls should be tormented," said Henry, "is what no one at all acquainted with *human nature* in a civilized state can deny" (I.14.111). And later, as Catherine is reading the laundry list in her bedroom during her first night at the abbey: "*Human nature* could support no more. A cold sweat stood on her forehead, the manuscript fell from her hand, and groping her way to the bed," she ends up falling asleep (II.6.174). Likewise, in *Sense and Sensibility*, Austen presents John Dashwood's declaration on human nature as ironic, as it shows him accusing Elinor of not understanding it, although it is he who misunderstands. Here, he sees Elinor's interpretation of human nature as overly pessimistic; his is optimistic about Edward's chances of being reinstated as heir by his mother: "'Ah! Elinor,' said John, 'your reasoning is very good, but it is founded on ignorance of *human nature*. When Edward's unhappy match takes place, depend upon it his mother will feel as much as if she had never discarded him; and therefore every circumstance that may accelerate that dreadful event, must be concealed from her as much as possible. Mrs. Ferrars can never forget that Edward is her son'" (*SS*, III.5.335–6).

The term appears only thrice in *Pride and Prejudice,* first associated with Mary's amateur moralizing: "They [Elizabeth and Jane] found Mary, as usual, deep in the study of thorough bass and *human nature;* and had some new extracts to admire, and some new observations of threadbare morality to listen to. Catherine and Lydia had information for them of a different sort" (I.12.67). Mary has earlier noted that she is convinced that pride "is very common indeed; that *human nature* is particularly prone to it, and that there are very few of us who do not cherish a feeling of self-complacency on the score of some quality or other, real or imaginary" (I.5.21). Later, Mr. Bennet says, meaning the opposite, that "*human nature* is particularly prone to fall into [being too severe upon oneself]," when Elizabeth counsels him not to feel too guilty for his part in Lydia's downfall (III.6.330).

In *Mansfield Park,* which uses the term perhaps more than any other of Austen's novels, Fanny is shocked and incredulous that "*human nature*" can have stooped so low as to allow the committing of adultery (II.15.511). Fanny's view of human nature seems to be facing a challenge: it has been too lofty, too idealized. What the reader might see as a very common sin, Fanny hardly can believe a human being can commit.

Near the close of the same novel, Austen follows Mrs. Price's pedestrian discussion of carpet mending with one of the most serious meditations on human nature in all of her oeuvre. Even should we mollify the seriousness of the passage by recognizing Austen's couching of it all as the response of "a mind like Fanny's" (perhaps her way of telling the reader a hyperbole is coming up), readers must still admit that the paragraph is not a parody of prudery. Fanny, who has memorized Mary Crawford's vague letter, lines up evidence; she even makes a concession to Mary Crawford's being a "woman of character." Fanny is not exaggerating the trespass of Henry and Maria, but folding back the layers of subterfuge and euphemism to reveal the "sin of the first magnitude," which adultery could not otherwise be called in Austen's day:

> The horror of a mind like Fanny's, as it received the conviction of such guilt, and began to take in some part of the misery that must ensue, can hardly be described. At first, it was a sort of stupefaction; but every moment was quickening her perception of the horrible evil. She could not doubt, she dared not indulge a hope, of the paragraph [i.e., a mention of the affair in a newspaper] being false. Miss Crawford's letter, which she had read so often as to make every line her own, was in frightful conformity with it. Her eager defence of her brother, her hope of its being *hushed up*, her evident agitation, were all of a piece with something very bad; and if there was a woman of character in existence, who could treat as a trifle this sin of the first magnitude, who would try to gloss it over, and desire to have it unpunished, she could believe Miss Crawford to be the woman! Now she could see her own mistake as to *who* were gone, or *said* to be gone. It was not Mr. and Mrs. Rushworth; it was Mrs. Rushworth and Mr. Crawford. (*MP*, III.15.510; emphasis in original)

That night, as Fanny finds herself unable to sleep, she thinks about human nature again:

> She passed only from feelings of sickness to shudderings of horror; and from hot fits of fever to cold. The event was so shocking, that there were moments even when her heart revolted from it as impossible: when she thought it could not be. A woman married only six months ago; a man professing himself devoted, even *engaged* to another; that other her near relation; the whole family, both families connected as they were by tie upon tie; all friends, all intimate together! It was too horrible a confusion of guilt, too gross a complication of evil, for *human nature,* not in a state of utter barbarism, to be capable of! yet her judgment told her it was so. *His* unsettled affections, wavering with his vanity, *Maria's* decided attachment, and no sufficient principle on either side, gave it possibility: Miss Crawford's letter stampt it a fact. (*MP*, III.15.510–11; emphasis in original)

Although Austen thinks on the resilience of human nature in volume I, as Mrs. Grant combats Henry's pessimism about marriage ("and we are all apt to expect too much; but then, if one scheme of happiness fails, *human nature* turns to another; if the first calculation is wrong" [*MP*, I.5.54]), Austen uses the term, in the main, to refer to the fallenness, the tendency to error, common to all humans. Thus, as Edmund says to Mary Crawford at Sotherton, "You have given us an amusing sketch, and *human nature* cannot say it was not so. We must all feel at times the difficulty of fixing our thoughts as we could wish" (I.9.102). In fact, Austen the narrator seems to bolster Edmund's more negative view in the last chapters as Fanny's revulsion at the idea of adultery as outside the scope of human nature can be seen only as the hyperbole of an innocent teenager, if the narrator expects the audience to share with her (the narrator) a more mature understanding of such a liaison as unremarkable in an unprincipled couple.

On the other hand, Sir Thomas is counting on that negative view in his efforts to bring Fanny into conformity with his plans by sending her to Portsmouth, and he thus misunderstands what matters to Fanny, at least in part:

> Sir Thomas, meanwhile, went on with his own hopes and his own observations, still feeling a right, by all his knowledge of *human nature*, to expect to see the effect of the loss of power and consequence on his niece's spirits, and the past attentions of the lover producing a craving for their return; and he was soon afterwards able to account for his not yet completely and indubitably seeing all this, by the prospect of another visitor, whose approach he could allow to be quite enough to support the spirits he was watching. William had obtained a ten days' leave of absence, to be given to Northamptonshire, and was coming, the happiest of lieutenants, because the latest made, to shew his happiness and describe his uniform. (III.6.424)

Sir Thomas's aforementioned comment on human nature also presupposes fallenness and imperfectability: "It is perfectly natural that you should not have thought much on the subject, Mr. Crawford ... He [Edmund] knows that *human nature* needs more lessons than a weekly sermon can convey" (II.7.288).

The fact that Fanny has imagined human nature to be potentially very bad in a state of nature, what she calls "utter barbarism," shows at least that she does not partake of Rousseau's and Locke's views of humankind. She can imagine human nature being degraded by lack of civilization and education, but she can hardly imagine a civilized English person being capable of breaking one of the Ten Commandments.

Unlike in *Mansfield Park,* Austen does not use the term "human nature" extensively in *Emma,* where it serves as a foundation for an amusing aphorism concerning human curiosity: the narrator claims that "*human nature* is so well disposed toward those who are in interesting situations that a young person, who either marries or dies, is sure of being kindly spoken of" (*E,* II.4.194). Drama of any sort in the life of a young person evokes sympathy, and the audience does not distinguish between the comic or the tragic in having this reaction.

Persuasion also offers few examples of the term, but those Austen does include fall into the types we have already observed. When discussing Nurse Rooke's ability to gather information from several levels of society, Anne comments to Mrs. Smith:

> Women of that class have great opportunities, and if they are intelligent may be well worth listening to. Such varieties of *human nature* as they are in the habit of witnessing! And it is not merely in its follies, that they are well read; for they see it occasionally under every circumstance that can be most interesting or affecting. What instances must pass before them of ardent, disinterested, self-denying attachment, of heroism, fortitude, patience, resignation: of all the conflicts

> and all the sacrifices that ennoble us most. A sick chamber may often furnish the worth of volumes. (*P*, II.5.169; my emphasis)

Here Anne imagines human nature as coming in "varieties," but those varieties fall into the classes of vice and virtue, not merely follies but instances of ennobling heroism in the form of self-sacrifice.

The famous dialogue in chapter 11 of volume 2 divides human nature into the nature of man and the nature of woman ("It would not be the nature of any woman who truly loved" [*P*, II.11.253]). But at the end of the chapter, Anne uses the term to describe humanity in general: "I mean, that I was right in submitting to her [Lady Russell], and that if I had done otherwise, I should have suffered more in continuing the engagement than I did even in giving it up, because I should have suffered in my conscience. I have now, as far as such a sentiment is allowable in *human nature*, nothing to reproach myself with; and if I mistake not, a strong sense of duty is no bad part of a woman's portion" (II.11.268). This last usage in Austen's published work constitutes the epitome of the author's view of human nature. It evokes the conscience as an essential part of the human being and acknowledges the limits of self-absolution. Anne says the sentiment she is expressing must be understood within the bounds of the Christian understanding from the Epistle of St. John that no human beings can hold themselves to be sinless: "If we say that we have no sin, we deceive ourselves, and the truth is not in us. If we confess our sins, he is faithful and just to forgive us our sins, and to cleanse us from all unrighteousness. If we say that we have not sinned, we make him a liar, and his word is not in us" (I Jn 1:8–11). Anne is being very careful about her phrasing, as she also refers to the biblical injunction to honour one's father and mother. Her conscience would have suffered if she had broken this commandment,[39] which we will examine more carefully in relation to the end of *Northanger Abbey* shortly. Anne interprets the commandment as including someone who "was in the place of a parent" to her, a very traditional approach to understanding the law, especially since Lady Russell was her godmother.

When Austen speaks of the varieties of human nature, then, she does not mean wholly different species of human beings, but tends to refer to different acquirements of virtue. The displays of virtue and vice, wisdom or folly, have to do with the character's intellectual ability and so could be said to have to do with the mind, but they also reveal the development of the ability to examine oneself according to the laws of the Bible and of Christianity. The Examen, which Austen owned, later giving a copy to her niece to prepare her for reception of Communion, is an act of meditation that is intended to help train the will, according to the dictates of conscience. The Austen family's practice was to include a brief Examen every evening in their prayers.[40] Because of the attention paid to the mind and the heart as well as the will and the passions in the Examen, it is very clear that Austen does not think of the human being as a mind in a body, a very common duality today. To understand Austen's view of human nature, modern readers should become familiar with the complex understanding of the composition of the human being, as reflected in the views of Austen's favorite author of sermons, Thomas Sherlock.[41] Sherlock speaks of this construction when he defends the idea of faith in the heart as well as in the intellect, asking his reader to consider how Scripture presents the makeup of the human:

> If faith be only an act of the understanding formed on due reasons and motives, how comes it to be described in Scripture as having its seat in the heart? The Apostle [St. Paul] in the text cautions against "an evil heart of unbelief": and the same notion prevails throughout the books of Scripture, and is as early as our Saviour's first preaching, in explaining the parable of the sower to his disciples, Luke vii. He tells them,
>
> "Those by the way-side are they that hear: then cometh the devil, and taketh away the word out of their hearts, lest they should believe and be saved": v.12. So again, "That on the good ground are they which in an honest and good heart should hear the word, and bring forth fruit with patience": v. 15. The first sort are those who had an evil heart of unbelief: the second are those who, as the same Apostle to the Hebrews expresses it, chap x. had a "true heart in full assurance of faith." In the Acts of the Apostles, Philip tells the Eunuch, that if he "believed with all his heart," he might be baptized: viii. 37. And Barnabas exhorts the Antiochians, that "with purpose of heart they would cleave unto the Lord"; which is only a periphrasis for faith: xi. 23. The Apostle to the Romans has *ex professo* determined this matter: "If thou shalt confess," says he, "with thy mouth the Lord Jesus, and shalt believe in thine heart that God hath raised him from the dead, thou shalt be saved": x.9. In the following

> verse he gives this general reason for his assertion: "For with the heart man believeth unto righteousness, and with the mouth confession is made unto salvation."
>
> Since then the Scripture, read to you for the text, contains an exhortation to faith, which supposes a man's faith to be influenced by his affections and inclinations; which is not always true, if we consider faith merely as an assent of the mind to a credible proposition: since there are also such things ascribed to faith in Scripture, such promises made to it, as cannot belong to it in this acceptation: since faith, thus considered, is a bare act of the mind; but the faith of the gospel is described as having its seat and operations in the heart of man: it is necessary, for the right understanding of the text, to inquire.[42]

Sherlock takes into account the "affections and inclinations," not just reason, because the Bible speaks of these other parts of the human being. Another sermon writer Austen admired, Thomas Jefferson, appealed to God in one of the prayers we know she read for "the hearing Ear, and the understanding Heart."[43] The modern reader might be inclined to imagine the human being as a body, a mechanical part, governed by a central computer, the brain. In contrast, Austen's readers understand the human being to have a nature that bridges the divine and the earthly, and to be composed of body and soul – the latter, an immortal part, is the form of the body but is not localizable in the brain, and encompasses the conscience and the heart as Sherlock defines it. However, it is not at all the same thing as the passions, which are also part of the human being. All these different elements must be present to represent human nature as Austen would have understood it.

The Role of the Austen's Conclusions in Speeding Truth

As the vilest Writer has his Readers, so the greatest Liar has his Believers; and it often happens, that if a Lie be believ'd only for an Hour, it has done its Work, and there is no farther occasion for it. *Falsehood flies, and the Truth comes limping after it*; so that when Men come to be undeceiv'd, it is too late; the Jest is over, and the Tale has had its Effect.

(Jonathan Swift, *Examiner*)

Austen admires truth that does not limp slowly on foot but that has wings. Her short note to her sister attesting to her valuing of truth, cited near the beginning of this chapter, reveals that she believes the conclusion plays a special role in the novelist's task. Her thought is most aligned with critic René Girard, who understood the conclusion of the novel as indispensable in revealing the trajectory of the whole.[44] Thus it behooves the reader of her novels to pay special attention to the closures. My investigation has revealed to me the complexity of those closures – indeed, a book that covered every rhetorical strategy, that closely read every telling sentence, that enumerated every moment of irony (and of ironized irony), would be of enormous length. Austen's art is compact, but when readers begin to unravel that compactness, the depth and breadth of her ambition as a writer spread out before them like an unending vista. The plan of this book is to highlight one strategy per novel, with some reference to Austen's use of the same strategy in her other conclusions, references that could easily have become whole chapters themselves.

Solon said to Croesus, "Count no man happy until the end is known," the reason being that tragedy or unhappiness could strike at any time before the final curtain.[45] For Austen, the final curtain is not death, as it is for Frank Kermode and Margaret Atwood, for example, but marriage.[46] The traditional ending for a comedy, marriage is an antideath ending, one might say. Although many critics would like to equate the two – seeing the heroines dwindling into wives, or the men losing their edge to welter in bourgeois morality as a kind of death to the fun and pleasure arising from earlier tensions and exercises of wit – comic writers are not aiming at an end that terminates in oblivion, but one that confirms the existence of joy, life, and understanding. For Austen, in the tradition of Shakespeare, speaking overmuch about love puts its sincerity into question. Therefore, she must assure the reader in a way that is not fulsome or clichéd, in a way that is not "talky," but that makes full use of the suggestive properties of silence and ironic narrative. The primary end that is known in her novels is how the heroine lives her married life with her chosen spouse. For Austen, the truth about human nature lies in the ability to understand, once we look at different ways of becoming happy, that her heroines have chosen the best path available to them. The discernment she asks of her readers in her endings shows that she expects us to have entered into her way of imagining the lives of her characters such that we can understand swiftly the irony, the ironizing of the irony, the jokes, and the satirizing of novelistic conventions. Because she can indulge in parody and even tease her protagonists does not mean that she hates humanity or even that she has created characters with failings in order to mock them and deconstruct her society's idea of the family. Austen knows well how to "deconstruct" a character's self-image or a literary cliché she clearly finds laughable. When reading her endings, we need to be able to distinguish between two types of language the narrator uses, satire and raillery. She is teasing Elinor or Fanny or Anne, just as Henry Tilney teases Catherine Morland, as Edward Ferrars teases Marianne Dashwood, or as Aunt Gardiner teases Elizabeth Bennet. In all these cases, even if there might be a difference of opinion, the language of teasing is a step towards intimacy; as Henry Tilney says in his first dance with Catherine Morland in *Northanger Abbey*, "Thank you; for now we shall soon be acquainted, as I am authorized to tease you on this subject whenever we meet, and nothing in the world advances intimacy so much" (I.3.22).

Austen is able to write in such an elliptical and protean style at the conclusions of her novels because she presumes she has created this type of intimacy Henry desires, a mutual understanding that does not always need words. Eleanor Tilney teaches the reader as well as Catherine not to misunderstand this style of communication. When Henry has been mockingly speaking of descending to women's level of understanding, his sister reprimands him: "You know what you ought to do. Clear your character handsomely before her. Tell her that you think very highly of the understanding of women." And when Henry continues to speak jestingly, Eleanor turns to Catherine to do the explaining herself: "We shall get nothing more serious from him now, Miss Morland. He is not in a sober mood. But I do assure you that he must be entirely misunderstood, if he can ever appear to say an unjust thing of any woman at all, or an unkind one of me" (*NA*, I.14.115). Such an explanation of Henry's saying the opposite of what he believes demonstrates that intimacy prepares the listener for rapidity of comprehension, and in the case of Austen's endings, that is comprehension of her illustration of human happiness. Though a valuable study on Austen's stylistic economy, Anne Toner's recent work discusses the author's exploitation of it to represent thought, without pointing the reader to what Austen hopes to achieve by its use: that very intimacy that will make the reader's comprehension rapid as Austen brings her heroines' stories to a close.[47] Turning to her conclusions in a sense forces our hand concerning the understanding of happiness, because multiplicity of potential meaning is about to come to an end. But is Austen like a modern critic who finds that the only truth is not to confirm a truth at all? It seems far more probable that Austen is like Henry in her conclusions, and the reader is like a Catherine being invited to be more like Eleanor. To where does this flippancy and pretense of disregard lead? The whole novel itself must be the feedback mechanism that allows the reader to comprehend the finale with the right disposition to the information unfolded there. Once you are Eleanor, you do not misunderstand.

In the ensuing chapters, I will be noting and analysing Austen's habits in her conclusions. Some of these habits are moral and thematic: she is interested in the heroine's marriage as a trial of the parent-child relationship and in the poetic justice she as novelist can affirm might take place in the sublunary region in which her characters dwell, the everyday world with its inequities in justice and in social divisions. Some habits are consistent narrative choices: for instance, Austen always omits dialogue from the main characters in the final chapters. We never hear her heroine or hero speak in the conclusion; her narrative voice always steps forward and takes centre stage. Austen also always includes some type of forward projection or prophecy in the conclusion.

Some of these habits are rhetorical: Austen employs Socratic irony, analepsis (which I call forced retrospection), metalepsis, apophasis, and even poetic techniques like alliteration. Austen is no unconscious rhetorician. In addition to the works of other classically trained authors, she had read Hugh Blair's sermons, which exemplified classical rhetorical strategies, and she knew his *Rhetoric* at least, and may also have been acquainted with the rhetorical guides of other authors available in her time.[48] Nevertheless, I do not cite Blair in regard to the rhetorical tropes Austen employs, mostly because he does not discuss apophasis or irony in his book, techniques that she uses in abundance. In addition, although Blair does briefly define metalepsis, he does not mean by it what modern critic Gérard Genette means, and it is Genette's usage that I find accords most closely with Austen's practice.[49] I make use of Genette's expansion of metalepsis's definition because Austen uses a strategy that is exactly like it in her endings, and not the more limited approach defined by Blair. She of course never names any of these strategies herself. Although I believe it is important for modern readers to recognize that Austen, at least when it came to her knowledge of rhetoric, was familiar with Blair's manual, the juvenilia make abundantly clear that she learned by observation of other authors in her youth. She does not use these strategies only in her later works. However, perhaps more importantly, Miriam Wolff points out the connection between Blair's rhetoric and his understanding of the happiness of the moral person as a form of justice available in this world: "Blair professes that 'The distribution of the goods of fortune, indeed, may often be promiscuous, that is, disproportioned to the moral characters of men, but the allotment of real happiness is never so.'"[50] Austen carefully proportions the type of happiness available to her characters in keeping with their moral characters. Her rhetorical strategies are closely bound to her portrayal of the verisimilar and to her conveyance of truth.

Jane Austen's novels speed truth into the world at the expense of both the traditional "fairy tale" ending and "realist" pessimism. As Lloyd Brown asserts, "the attack on the creaking machinery of the 'happy ending' is related to ... [a] major feature of Jane Austen's comic conclusions – a realistic reappraisal of the right insistence on rewarding virtue and punishing evil."[51] If she admits into the world of "perfect felicity" the shades of future worries and the knowledge that one's own and one's spouse's troubling relatives will continue to irritate and discomfit in the future, she is not in a post-Marxist, post-Nietzschean world, like Foucault espousing the "rightful multiplicity of language games," suspending "all judgments of right and wrong."[52] To do so would be to homogenize the lies of John Thorpe, the braggadocio of Mr. Collins, the inconstancy of Henry Crawford, with the playful wit of Elizabeth Bennet or Henry Tilney. When serious falsehood and playful saying "What you do not mean"[53] are confounded, readers become "such dull elves as have not a great deal of ingenuity themselves," to misquote Sir Walter Scott, as Austen does in a letter to her sister.[54] The truth she espouses is that her main characters, no matter how much they are unable to say straightforwardly what they mean, no matter how much they might revel in saying the opposite of what they mean, can experience a felicity that is perfect, despite all these defects.

Jane Austen has been told for years how she went wrong in her endings. I venture forward with the conviction that her books themselves teach us how to read them. To read for what we want to find is to wish for a book to be a mirror, but Austen thinks of a book as a launched arrow, and in the following pages, I hope to help readers learn how to allow themselves to be her target.

CHAPTER TWO

"Abjuring All Future Attachments": Teaching the Reader to Desire the Right Object in *Lady Susan*

Second attachments play a role in most of Austen's conclusions.[1] Because she focuses on happiness through marriage as a telos, the problems of change through maturation and infidelity are ever-present threats to the young people about to enter the married state. Austen's epistolary novella, *Lady Susan*, an early work written when she was around nineteen, sets the stage for Austen's later presentations of these problems (even though she almost always considers them in the more youthful short stories). Although the letters in the novella focus mostly on the titular heroine, or anti-heroine, the narrative closure concerns the reasons why Susan loses Reginald De Courcy to her daughter Frederica, and makes marriage to Reginald the desirable end goal that Susan fails to attain. Yet Reginald has wanted Lady Susan, and Austen enjoys having the reader think about the length of time it takes for a sincere lover to recover from an ill-fated relationship. It most certainly is not an eternity. One could recall Frank Kermode's invocation of death and apocalypse in *The Sense of an Ending* to read *Lady Susan*'s closure: Austen's narrative voice steps in as judge and declares human affections incapable of the eternal, although blind humans habitually claim eternity as the arena for their passions.[2] For Austen, the end times are, conversely, comically near.

Years before she poked fun at Edward Ferrars's and Edmund Bertram's changing affections, Austen invented Reginald De Courcy, who, in *Lady Susan*'s conclusion, is "talked, flattered, and finessed into an affection" for Frederica.[3] Like Harriet Smith in *Emma* and Edmund Bertram in *Mansfield Park*, Reginald is able to be in love with several people within the span of one year. "Abjuring all future attachments," Reginald is a clichéd disappointed lover but also becomes one of the objects of Austen's satire not only because of the incommensurateness of his hyperbolic reaction to his fortunate loss, but also because he is consoled within the year by a new attachment. Austen always considers time as a subject in the close of her novels, and this early piece is no different. How long is "ever after" for her characters? At the outside, forever is twelve months.

Austen gives Reginald De Courcy the traits that make him sympathetic and deserving of a happy ending while also mocking and satirizing his idea of his heart's own stability. Because Austen will regularly return in every one of the later novels to Reginald's character type – a young person who forms a second attachment after thinking it impossible – it is worth examining how Austen thinks this trait affects the reader's judgment of the character. In almost all the cases of second attachments Austen provides, the person who marries his or her second love is not condemned but nonetheless is held up to some mockery. Second attachments allow a good window into Austen's methods of balancing both affirmation and irony. Good characters are not perfect; human intentions often bend or change with the passage of time, and yet fidelity and mutual respect are still possible.

In the completed novels, Austen tends to make the protagonists' love interests more substantial than she does in *Lady Susan*, though they always rank second to the heroine, or third, or even lower, in their allotment of narrative space and dialogue. In this novella, the flatter portrait of Reginald is partly the result of her allowing him less narrative space than she allots to his manipulators. Nonetheless, Austen repeats some characteristics of this early central male character in both central and secondary male and female characters in her later novels. Reginald is a prototype of Marianne Dashwood and Edmund Bertram, who are self-deluded about the value of the objects of their infatuation. Reginald has in common with Harriet Smith being easily influenced by others into an affection he cannot see is manufactured. He also resembles Edward Ferrars, who, because of youth and inexperience, attaches himself to a deceitful hypocrite but later falls in love with a good woman of excellent understanding. Comparing Reginald to Austen's later inconstant hearts allows us to see that in the juvenilia she already distinguishes among kinds of inconstancy and that she is also working on the reader's powers of detection to establish Reginald as the hero of the novella (though he clearly is not the protagonist), whose happy ending is not altogether undeserved in spite of his shifting affections. Without fail, that negotiation forms a part of her novelistic conclusions.

The Comedy of Abjuring Future Attachments: Lack of Self-Knowledge

Inconstancy forms the theme of much of Austen's comedy in the juvenilia. That characteristic is interesting to her probably because it is the greatest threat to love and marriage, both of which are necessary to the narrative conclusions in her later works. But it clearly also interests her because it is comically deflating, revealing the human "'follies and nonsense, whims and inconsistencies'" that divert Elizabeth Bennet, as she tells Mr. Darcy, and that he will subsequently christen "'those weaknesses which often expose a strong understanding to ridicule'" (*PP*, I.11.63). She will even deflate the romantic musings of her later heroine Anne Elliot, whose constant love is so moving to the reader. Famous for Anne and Captain Harville's discussion of male and female constancy, does *Persuasion* not also include a soupçon of mirth in the narrator's description of Anne, who, she suggests, might be feeling differently about Mr. Elliot after the concert in Bath had there been no Frederick Wentworth?

> How she might have felt had there been no Captain Wentworth in the case, was not worth enquiry; for there was a Captain Wentworth; and be the conclusion of the present

> suspense good or bad, her affection would be his for ever. Their union, she believed, could not divide her more from other men, than their final separation.
>
> Prettier musings of high-wrought love and eternal constancy, could never have passed along the streets of Bath, than Anne was sporting with from Camden Place to Westgate Buildings. It was almost enough to spread purification and perfume all the way. (*P*, II.9.208)

It seems even Anne is not completely incapable of being consoled, because, the author implies, it is human nature to seek consolation. Surely if Austen can tease Anne Elliot on the subject, her mockery of Reginald should not sink him forever in the reader's eyes.

Yet inconstancy is not always comical; it is often the source of the greatest unhappiness Austen's characters experience. The conclusions of all the novels unite a heroine and a spouse whom the reader can believe will never be inconstant. Joyce Tarpley has shown that constancy is necessary in Austen's scheme of the virtues.[4] Readers cannot believe in the happy endings if they suspect either spouse will be unfaithful.

The theme of a battle between constancy and inconstancy was popular in music and poetry in Austen's youth. Jeanice Brooks has studied some songs Austen had in her own collection or is known to have played and sung before she wrote the later Chawton novels, showing Austen's familiarity with a popular and conventional tension between sentimentalism and pragmatic cynicism in solo pieces and duets that dramatize the two points of view on love and constancy.[5] In the juvenilia, Austen is already experimenting with this dissonance, which often forms the groundwork for her wildly comic plots (as in "Frederic and Elfrida" when Charlotte commits suicide because she has plighted her troth to two different men in the same day).[6] Reginald, Lady Susan, and Sir James Martin all shift fidelities in the course of *Lady Susan*. The nature of their instability is, however, different. Lady Susan, for instance, is never in love at all, but is in what is probably an adulterous relationship with Lord Manwaring during her official period of mourning for her husband. She toys with Reginald until she decides to become engaged to him, but she then marries Sir James Martin. Reginald's "abjuring all future attachments" shows his desire to be constant, but his family, like Lady Susan, is able to change his mind. The culminating comic marriage is a result of connivance rather than a simple shift in affections from an unattainable to an attainable object.

Austen always parodies the impermanence of romantic affections that seem to be indelible to the afflicted lover. And yet she is able to preserve Reginald from the suspicion of being habitually inconstant. He does not even fall in love spontaneously. The manipulators who want to finesse Reginald into marriage all look with a kind of indulgent humour on his conviction of his own stability, whether it be Lady Susan herself, or Reginald's sister and mother. Austen participates in the ancient ascription of *astutia*, or cunning cleverness, to the women, who use their intelligence to entrap the man.[7] This tactic makes Reginald into a gull, but not into a seducer or a cad.

In *Lady Susan*, the recovery from disappointed hopes seems to be a good thing for the character and for the resolution of the plot, as it is for Marianne Dashwood in *Sense and Sensibility*. Austen does not seem to admire fidelity to a worthless object. Indeed, in *Lady Susan*, she seems to celebrate the escape of both Reginald and Frederica from Lady Susan's grasp. For what would it mean for Reginald to keep Lady Susan? After all, she herself does not seem to be in love with him, or her late husband, or Sir James, and her attraction to Manwaring might be called something other than love. Attachments of the heart are not for her (as they will not be for the unsuspecting Emma Woodhouse many years later). Yet Austen's flippancy in resolving the narrative in this strange manner in no way signals a pessimism about future marriage. Surprisingly for modern audiences, the opposite is the case. Austen's delight in her anarchic, amoral heroine is not approval, and her creation of a hero who is able to be "finessed" into affection for another does not signal disapproval.

The characters in the later novels are all more fully drawn, although Edward Ferrars spends a good deal of his novel offstage. Unlike Reginald, however, they are all animated by their sincere affection for the women they eventually marry. Austen grants Reginald De Courcy the additional attractions of a Mr. Darcy or Captain Wentworth in the form of wealth, and of Mr. Knightley in his property. The usual effect of money and property on the Austen hero's alpha-male status, however, does not seem to secure for Reginald the affection of the novella's readers. In spite of his wealth and status, Reginald De Courcy as a sentimental hero will never win hearts as Mr. Darcy does. And that is because of his inconstant heart. Yet this seems to be a risk with the hero's status and reputation among her readers that Jane Austen is willing to take – and more than once, to boot.

Reginald, like many eighteenth-century heroes and their prototypes in Plautus and other classical comedies, is fascinated by an older woman who is a "cool, accomplished taker."[8] These merry widow stereotypes traditionally lose their hold on the fluctuating emotions of young bachelors, who end up marrying a younger, innocent spouse. As Jay Levine has shown, Lady Susan herself serves as the comic blocking character of the widow.[9] Ann Raia has pointed out that in Roman comedy, the innocent spouse is necessary. Called the *puella*, "as a character she is much less interesting dramatically than the *matrona* or the meretrix, but her … marriageability often furnishes the requisite 'happy ending.'"[10]

Unlike Wycherley and Etherege, who also employed such characters, Austen is so motivated by a desire to exploit or explode conventions for her own purposes that she makes Lady Susan's designs on Reginald the centre of the plot rather than just a block to the central development. Reginald's plan to resist the charms of the famous flirt fails almost immediately. The hero's repeated failure to see through Susan's self-fashioned persona is central to the comedy of the work as a whole and is the main source of tension in the plot. In contrast, the romance of the younger couple is so underplayed as to be almost invisible. In foregrounding Susan, Austen also places squarely before the audience the foolishness of the "hero," who is at least at first a conventional "Love Heretic."

The Love Heretic

The Love Heretic is a character descended from troubadour and romance prototypes, known to Austen through several authors. Among the most important is Shakespeare, who in *Much Ado About Nothing*, as one example, makes the hero of the comedy, Benedick, a Love Heretic. Benedick is sure that he will never fall in love and that he cannot be taken in by reports of a woman's excellence. Beatrice, the heroine, is also a Love Heretic, famously declaring, "I had rather hear my dog bark at a crow than a man swear he loves me" (I.i.125–6). The Love Heretic enters the drama in order to be cured in the end. Love Heretics are always caught. Benedick, for one, declares, "When I said I would die a bachelor, I did not think I should live till I were married" (II.iii.263–4) as an excuse for changing his mind.

Reginald is a classic example of this type, trespassing into the realms of Cupid with a ridiculous sense of his own imperviousness to attraction. When his father writes to him of his worries about Reginald's attachment to lady Susan, Reginald replies huffily, "Equally low must sink my pretensions to common sense if I am suspected of matrimonial views in my behaviour to her. Our difference of age must be an insuperable objection, & I entreat you, my dear Sir, to quiet your mind, & no longer harbour a suspicion which cannot be more injurious to your own peace than to our Understandings" (24–5). The purpose of employing a Love Heretic in a comic plot is to make the comic ending depend on his or her conversion.

The ending of *Lady Susan* will derive its comic force from the ways in which Austen examines Reginald's succumbing to love and marriage.

Lady Susan, too, is a Love Heretic who will get caught in her own toils, eventually having to marry Sir James Martin. She, however, never converts. She declares to Mrs. Johnson,

> I like [Reginald] on the whole very well; he is clever & has a good deal to say, but he is sometimes impertinent & troublesome. There is a sort of ridiculous delicacy about him which requires the fullest explanation of whatever he may have heard to my disadvantage, & is never satisfied till he thinks he has ascertained the beginning & end of everything.
>
> This is *one* sort of Love, but I confess it does not particularly recommend itself to me. I infinitely prefer the tender & liberal spirit of Manwaring, which, impressed with the deepest conviction of my merit, is satisfied that whatever I do must be right; & look with a degree of contempt on the inquisitive & doubtful Fancies of that Heart which seems always debating on the reasonableness of its Emotions. Manwaring is indeed, beyond compare, superior to Reginald – superior in everything but the power of being with me! Poor fellow! he is quite distracted by Jealousy, which I am not sorry for, as I know no better support of Love. (30)

Susan has never had any idea what love is, and the narrator confirms that she never will: in the second-to-last paragraph, the author sums up the unknowability of her protagonist's future state in a way that makes it utterly knowable: "Whether Lady Susan was, or was not happy in her Second Choice – I do not see how it can ever be ascertained – for who would take her assurance of it, on either side of the question? The World must judge from Probability. – She had nothing against her, but her Husband & her Conscience" (77). Here, the narrator pretends to be unreliable, a pose Austen will adopt in most of the later novels, especially at the conclusion, but the sideways "Knight's move," as Vladimir Nabokov named it, in the last sentence above associates happiness with a wise choice in marriage and a clear conscience. The probability that Lady Susan will ever have either is very low. Susan serves as a Love Heretic in order to be caught not by love, but by marriage. Austen's heroine and hero will both renounce their opposition to marriage; that is the telos towards which Austen aims the action.

Lady Susan occupies most of the narrative space of the novella, and she also has almost all the funny, smart lines. Jay Levine has already explained why the latter fact, at least, is not an indication of the author's approval. Nonetheless, in foregrounding a traditionally secondary character – the predatory widow – through Lady Susan's dominance of the epistolary correspondence, Austen consigns our perceptions of Reginald De Courcy – a traditionally central sentimental hero – to the words and judgments of others. That tactic seems to be a major problem in the novella. However, at the same time Austen elevates him to the position of hero because he is the man Susan Vernon wishes to conquer. The conclusion must be the location where the extent of Susan's power is made clear if she is a triumphant heroine.

Narrative Space

Important features in our estimates of the characters in Austen's novels are how much she allows them to speak for themselves and how much she shows of their internal meditations. One could say such issues pertain mostly to the "middle" of the novel. But they are nonetheless important to the reader's assessment of the conclusion. Does Reginald have interiority, and, perhaps more importantly, does Austen grant him sufficient narrative space for the reader to consider him a hero? James Wood argued that Emma is a heroine who interprets and discovers salutary truths, a new kind of heroine.[11] Emma is central to her novel in great part because so much of the action is perceived through her eyes: her voice even dominates much of the coloured narrative. Reginald's voice, however, does not occupy sufficient space in Austen's letters to allow him to be the reader's main source of information about himself or to strike readers as having the kind of interiority Austen's later heroines (and some of her heroes) will have. The correspondence in *Lady Susan* is carried on almost exclusively by the women in the story and, even more interestingly, by the older women rather than the younger generation.[12]

This challenge to the reader is more complex in Reginald's case than in the cases of the later heroes whom he resembles most, Edward Ferrars and Edmund Bertram. That Austen chooses to present him this way is fascinating: he cannot be an object of amorous interest to his relations who write about him or to him, and he is not one for Lady Susan, who sees him more as an enemy to be conquered than as someone to whom she is irresistibly attracted. This is indeed a disadvantage as far as moulding the reader's attachment to the character is concerned. However, the reader must care about his fate if the ending of the novella is to be satisfying or entertaining.

One main theme of *Lady Susan* is the way in which our sentiments can be controlled by others' language about us. We are never able to ascertain from her own lips the amount of interest Frederica has in Reginald, and the narrator does not intrude to make the reader watch her admiring or loving him as she does when she portrays Elizabeth Bennet, Fanny Price, or Anne Elliot watching and interacting with Mr. Darcy, Edmund Bertram, or Frederick Wentworth. The heroine's and other women's perspective on these men is, in part, what ratifies their desirability in the reader's eyes. It is up to Catherine, who is an acute observer if not always a clever strategist, to let us know through her letter to her mother that Frederica is smitten with Reginald:

> "I am very glad to find that my description of Frederica Vernon has interested you, for I do beleive her truly deserving of your regard; & when I have communicated a notion which has recently struck me, your kind impressions in her favour will, I am sure, be heightened. I cannot help fancying that she is growing partial to my brother, I so very often see her eyes fixed on his face with a remarkable expression of pensive admiration! – He is certainly very handsome – & yet more – there is an openness in his manner that must be highly prepossessing, & I am sure she feels it so. – Thoughtful & pensive in general, her countenance always brightens into

> a smile when Reginald says anything amusing; & let the subject be ever so serious that he may be conversing on, I am much mistaken if a syllable of his uttering, escape her. – " (34)

Aside from assuring us that Reginald is handsome, Catherine attests to the kind of openness of manner Austen seems to find very winning in such characters as Catherine Morland and Emma.

In letter 24, Catherine tells her mother she is observing Frederica and Reginald, and sees no hope of her affection being returned. In letter 25, it is in fact Lady Susan who confirms that Frederica has fallen in love with him: "'Her idle Love for Reginald, too; – it is surely my duty to discourage such romantic nonsense. – All things considered therefore, it seems encumbent on me to take her to Town & marry her immediately to Sir James'" (58). This is an interesting way to frame the fact of the daughter's affection for Reginald. Though it is brief, it shapes the reader's knowledge of the characters in several ways. We see that for Susan, the most sensible thing one can do if one's daughter is suffering the pangs of unrequited love is to marry her off to someone else she insists she does not want. And this though even Fordyce in his letters to young women will advise young ladies that their obligation to obey a parent ceases when they are urged to marry without affection.[13] It does not seem to occur to Susan that Frederica would gain almost as much from a marriage to Reginald as she would from a marriage to Sir James; if Susan's only goal is unromantic sense, it should be fine to make the substitution. The dismissive lines constitute one proof that Susan does indeed see something of value in Reginald personally and wants him for herself. Allowing the reader to see that Lady Susan perceives her daughter as her rival, and her affections as dangerous to her own mission, is a prime way in which Austen can ratify Reginald's worth in the eyes of her protagonist. In this circuitous way, Austen also builds up Reginald's "hero credentials" because he is now admired and loved by the persecuted daughter and becomes an object of female rivalry. Frederica's acquisition of Reginald as a husband signals the defeat of her mother as no other element in the plot can in the narrative close.

Sincerity and Self-Knowledge

Reginald's ability to know himself and to recognize errors elevates his status as hero. That Reginald's opinion of Frederica undergoes a dramatic change from his initial prejudiced view (reminding readers of the shift in Mr. Knightley's prejudiced view of Harriet Smith and also of Mr. Darcy's dismissive initial evaluation of Elizabeth Bennet) proves that Austen thinks of him as a dynamic character who is able to re-evaluate and attempt to be fairer, even when he is not being manipulated. Such growth satisfies E.M. Forster's definition of a round character, but the requirement in general applies to heroes and heroines of any *Bildungsroman*.[14] Reginald, a seemingly flat character, is able, after Frederica's appeal to him, to reject the contemptuous opinion of her that he expressed in his first letter to his sister: he has become convinced of her good character and innocence.

That conviction is one of the tensions that propels him towards the final breakup with her mother.

What Reginald first says of his future wife at the outset of the novella comes from others' reports, as does his opinion of Lady Susan: "'I am glad to find Miss Vernon does not accompany her Mother to Churchill, as she has not even Manners to recommend her, & according to Mr. Smith's account, is equally dull & proud. Where Pride & Stupidity unite there can be no dissimulation worthy notice, & Miss Vernon shall be consigned to unrelenting contempt; but by all that I can gather, Lady Susan possesses a degree of captivating Deceit which it must be pleasing to witness & detect'" (8–9). Reginald enters the story as a satirist who wants to be a detective who ferrets out deceit. He prides himself on being observant – rather like Elizabeth Bennet – and expressly announces that Frederica will not interest him because she, pridefully stupid, will be incapable of the cunning and lies his skills will help unmask.

The actual result of this challenge to his own detective skills is disastrous to the audience's perception of him as an admirable and manly character: Reginald becomes a comic object because his emotions are in fact easily swayed. He is incapable of seeing through feminine wiles when they are exerted in his direction. This vulnerability makes him too gullible to be a hero. Perhaps the audience begins to desire that he should fail in the end as punishment for his stupidity. He is laughable, whereas Mr. Darcy's immunity to the flattering attentions of Caroline Bingley shows him to be worthy of respect. Self-love does not make *him* anyone's gull.

And yet Austen takes pains to show that, in spite of Reginald's protestations to the contrary, he is tenderhearted. He is gallant and sincere, characteristics he shares with Mr. Darcy, among other admirable characters in Austen's oeuvre. Being able to evoke an emotional reaction in Reginald is one of the things that not only pleases Lady Susan, giving her a sense of power, but also attracts her to him. Lady Susan tells Mrs. Johnson,

> "Oh! how delightful it was, to watch the variations of his Countenance while I spoke, to see the struggle between returning Tenderness & the remains of Displeasure. There is something agreable in feelings so easily worked on. Not that I envy him their possession, nor would for the world have such myself, but they are very convenient when one wishes to influence the passions of another. And yet this Reginald, whom a very few words from me softened at once into the utmost submission, & rendered more tractable, more attached, more devoted than ever, would have left me in the first angry swelling of his proud heart without deigning to seek an explanation! – " (57)

Susan does not like it when "this Reginald" is angry with her because the irascible emotion provides him with a defence against her influence. But she is telling the reader something very important here as regards Reginald's future with Frederica, something we should bear in mind when interpreting the conclusion: he has a propensity to be tender and devoted. The reader judges these qualities to be good, although we evaluate them positively for very different reasons than for their convenience to Lady Susan's designs. She wants to punish him for his pride by dismissing him or "'marrying & teizing him for ever'" (57), but considers both courses of action "'too violent.'" Her harshness contrasts with his softness in this contretemps, but it is Reginald's aptitude to make peace and not Lady Susan's unappeased desire to punish that appears the more amiable quality. If there is to be a happy ending, it turns out that Reginald's values, and not Susan's, must be affirmed.

Malleability and Firmness

Should men be intractable and implacable, as Mr. Darcy announces himself to be near the beginning of *Pride and Prejudice*? Should they nurse resentment, as Frederick Wentworth does for almost a decade? Should a man be firm in defying his older relations, as Mr. Knightley claims he would be (if he had them)? Or should he be pliable, as we see Edmund Bertram is (excepting his resolution to be ordained) until he finds out the truth about Mary Crawford's beliefs regarding the seriousness of adultery? As a youthful writer, Jane Austen is already experimenting with the kinds of faults a hero can be permitted to have in a novel before he finds himself disqualified from that role. How imperfect can a character be before he or she falls off the scale of acceptable conduct? Austen seems to want to avoid with both her male and female characters the creation of "Pictures of Perfection" that she will later claim make her "sick and wicked."[15] However, this desire to create mixed characters requires some skilful navigation. The difference between being stupid or deluded, on the one hand, or actually approving of vice, on the other, seems to create the dividing line. In the conclusion of *Lady Susan*, Austen's narrative voice enjoys her own recklessness and defiance of sentimental convention yet indulges the reader in a happy ending achieved by the defeat of vice: "Frederica was therefore fixed in the family of her Uncle & Aunt till such time as Reginald De Courcy could be talked, flattered, & finessed into an affection for her – which, allowing leisure for the conquest of his attachment to her Mother, for his abjuring all future attachments, & detesting the Sex, might be reasonably looked for in the course of a Twelvemonth. Three Months might have done it in general, but Reginald's feelings were no less lasting than lively" (77). Here the narrator assuredly invites the reader to laugh at Reginald. His "lasting" and "lively" feelings make him a woman-hater for slightly longer than most men in his situation.

But Austen gives with one hand and takes away with the other: she does assure us that Reginald has more lasting feelings than most. The sad truth, however, seems to be that a few months at the outside are all that is necessary for most men to find consolation elsewhere. "Fixed," "family," "flattered," "finessed," "affection for": Austen expertly lines up her alliterated words to suggest the way families deal with their wayward young people. The fricative "f" in this rhetorical flourish is a sound that poets often use to convey scorn and disdain. However, is Reginald's susceptibility to these machinations not proof that his character is neither stubbornly vindictive nor spiteful? Frederick Wentworth outlasts him, but would Frederick not have been happier if he had surrendered to his curiosity to know what had happened to Anne, to his actual desire to sound out her intentions again, a year or two after their separation?

Reginald De Courcy has two options and chooses ill for himself. It is up to others to choose for him if he is to be rescued. The narrator seems to think landing in this situation is not a bad thing – it is a funny thing. Indeed, Reginald makes himself ridiculous with his preposterous claims to a "lasting and lively" love with the devious Lady Susan when he will marry her daughter less than twelve months later. It is ludicrous that he inveighs against the female sex when he will be content to settle down with a member thereof so expeditiously. The narrator of *Lady Susan* is as derisive about the "plans and decisions of mortals" as the narrator of *Mansfield Park* will be. Human security about the state of one's own emotions is one of the main targets of her satire, but she treats such self-assurance as merely a folly, not a vice.

Though Reginald is foolish, and temporarily disgusted with women in general because of one woman in particular, no one in the novella thinks he deserves everlasting punishment, or even that he is unusually bad. They are, rather, happy in their knowledge that he is a manageable young man who will recover. Letter 40, from Lady De Courcy to Catherine, overtly declares her intention to manipulate her son:

> Reginald is returned, not to ask our consent to his marrying Lady Susan, but to tell us they are parted forever! ... He is so very low that I have not the heart to ask questions; but

> I hope we shall soon know all. This is the most joyful hour he has ever given us since the day of his birth … Pray bring all my Grand-Children; & your dear Neice is included, of course; I long to see her. It has been a sad, heavy winter hitherto, without Reginald, & seeing nobody from Churchill. I never found the season so dreary before; but this happy meeting will make us young again. Frederica runs much in my thoughts, & when Reginald has recovered his usual good spirits (as I trust he soon will), we will try to rob him of his heart once more, & I am full of hopes of seeing their hands joined at no great distance. Yr. affec: Mother, C. DE COURCY. (73)[16]

When assailed, will Reginald's persevering devotion to Lady Susan crumble? Yes. But aside from this potentially damning detail, Austen affirms other positive qualities his mother values in Reginald: "'his usual good spirits,'" whose absence have made the past season a "'sad, heavy winter'" for his parents.

Infinite malleability is not a good quality in any person, and so, in the later novels, the less easily swayed characters of Fitzwilliam Darcy and George Knightley, and perhaps Henry Tilney, will stand out among Austen's heroes as men whose future constancy may be presumed. Frederick Wentworth, Edward Ferrars, and Edmund Bertram have demerits, but all seem inclined to faithfulness once settled, and Frederick has the additional virtue of reorienting his heart to his old love once he realizes she is the greater prize than the younger women flinging themselves at him. The assurance of male constancy is, for Austen, a quality that is paramount in her happy endings for her heroines. However, among these, Austen singles out only George Knightley as having the quality of alleviating tedium and sorrow by his presence. In this he is like Reginald De Courcy. She makes Reginald a complex character through these tactics of indicting his weakness and yet assuring us of his general liveliness and virtuous tendencies. She accomplishes this narrative feat by a kind of subterfuge in plain sight. Although he is too easily won over by charm, he is a good-natured companion. Although he is inclined to be cheerful, he has a temper roused by indignation at injustice and falsehood. One could say that, for Austen, as will be the case with Mr. Darcy and Mr. Knightley, a certain amount of prickliness or charmlessness is a better indicator of a man's choosiness than is facile charm, the allure of a Willoughby or a Wickham. However, Reginald is far more easily deceived than are the heroes of *Pride and Prejudice* and *Emma*.

Being gullible, Reginald is unable to extricate himself by his own powers of perception and judgment. On the other hand, he is self-aware enough to realize eventually that this lack of self-sufficiency is his predicament. In letter 36, where he declares to Susan his renunciation of her, Reginald accuses her of misbehaviour and ascribes his escape to the help of others, not his own discernment:

> "That you have corresponded with him [Manwaring] ever since your leaving Langford – not with his wife – but with him – & that he now visits you every day. Can you, dare

> you deny it? & all this at the time when I was an encouraged, an accepted Lover! From what have I not escaped! I have only to be grateful. Far from me be all complaint, & every sigh of regret. My own Folly had endangered me, *my Preservation I owe to the kindness, the Integrity of another."* (69–70, my emphasis)

Reginald, if not as good at detecting hypocrisy as he originally thought he was, is at least grateful for his eventual enlightenment. His admission here demonstrates a maturity well beyond the grasp of all of Austen's fools, and it reads like the self-castigating illuminations of Austen's later heroines Elizabeth Bennet and Emma Woodhouse.

Reginald thus ends his relationship with Lady Susan with these words:

> After such a discovery as this, you will scarcely affect further wonder at my meaning in bidding you Adieu. My Understanding is at length restored, & teaches me no less to abhor the Artifices which had subdued me than to despise myself for the weakness on which their strength was founded. R. DE COURCY. (70)

Reginald ascribes both his falling in love with Susan and his disabuse to outside forces. What is missing is free consent and spontaneous affection inspired by real goodness. He has pursued a false good, which he had ceased to know was false. It is remarkable that, given his inclination to anger, Reginald does not directly insult Lady Susan but rather faults himself for the weakness the author has made him suffer. This manly acknowledgment of his own deficiency is another quality that elevates the otherwise lamentably weak De Courcy.

The Narrative Conclusion

As she does in the conclusion of all the later novels, in *Lady Susan* Austen detaches us from the protagonist by eliminating her spoken word and, indeed, her written word. But what is the narrator's attitude towards Reginald? In the conclusion, Reginald is still, as before, the passive victim of persuasion in the form of flattery and finessing. The affection thereby produced seems almost the same as his feelings for Susan, a delusion manufactured by persuasion. Reginald's love for Lady Susan vanishes not because of a spontaneous affection for Frederica, although he had already become her champion earlier in the action, but because he can be worked on, just as Susan had noted.

Through the sincere affection Frederica has conceived for Reginald, Austen has already confirmed that not all love is the result of flattery and finessing. But does the young Jane Austen think love is always evanescent? Is the later Mary Crawford ventriloquizing Austen herself when she chillingly predicts the inevitable subsidence of Henry's passion for Fanny? "'I know that a wife you *loved* would be the happiest of women and that even when you ceased to love, she would yet find in you the liberality and good-breeding of a gentleman,'" Mary declares to the incredulous Henry

(*MP*, II.12.343). Austen tempers this cynical view with ironically showing that love is more permanent than cynics suppose: both the Crawfords unhappily discover that real love, fixed on a good object, does not evaporate as rapidly as they imagine it will earlier in the novel. Edmund's supposedly everlasting love for Mary endures only briefly because it is based on an illusion, as is Reginald's. In *Lady Susan,* Austen imagines Reginald as that good object Susan has lost and Frederica has gained.

Reginald's feelings are real, even if devoted to an imaginary object; they are also intense, but Austen expects her readers to agree with her that intensity does not equal longevity. Her one concession to the great strength of Reginald's feelings is her playful suggestion that he will require a twelvemonth at the outside to recover from his renunciation of Susan and to attach himself to Frederica. Of all the poseurs in Austen who acquire another's affection through pretense, only Willoughby in *Sense and Sensibility* has the equivalent honour of inspiring a prolonged devotion. Though Austen gives no dates, she shockingly indicates that Marianne marries Colonel Brandon before transferring her heart entirely to him. Critics run the gamut from believing this twist a supremely unjust and soul-crushing imposition of boring morality on the winningly emotional Marianne to Austen's finishing touch on the real heroine of the novel, who gets the reward of the morally best and most independently moneyed single man.

Marianne's case is more complicated than Reginald's. Willoughby shares with Henry Crawford the distinction of being the most complex of Austen's charming villains, and he does indeed love Marianne – as far as he is capable of loving. There is good in Willoughby, though he is not what she believes him to be. But, the narrator tells us, "Marianne Dashwood was born to an extraordinary fate. She was born to discover the falsehood of her own opinions, and to counteract by her conduct her most favorite maxims" (*SS*, III.14.429). Austen rewards faithful, single-hearted lovers like Elinor Dashwood and Fanny Price with their hearts' desires, but no one would call it a punishment for Edward Ferrars to end up with Elinor instead of Lucy Steele, or for Elizabeth Bennet to end up with Mr. Darcy instead of Mr. Wickham or the only mildly interesting Colonel Fitzwilliam. Although Austen sees a value in an unchanging first love, which she will ratify in the last completed novel, she also does not think being an inconsolable spinster or widower is a happy fate. It is better to have done with the illusion and marry the really virtuous person, even if he or she is less fascinating. The glamour partly derived from the characters – Reginald, Marianne, Elizabeth, or Fanny – seeing a reflection of themselves in their love objects, or imagining the charming character as adhering to their own principles, when in fact Susan Vernon, John Willoughby, George Wickham, and Mary Crawford do not combine charm with love of truth and honour. What happens to love when the beloved object is revealed to be a sham? Austen clearly indicates the emotion takes time to dissipate, and the sore spot is still there. But she is not interested in having her characters pine after an unattainable object that is, moreover, unworthy. Edward Ferrars finds Elinor when he grows up and realizes Lucy is ignorant and selfish, and Marianne finds Colonel Brandon.

Yet Austen will have Reginald, like Edmund Bertram, marry after discovering an affection for his future wife. Readers often scorn Edmund but pardon Marianne. Austen affectionately satirizes both in the final chapters of their novels, but it is Edmund, like Reginald, who loves the person he is marrying.

Willoughby and Lady Susan both pretend to be virtuous to lure in their younger prey, who are sincere, even severe, about love and virtue. Susan has no time for "romantic nonsense." Her real beloved, Manwaring, has a name that is a homonym for "mannering," a word replete with connotations of acting, and she ends up married to the man she thought of as a punishment for Frederica – "But she *shall* be punished, she *shall* have him [Sir James]" (29). Reginald is spared such a marriage. Even if Austen deflates his romantic hyperbole, she attests to its sincerity. It is well for him that even strong affections can be directed to a more worthy object. Austen gives to him the last name De Courcy, which sounds like "de coeur," from the heart, even if its more direct French etymology is "de cour," from the court.[17]

"Abjuring all future attachments" is for Austen always a laughable act, as she knows the inconstancy of the human heart, even as a teenager, better than her characters do. However, the affectionate concern we see Reginald to be capable of in his brief interactions with the distressed Frederica is the most positive character trait he shares with Austen's later incarnation of the infatuated, moralistic, upright young man, Edmund Bertram: Reginald De Courcy has a heart.

CHAPTER THREE

Parental Tyranny and Filial Disobedience: Socratic Irony and Metalepsis in *Northanger Abbey*

To begin perfect happiness at the respective ages of twenty-six and eighteen is to do pretty well; and professing myself moreover convinced that the General's unjust interference, so far from being really injurious to their felicity, was perhaps rather conducive to it, by improving their knowledge of each other, and adding strength to their attachment, I leave it to be settled, by whomsoever it may concern, whether the tendency of this work be altogether to recommend parental tyranny, or reward filial disobedience.

(*Northanger Abbey*, II.16.261)

The narrator of *Northanger Abbey* is not deeply concerned about Catherine Morland's tears or the testing of Henry Tilney's devotion at the end of the novel's last chapter, knowing as she does that parental interference in a love relationship is a traditional method by which a narrative cements the lovers' devotion to each other. In this novel, the narrator allows a girl who does not seem born to be a heroine to nonetheless suffer the sentimental novel's pangs of a forbidden relationship, even when this heroine's own parents are the mildest of guardians. General Tilney's "parental tyranny" is so useful narratively that Jane Austen appears to recommend it, while she understands this recommendation might pose a problem to the moral of her story. In terms of the parent-child relationship, the narrator proposes two almost equally bad morals: recommending "parental tyranny" or rewarding "filial disobedience." This is a metalepsis of the type Austen will recur to at some point in every novel, but most particularly in her endings. "Metalepsis" is, according to Gérard Genette, "any intrusion by the extradiegetic narrator or narratee into the diegetic universe … or the inverse."[1] Cohn and Gleich explain that "metalepsis at the discourse level is (in the sense established by Genette) a kind of 'figure': it consists in the habit of certain narrators interrupting the description of the routine actions of their characters by digressions; it results in a light-hearted and playful synchronization of the narration with the narrated events."[2] Austen's narrator "intrudes" (if one can call it intrusion in the days before the storyteller was forbidden to interrupt his or her own story) to propose a bad moral to her reader, expecting the audience to understand her playfulness. She intrudes also to speak of her characters as real people, existing somewhere one could visit, in the real world. Outside of the worlds of tragedy and modern and postmodern art, metalepsis almost always indicates jocularity. It is, as Cohn and Gleich point out, playful. It often comes as a surprise to the reader and prompts a startled recognition that the author is transgressing the boundaries between the world she is telling about and the world in which she is telling.

As is always the case in her novels, Austen jokingly draws attention to her potential deleterious moral effect on her reader, placing her works, perhaps, among those Richard Sheridan's Lydia Languish and her maid Lucy hastily hide in *The Rivals*. (They stow away every popular novel when Lydia's guardian comes to visit unexpectedly and set out Fordyce's sermons as an acceptable text for his watchful eyes.) The narrator accuses herself in the end of *Northanger Abbey* of perverting the didactic end of a work, a function she had claimed for it in the famous defence of the novel in that book's earlier pages. What did she expect readers to make of the happy sort of frivolousness in this self-mockery? In undercutting the undercutting, Austen produces a kind of double negative effect, which aids her in creating the speed of delivery. Austen's strategy of metalepsis aids her in the creation of Socratic irony – "a pretense of ignorance and of willingness to learn from another assumed in order to make the other's false conceptions conspicuous by adroit questioning"[3] – to present to the reader what at first appears to be an immoral proposition. To Austen, the end of a novel seems incomplete without this tactic she almost invariably has recourse to: the apparent dismissal of her own work. What she means by this dismissal, in the Socratic tradition, is precisely the opposite. She is, in her own words, preparing to "speed truth into the world."[4]

That parents could be tyrannous, no English reader of Shakespeare could doubt. And it was not in fiction alone that such parents were to be found. Samuel Johnson, Austen's favourite writer in prose, had said of real parental tyranny in *Rambler* 148:

> The regal and parental tyrant differ only in the extent of their dominions, and the number of their slaves. The same passions cause the same miseries; except that seldom any prince, however despotic, has so far shaken off all awe of the public eye as to venture upon those freaks of injustice which are sometimes indulged under the secrecy of a private dwelling. Capricious injunctions, partial decisions, unequal allotments, distributions of reward not by merit but by fancy, and punishments regulated not by the degree of the offence, but by the humour of the judge, are too frequent where no power is known but that of a [parent].[5]

Johnson is pointing out the evils that can arise when one or two persons have unlimited power in the family. Injustice will prevail when no counterbalancing power checks a domestic autocrat. Children have no protection if everything takes place within the walls of the home, since their innocence does not matter to the arbitrary parent. This paragraph could certainly have inspired the creation of General Tilney, or of Mrs. Ferrars, Lady Catherine de Bourgh, Sir Thomas Bertram, Mr. and Mrs. Price, or even Sir Walter Elliot. Like Johnson, Austen sees very clearly the probability that parents will be prejudiced and unjust if they see no reason to be otherwise. Austen is deeply interested in the role of parents in her heroines' and heroes' lives, and she will create some of the most memorable tyrannical parents – and aunts – in English literature. The role of the comic narrative closure is in part ensuring that justice is meted out: Austen often focuses on the conversion or correction of unjust parents in those closures. In her portrayal of Henry Tilney's father, Austen joins a narratively useful stereotype, like Old Capulet in *Romeo and Juliet*, to a probable and realistic character.[6] Does her flippant final sentence evacuate moral seriousness from the conclusion of her novel or, rather, does it not make the reader confront the true problem facing Catherine Morland and even more particularly Henry Tilney: how can he, a clergyman, be more virtuous than his unvirtuous parent in his earnest pursuit of marriage when the unjust General has authority over his son?

In all her novels, Austen makes the acquisition of a parents' permission to marry a dramatic moment; it is often a last hurdle to be surmounted. However, not all her parents are tyrants. One would think that, with Mrs. Bennet's eagerness to marry off her daughters in *Pride and Prejudice*, for instance, consent would be a foregone conclusion, but Austen typically turns to such moments for drama specifically because the conclusion is not foregone. Even in *Pride and Prejudice*, Mr. Bennet might withhold his consent from the union of Darcy and Elizabeth – as he does conclusively in the case of Mr. Collins's proposal. He is justifiably worried about Elizabeth's future happiness.[7] Mrs. Ferrars relents a little towards Edward and Elinor; Sir Thomas, who once feared a union between his niece Fanny and one of his sons, now rejoices in it; poultry thieves jolt Mr. Woodhouse's fears of housebreaking enough for him to accept the marriage of Emma and Mr. Knightley; and Captain Wentworth's fortune and handsome appearance convince Anne Elliot's spendthrift father that he is as good a match as his least favorite daughter is going to make. Austen is always thinking of what will convince the parents of her heroine or hero to allow them to marry; she is always thinking of the impediments of fortune or disposition in her final chapters. Thus, it is impossible to understand Austen's endings unless one considers the relationship between parents and children, and what rules about parental consent or blessing prevailed in Austen's time.

Parental Consent: The Fifth Commandment and English Marriage Law

In *Northanger Abbey*, Mr. and Mrs. Morland at first withhold their consent from the marriage of Catherine and Henry, not because they dislike Henry, not because they are angry at the General, but because the General has a right to forbid his grown son to marry the lady he has chosen, the lady who has accepted his proposal. The last action of the novel is the overcoming of General Tilney's "unjust" opposition so that the marriage can take place. But Henry is not a minor, and Catherine's parents approve the match, so why can the General exercise such power? Would it not be a reasonable thing to disregard him – for Henry and Catherine both think he will never give his blessing – and go ahead with the wedding? Henry is not only a free adult but also a minister in the Church of England, a position that might be said to give him some power even over his own father as a spiritual authority. Why should Austen, in the last act of her drama, make him bend to conventional proprieties?

In spite of Austen's joking about proposing an immoral moral, this need for parental blessing as obstacle is both conventional and very real. She fashions the trajectory of the novel to present the reader with the need to iron out adult child–parent relationships even as she parodies the conventional place of parental obstacles in the novels of her day. There is no ending, no wedding, if General Tilney cannot be brought around to supporting Henry's decision to propose to Catherine. The final chapter begins with the Morlands' balking only at the General's forbidding of the marriage before granting their own consent. Austen reminds the reader that they are the mildest and most unsuspicious of parents; moreover, they know the General has done their daughter a wrong that some might consider unforgivable. Nonetheless, they sustain the view that a parent's consent is necessary. In their view, forging ahead with a marriage without it would be wrong. Therefore, because Catherine is a minor, the English Marriage Act of 1753 comes into play, as does the fifth commandment.

To what extent is Henry, already in his majority and already in charge of a parish, compelled to obey his father or obtain his blessing for his marriage? Austen says clearly:

> There was but one obstacle, in short, to be mentioned; but till that one was removed, it must be impossible for them to sanction the engagement. Their tempers were mild, but their principles were steady, and while his parent so expressly forbade the connection, they could not allow themselves to encourage it. That the General should come forward to solicit the alliance, or that he should even very heartily approve it,

> they were not refined enough to make any parading stipulation; but the decent appearance of consent must be yielded, and that once obtained – and their own hearts made them trust that it could not be very long denied – their willing approbation was instantly to follow. His consent was all that they wished for. (II.16.258–9)

Principle requires that the parents of the bride refrain from granting their consent to the marriage if even one parent of the groom disapproves. That principle is, primarily, a biblical one. It was also a legal one: because of the aforementioned 1753 Marriage Act, it was illegal for any person under the age of twenty-one to marry without the consent of their parents,[8] and a clergyman performing such a ceremony was liable to fourteen years transportation if found guilty. But the legal principle was itself based on the commandment "Honour thy father and thy mother" (Ex 20:12).[9] The primal obligation of obedience and respect from child to parent is enshrined in the Decalogue, which was a foundational text in Austen's England. Lisa O'Connell has recently shown how critical the debates over marriage, free consent, and filial obligations were to the development of the marriage plot that so dominates the nineteenth century.[10] Austen's work is part of this focus on the religious and legal meaning of marriage.

In this final chapter of *Northanger Abbey*, Austen is balancing her own need for drama – a final obstacle to be overcome before the happy union of Catherine and Henry – with an investigation into a problem that concerned her throughout her career, even up to *Persuasion*. At what age does a child cease to have an obligation to obey parents? When does filial obligation cease to be the "primary directive"? For Austen, it seems to end only when the parent himself or herself ceases to impose it, whether that be General Tilney near the beginning of Austen's writing career or Lady Russell and Sir Walter Elliot close to its end. No Austen heroine marries without her own parents' consent, and Edward Ferrars is the only other hero with a still-living parent who objects, and even she is mollified.

Surprisingly to modern readers, Henry and Catherine do not resent the necessary separation the General's angry stubbornness enforces upon them: "The young people could not be surprised at a decision like this. They felt and they deplored – but they could not resent it; and they parted … Henry returned to what was now his only home, to watch over his young plantations, and extend his improvements for her sake, to whose share in them he looked anxiously forward; and Catherine remained at Fullerton to cry" (II.16.172). Henry does not go home to Northanger. This is not because Henry chooses not to return, but because his father forbids it. Henry has already earned his heroic stature with the reader by his angry defiance of the General, but he does not increase it romantically by direct disobedience after the Morlands lay down the law. Respect for Catherine's situation, and for her parents, seems to move him more than respect for his own father. In fact, in a touching moment of the narrative, Austen depicts him remodeling his house to Catherine's taste, looking forward "anxiously" to her living there, all the while thinking the General's will to be unalterable. Catherine's tears attest to her desire to be with him. They want to be with each other, but they remain apart. Why? Because Catherine, a minor until she is twenty-one, is legally obligated to obey her parents in regard to marriage, and they on principle will not defy the General's ban on that marriage.[11]

The Morlands are not so rule-bound that they do not allow Catherine to receive letters from Henry, as we are subtly informed: "Whether the torments of absence were softened by a clandestine correspondence, let us not inquire. Mr. and Mrs. Morland never did – they had been too kind to exact any promise; and whenever Catherine received a letter, as, at that time, happened pretty often, they always looked another way" (II.16.259). Henry and Catherine's engagement may be informal as long as his father withholds consent, but it is enough for the Morlands that the two are sincerely committed. However, other, more proper, parents might not have allowed this correspondence. Austen often uses as a plot device the understood impropriety of letter writing between unmarried persons: in *Emma,* between Jane Fairfax and Frank Churchill; in *Mansfield Park,* between Henry Crawford, using his sister as his proxy, and Fanny Price (and also between Edmund and Fanny, but that is more of a grey area). In *Sense and Sensibility,* Marianne writes to Willoughby, although they are not engaged, but her doing so seems proof to her family and others that they are indeed engaged. In *Pride and Prejudice,* when Mr. Darcy writes to Elizabeth Bennet after her refusal, he justifies the letter and attempts to keep any word of affection out of it, yet it is still a breach of etiquette, although in his case it is not direct disobedience to a parent. He hand-delivers the missive to her, as Frederick Wentworth does his to Anne Elliot, in such a way that will ensure no one else observes it.

Some parents, more scrupulous about these standards than the Morlands, might even have confiscated the letters. Modern readers might smile upon the Morlands because of their mildness, but the narrator also shows them to be rigorous about not acting as the parents of a young woman chasing a fortune might do. Readers are to understand they are morally good people in part *because* they await the General's decision. However, to return to biblical injunctions, writing letters is not expressly forbidden – perhaps for the simple reason that in the time of the Exodus, few people would have been literate.

In Judaic and Christian law, when does the obligation to obey one's parents cease? The modern reader might feel there is no such obligation, or believe it ceases when the young person is no longer living under the parental roof, or when one can vote or drive. This is to misunderstand the history of the commandment entirely, for it has nothing to do with the child's financial dependence upon the parent. In Ephesians, St. Paul says this is the first commandment to have a promise attached to it, emphasizing its importance. In the 2016 film *Love and Friendship*, based on *Lady Susan*, writer/director Whit Stillman has Lady Susan manipulate her daughter by invoking this central teaching on family relationships in the Judeo-Christian tradition (and reveals her own Romish leanings by nominating this the fourth commandment, as it is in the Roman Catholic tradition as well as the Lutheran).[12] The Morlands understand that Henry is bound by this obedience even though he is a grown man and has independent means. As a Christian minister, he would be even more aware than the English layperson of its import, although he initially seems more disinclined than the Morlands to think of it at this juncture. It might even seem that he complies more out of deference to the Morlands' authority than out of deference to General Tilney's, but he complies nonetheless.

Shortly after *Northanger Abbey* came out, an early reviewer compared another Austen novel to it unfavorably in terms of the two novels' approaches to filial obedience in just this question of marriage and filial duty. In March 1818, *The British Critic* spoke of *Persuasion* as inferior to the novel published in tandem with it, *Northanger*, and objected to the "moral" of *Persuasion*, "which seems to be, that young people should always marry according to their own inclinations and upon their own judgment."[13] That is a response to Austen's ironic claim in the last chapter of *Persuasion*: "Who can be in doubt of what followed? When any two young people take it into their heads to marry, they are pretty sure by perseverance to carry their point, be they ever so poor, or ever so imprudent, or ever so little likely to be necessary to each other's ultimate comfort" (*P*, II.12). Here, Austen uses the rhetorical device of hypophora to answer her own question that she has just raised. Hypophora is the rhetorical technique of answering what at first appears to be a rhetorical question, or at least a question the speaker does not intend to answer. Austen asks, "Who can be in doubt of what followed?" but she does not wait for an answer. She immediately exempts Anne and Frederick from the pejoratives lined up in this provocative sentence. The reviewer's disapproval proves that her initial sentence drew his attention more than her qualification of it did. Modern readers might not read that sentence as her contemporary audience would have: for Austen it is probably far more explosive and potentially dangerous. It is clear that her audience would also have watched Henry and Catherine's response to their parents' injunctions with a critical eye and judged them on the basis of their reactions to his unjust father's resistance to their engagement.

Fordyce in his famous sermons (which Austen knew well) provides an example of some of the most famous advice of the era on the matter of filial obedience:

> Of filial duty in all its branches she will naturally acquit herself best, who has the deepest sense of religion. "Keep thy father's commandments, and forsake not the law of thy mother. Bind them continually upon thy heart, and tie them about thy neck. When thou goest, it shall lead thee; when thou sleepest, it shall keep thee; and when thou wakest it shall talk with thee. Whoso revileth his father or his mother, his lamp shall be put out in obscure darkness. The eye that mocketh at his father, and despiseth to obey his mother, the ravens of the valley shall pick it out, and the young eagles shall eat it." Jesus was subject unto his parents. "Children obey your parents in the Lord; for this is right. Honour thy father and mother (which is the first commandment with promise) that it may be well with thee, and thou mayest live long on the earth." All this a Christian daughter has read with attention, and reflects upon with awe. It corresponds, in substance, with the instinct of nature, which it contributes

> at once to corroborate and exalt. She who truly reverences her parent in heaven, would tremble at the thought of dishonouring his representatives on earth. From their authority she has acquired the idea of his; and this last, including all that can be conceived of great and good, is the commanding idea of her life.[14]

Austen never shows Catherine reading sermons, even in her youthful exposure to *Elegant Extracts* and other works. However, the two young people's lack of resentment of the General's tyrannical interference, which the narrator insists on, needs to be explained to an audience confronted with it after a lapse of two hundred years. Fordyce's standards are not in any way out of the ordinary and present a norm for the period. Georgian Englishmen and women were taught, based on St. Paul's portrayal of earthly governance as a reflection of divine authority, that those placed in authority were God's substitute, at least in some way. The Reverend Edward Hull in *The Duty of Obedience to Civil Governors*, published in 1819, cited all the usual texts so important in the English resistance to the Age of Revolution, in particular Romans 13:1, 2: "Let every soul be subject to the Higher Powers, for there is no power but of God: the powers that be are ordained of God: whosoever, therefore, resisteth the power, resisteth the ordinance of God."[15] Parents, too, had biblical and natural law to rely on for their authority. As the Bishop of Exeter had argued a century earlier,

> Before the 5th Commandment was given by *Moses*, and much before it was repeated and reinforc'd in the *New Testament*

> there had been many *Fathers without natural Affection*, who had extremely exceeded their Paternal Commission, and grosly abus'd their Paternal Power, to the great Hurt, Vexation, Ruin, Destruction, and even Death of their Children; and yet all the Precepts we meet with either in the Law or the Gospel, relating to the Behaviour of Children to their Parents, are to this tenour; *Honour thy Father and Mother; who so Curseth Father or Mother let him die the Death; Children obey your Parents in all things, for this is Right, &c.* Not one Word or Hint do I remember in the whole Bible, directing, or giving allowance to Children, to strike, cast off, and much less to kill their Parents, in Case of their Cruelty, Madness or Rage, or for any Provocation whatsoever.[16]

To disobey or give offence to a parent was a very grave sin, as Austen would have seen illustrated in the remarkable episode of Samuel Johnson's self-imposed penance narrated by James Boswell in his biography of the great eighteenth-century sage, a book Austen knew. In 1784, Johnson, at age seventy-five, still felt guilty for having disobeyed his father once at the age of twenty-five. He undertook to expiate before God and man this only disobedience to his father of which he was aware: "During the last visit which the Doctor made to Lichfield, the friends with whom he was staying missed him one morning at the breakfast-table … He had set off from Lichfield at a very early hour, without mentioning to any of the family whither he was going. The day passed without the return of the illustrious guest, and the party began to be very uneasy on his account, when, just before the supper-hour, the door opened, and the Doctor stalked into the room."

Dr. Johnson did not always offer explanations of his odd behavior, but in this case, he spoke of his reasons very feelingly:

> A solemn silence of a few minutes ensued, nobody daring to inquire the cause of his absence, which was at length relieved by Johnson addressing the lady of the house ...: "Madam, I beg your pardon for the abruptness of the departure from your house this morning, but I was constrained to it by my conscience. Fifty years ago, Madam, on this day, I committed a breach of filial piety, which has ever since lain heavy on my mind, and has not till this day been expiated. My father, you recollect, was a bookseller, and had long been in the habit of attending Uttoxeter market, and opening a stall for the sale of his books during that day. Confined to his bed by indisposition, he requested me, this time fifty years ago, to visit the market, and attend the stall in his place. But, Madam, my pride prevented me from doing my duty, and I gave my father a refusal. To do away the sin of this disobedience, I this day went in a post-chaise to Uttoxeter, and going into the market at the time of high business, uncovered my head, and stood with it bare an hour before the stall which my father had formerly used, exposed to the sneers of the standers-by and the inclemency of the weather; a penance by which I trust I have propitiated heaven for this only instance, I believe, of contumacy towards my father."[17]

Johnson's act of penitence stands commemorated in his statue in Lichfield. Boswell's readers were moved by this tale of filial piety, not to the ridicule of Johnson's initial onlookers, but to reverence, seeing that so great (and so old) a man should feel so deeply an offence against a parent who was not even alive any longer. In his seventies, Johnson could remember with pain only one instance of disobedience to his father. Henry Tilney is about the young Johnson's age and thus no longer a minor. Austen knows that he is not bound by the law to respect his father's word on the matter; he is bound by his Christian duty, as all of Austen's readers would have understood.

Austen is thinking of exactly this kind of expected obedience in the final pages of her novel; the hero and heroine's last test is one of patience and obedience, and they pass it. The reader, setting aside questions about whether or not Henry actually loves Catherine, or whether or not the General is a symbol of oppressive patriarchy, can see what occurs in the plot more clearly. Instead of eloping, Henry and Catherine wait. Austen then rewards them with the *deus ex machina* of Eleanor's fortuitous marriage, which mollifies the General, so he gives Henry leave "to be a fool if he liked it" (*NA*, II.16.260). In fact, the disobedience of Henry consists only in the proposal, and the disobedience of Catherine only in receiving and writing letters of which she must know Henry's father would disapprove, despite there being no explicit injunction against them. Austen clearly approves of both actions, in spite of their irregularity, so she seems to take a position resembling an Aristotelian mean. The "Great Forbidder," General Tilney, is reduced comically to a convenient plot device for the author, and the not very disobedient children mildly await his paternal nod before their union, their love made stronger by his opposition and their forced separation. Rather than destroying the young people's chance for happiness, General Tilney creates it and provides the opportunity for the comic ending of the novel. Remarkably, the narrator seems to justify the General's unreasonable behaviour for two reasons: first, it is expedient for her to have a misfortune befall her hero and heroine, and, second, a parent with divine authority behind him is for her the best kind of insuperable obstacle that allows her to prove her protagonists' devotion. It seems the novel, if readers are to take a stand on the narrator's final dilemma, recommends parental tyranny.

Yet it also seems to reward filial disobedience. The conclusion features the famous meta-narrative declaration by the narrator: "The anxiety, which in this state of their attachment must be the portion of Henry and Catherine, and of all who loved either, as to its final event, can hardly extend, I fear, to the bosom of my readers, who will see in the tell-tale compression of the pages before them, that we are all hastening together to perfect felicity" (*NA*, II.16.259). Austen, however, is playing with temporal extensions in this final chapter, as she imagines the reader's lack of concern over the young couple's fate. She makes Catherine and Henry wait longer than they have actually known each other (that is, February through April) to be married (from the proposal in April to an indeterminate date in the fall after Eleanor's late summer wedding).[18] Catherine, Henry, and Eleanor's filial piety must be proven for them to deserve a reward from poetic justice, and extension in time is necessary for their trial. It is not, however, necessary to the reader's, and Austen clearly thinks about and distinguishes between the readers' frame of mind regarding the time left to finish the book in their hands and the time necessary for her characters to accomplish the task she has set for them in the plot. Austen produces more life-like and mixed characters with this last attention to her heroine and hero's actions in response to their parents' commands, but she also plays with the reader's plain sense that this is a fiction and her metaleptic claims to know the characters themselves as real people.

In the end, the novel does reward its hero and heroine, but only after what is considered bad in their behaviour is mitigated by the author. Catherine never deliberately disobeys an order given by her parents; Henry's argument with his father is over the two things that had long been exceptions to the general rule of filial obedience: cooperation in wrong-doing and the choice of a spouse. As Fordyce says in his sermon "On Good Works," in these cases no parent has the right to give such commands, and the child must not obey:

> I will suppose the worst: that they [the parents] are really hard-hearted, and unnaturally rigid. To bear it well will require all the fortitude of faith. Here then is an opportunity for displaying your principles in their utmost power. You are called forth to the conflict, as to a field of battle, where even your sex may reap immortal laurels. She is a heroine indeed, whose regard for her parent no unkindness can conquer.
>
> But they would force you to sacrifice your happiness to a man whom you cannot love. There your submission must stop. No rules of duty can oblige you to involve yourself in misery and temptation, by entering into engagements to love and to honour, where your hearts withhold their consent.[19]

What Henry rightly considers morally wrong is to jilt Catherine when, along with his family, he has given her every expectation that he will be offering marriage to her. His father has also led Catherine to believe that she would be an honoured daughter-in-law:

> Turned from the house, and in such a way! Without any reason that could justify, any apology that could atone for the abruptness, the rudeness, nay, the insolence of it. Henry at a distance – not able even to bid him farewell. Every hope, every expectation from him suspended, at least, and who could say how long? Who could say when they might meet again? And all this by such a man as General Tilney, so polite, so well bred, and heretofore so particularly fond of her! It was as incomprehensible as it was mortifying and grievous. From what it could arise, and where it would end, were considerations of equal perplexity and alarm. … What could all this mean but an intentional affront? (II.13.233–4)

In the face of this extreme behaviour, Catherine blames herself: "By some means or other she must have had the misfortune to offend him [General Tilney]. Eleanor had wished to spare her from so painful a notion, but Catherine could not believe it possible that any injury or any misfortune could provoke such ill will against a person not connected, or, at least, not supposed to be connected with it" (II.13.234). The danger of being driven from the abbey without even the money to go home occurs to her and to Eleanor: "Catherine had never thought on the subject till that moment, but, upon examining her purse, was convinced that but for this kindness of her friend, she might have been turned from the house without even the means of getting home; and the distress in which she must have been thereby involved filling the minds of both, scarcely another word was said by either during the time of their remaining together" (II.13.237). This realization undermines her earlier proud declaration that she should not send letters to Eleanor announcing her safe arrival back home: "No, Eleanor, if you are not allowed to receive a letter from me, I am sure I had better not write. There can be no doubt of my getting home safe" (II.13.236). At this point, Eleanor's distress produces Catherine's promise to write – again, not a direct disobedience on either's side, but something Catherine thinks might compromise Eleanor's duty to her father. Eleanor's profound reluctance and embarrassment when carrying out the General's commands in fact shows that she is unwillingly participating in what she thinks is a bad deed, forced to be an agent because of her obligation to him as his daughter.

Although Catherine fears that Henry will calmly go along with his father – and the reader knows this is his usual accepting attitude of both his father's and his elder brother's wrongdoing – she does not expect an outright defiance even if he should be resentful, because of his filial obligation:

> How Henry would think, and feel, and look, when he returned on the morrow to Northanger and heard of her being gone, was a question of force and interest to rise over every other, to be never ceasing, alternately irritating and soothing; it sometimes suggested the dread of his calm

> acquiescence, and at others was answered by the sweetest confidence in his regret and resentment. To the general, of course, he would not dare to speak; but to Eleanor – what might he not say to Eleanor about her? (II.14.239)

Catherine's stay at Northanger has produced no ghosts or skeletons, but it has produced a correct conviction that the General is a tyrant and that Henry and Eleanor order their lives so as not to irritate him in any way.

However, both the younger Tilneys feel that they are tainted by their perceived cooperation with the General's ugly behaviour. Eleanor is forced into doing something she knows is wrong, and Henry refuses to cooperate:

> A very short visit to Mrs. Allen, in which Henry talked at random, without sense or connection, and Catherine, rapt in the contemplation of her own unutterable happiness, scarcely opened her lips, dismissed them to the ecstasies of another tete-a-tete; and before it was suffered to close, she was enabled to judge how far he was sanctioned by parental authority in his present application. On his return from Woodston, two days before, he had been met near the abbey by his impatient father, hastily informed in angry terms of Miss Morland's departure, and ordered to think of her no more.
>
> Such was the permission upon which he had now offered her his hand. The affrighted Catherine, amidst all the terrors of expectation, as she listened to this account, could not but rejoice in the kind caution with which Henry had saved her from the necessity of a conscientious rejection, by engaging

> her faith before he mentioned the subject; and as he proceeded to give the particulars, and explain the motives of his father's conduct, her feelings soon hardened into even a triumphant delight. The general had had nothing to accuse her of, nothing to lay to her charge, but her being the involuntary, unconscious object of a deception which his pride could not pardon, and which a better pride would have been ashamed to own. She was guilty only of being less rich than he had supposed her to be. Under a mistaken persuasion of her possessions and claims, he had courted her acquaintance in Bath, solicited her company at Northanger, and designed her for his daughter-in-law. On discovering his error, to turn her from the house seemed the best, though to his feelings an inadequate proof of his resentment towards herself, and his contempt of her family. (II.15.253–4)

Henry's father has forbidden him to think of Catherine, and it is this express command that Henry disobeys. Catherine sees his proposal half an hour before as a "kind caution" – that is, he does not fully involve her in his own disobedience when he asks for her consent to an engagement. But once her faith is plighted, Catherine does not imagine retracting it. In a moment so unusual for Catherine, the reader must notice it, "her feelings soon hardened into even a triumphant delight." Both Catherine and Henry now realize they have better moral standards than General Tilney, and Henry has withheld important information from Catherine before seeking her promise to marry him. Here Austen shows how the marriage bond is beginning to take its precedence over the filial one, and also how much more seriously engagements were taken as promises at the time. In this second-to-last chapter, Austen is not scrambling to concoct an ending; she is bringing to a head the whole central problem she has created in the Tilney family: the habitual deference to the General as parent, turning him into a tyrant:

> Henry, in having such things to relate of his father, was almost as pitiable as in their first avowal to himself. He blushed for the narrow-minded counsel which he was obliged to expose. The conversation between them at Northanger had been of the most unfriendly kind. Henry's indignation on hearing how Catherine had been treated, on comprehending his father's views, and being ordered to acquiesce in them, had been open and bold. The general, accustomed on every ordinary occasion to give the law in his family, prepared for no reluctance but of feeling, no opposing desire that should dare to clothe itself in words, could ill brook the opposition of his son, steady as the sanction of reason and the dictate of conscience could make it. (II.15.257)

As others have noted, it is only after Catherine, a cherished outsider, has been exposed to and injured by his father's tyrannical rule that Henry can see it for what it is. I recur to Johnson's account of the higher degree of absolutism possible in the privacy of a home rather than in the publicity of a kingdom: "Capricious injunctions, partial decisions, unequal allotments, distributions of reward not by merit but by fancy, and punishments regulated not by the degree of the offence, but by the humour of the judge, are too frequent where no power is known but that of a [parent]." General

Tilney was "prepared for no reluctance but of feeling" – that is, he knows Henry will not condone this kind of behaviour and perhaps even knows Henry is sincerely attached to Catherine, but he does not care in the least. Henry's opposition is, however, "steady as the sanction of reason and the dictate of conscience could make it." Austen's choice of words draws the reader to note that, in this conflict, it is the son, not the father, who has goodness on his side. Thus, in spite of the Bishop of Exeter's argument to the contrary, Austen does believe there are situations in which a child may, perhaps must, disobey a parent. By placing Catherine in their midst, she has applied the shock that will shake up the Tilney family enough to permit both Eleanor and Henry to claim the independence of adults without outraging religious obligations.

Austen continues to use strong terminology associated with virtue as Henry's narrative proceeds: "In such a cause, his anger, though it must shock, could not intimidate Henry, who was sustained in his purpose by a conviction of its justice. He felt himself bound as much in honour as in affection to Miss Morland, and believing that heart to be his own which he had been directed to gain, no unworthy retraction of a tacit consent, no reversing decree of unjustifiable anger, could shake his fidelity, or influence the resolutions it prompted" (II.15.257). "Conviction," "justice," "honour," "fidelity," "resolutions": all these words, applied now to Henry, elevate him above the merely charming and funny suitor, at times worryingly heedless of the rights and wrongs of his elders' doings, and turn him into a moral force. Austen also reminds the reader that Henry's courtship of Catherine was at least in part a response of obedience to his father's order: "believing that heart to be his own which he had been directed to gain." Thus, it is filial duty that has put him in the position of moral peril in which he now finds himself. No other Austen hero is placed in a similar predicament. It seems to have been Austen's design from the beginning to make Henry, the master of parody, undergo a test of his sense of justice, his moral seriousness.

Henry's announcement of his purpose to ask Catherine to marry him is thus a direct disobedience to his father's unjust request but is, ironically, obedience to his father's earlier wishes: "He steadily refused to accompany his father into Herefordshire, an engagement formed almost at the moment to promote the dismissal of Catherine, and as steadily declared his intention of offering her his hand. The general was furious in his anger, and they parted in dreadful disagreement. Henry, in an agitation of mind which many solitary hours were required to compose, had returned almost instantly to [his estate at] Woodston, and, on the afternoon of the following day, had begun his journey to [Catherine's home in] Fullerton" (II.15.257).

The concluding chapters of the novel might seem, as I have said in regard to Catherine's parents, to produce an Aristotelian mean between rigorous deference to parents and lax interpretation of social mores, but what Austen is more likely trying to do is make Henry negotiate between what is due to the General as a father and what is due to God and to Catherine, who, it appears, are on the same side. When Moses Maimonides and John Calvin, among others, confronted the implications of the fifth commandment (or fourth in the Catholic tradition, up to and including Lutheran reformers such as Melanchthon), they came up against marriage and the other laws of God. When we see Eleanor's emotional distress over obeying her father's command, and Henry's refusal to do likewise, we are not seeing a mere repetition of novelistic convention – though it is also that – but rather an early foray (perhaps amended years after the book's initial composition) into the difficult territory of the moral relationships between parents and children that Austen will challenge herself with in every novel. In *Northanger Abbey*, the encounter between parent and child is the most explosive, but we should not forget Mrs. Bennet's threat not to see Elizabeth again if she refuses to marry Mr. Collins, or Elinor Dashwood's dilemma of having to defer to her mother when she has greater good sense. Austen shows that Emma must pamper and protect her valetudinarian father and await his cooperation if she is to marry Mr. Knightley, and the meek Fanny Price stands up to Sir Thomas when the right of refusing a man she does not like is on her side. Anne Elliot judges with approval her choice eight years before to bend to her godmother Lady Russell's will, but later asserts her own right to make an independent choice.[20]

"And the Conclusion Must Be Delightful Too"

Though, in all her conclusions, Austen highlights the tendency of her work towards recommending immorality, drawing attention to her stories' difference from the didactic novel's unmixed characters and use of poetic justice, she also tends to undercut this mischievous suggestion. Even, and perhaps especially, in her conclusions, Austen makes fun of her heroines and heroes, puncturing lovers' hyperboles and self-deceptions, and allowing them little foibles that arise from normal self-interest. This last characteristic occurs in every novel, up to and including *Persuasion*. These weaknesses or foibles are not generally a complete descent into the amoral but often consist of Austen's observation of the milder forms of vice in even her good characters, whose wrongdoing is always eclipsed by that of the villains. Austen's narrator will express deep irony about this world's tendency to reward selfishness and malice, as we see the more vicious characters tending to prosper and the unreasonableness of expecting heroines or heroes to be paragons of selflessness. *Sense and Sensibility* features an explicit question about its own moral in the second-to-last chapter, as *Northanger Abbey* does at its close: "The whole of Lucy's behaviour in the affair, and the prosperity which crowned it, therefore, may be held forth as a most encouraging instance of what an earnest, an unceasing attention to self-interest, however its progress may be apparently obstructed, will do in securing every advantage of fortune, with no other sacrifice than that of time and conscience" (*SS*, III.14.426). This sentence is saturated with different levels of meaning and rhetorical ploys. The idea of prosperity as a crown, a blessing conferred as reward for virtue, is a notion familiar to any reader of the English eighteenth-century novel. The paragraph ends with what Vladimir Nabokov called "the Knight's move," a sentence structure

Austen uses to introduce irony. Like the knight in a chess game, the sentence at first appears a straightforward assertion, though we might be a bit baffled by the apparent support given to vice, but also like the knight on a chess board, the sentence veers to the side: "with no other sacrifice but that of time and conscience."[21] The verdict is devastating because the speaker at first appeared to support the wiles of the assiduously social-climbing Lucy Steele. But sacrificing conscience? The sentence ends with a radical shift whose suddenness and deflating contrast demand a burst of laughter. The high moral tone that makes Lucy an exemplar crushes her beneath its hyperbole turned to scorn. We hear again almost the very words that the narrator used to deflate Lady Susan at the end of her novella.

In the last completed novel, *Persuasion*, Austen has her hero wryly mock his own ego and admit his wrongdoing in the selfsame sentence: "'Like other great men under reverses,' he added with a smile, 'I must endeavour to subdue my mind to my fortune. I must learn to brook being happier than I deserve'" (II.11.269). Anne has already indulged herself in an interior laugh at his inconsistency, for he has announced that she could never change in his eyes, although she knows he recommenced their relationship by telling her family she was so changed he would not have known her again. In *Pride and Prejudice*, Elizabeth and Darcy actually discuss whether the moral of their story is damaged by the means they have used to attain their happiness.

In *Northanger Abbey*, Austen casts doubt on the filial qualities of Henry and Catherine, the sensitivity of Mrs. Morland,

and the potential for moral growth in General Tilney and Mrs. Allen, and compromises the seriousness of her closure by self-mockery, by an improbable and offstage *deus ex machina*. and by the exposure of the pettiness of her villains. She reveals that the demi-villain John Thorpe misinformed General Tilney of the Morlands' poverty out of spite. This act is what precipitates the General's own serious trespasses of evicting his guest Catherine from the home her guardians had confided her to, without proper supervision and financial aid to get her to Fullerton. Thorpe had earlier, in the glow of his friendship with Catherine's brother James and in a mistaken belief that he had secured Catherine's hand in marriage, told the General that the Morlands were wealthy and that Catherine was the even-wealthier Allens' heir. Now, rejected by Catherine and with Isabella deceived by Frederick Tilney and cut off from James Morland, Thorpe gets a little revenge. With these false views corrected and his vain spirits uplifted by Eleanor's marriage to a viscount, General Tilney relents towards Catherine and Henry:

> On the strength of this, the General, soon after Eleanor's marriage, permitted his son to return to Northanger, and thence made him the bearer of his consent, very courteously worded in a page full of empty professions to Mr. Morland. The event which it authorized soon followed: Henry and Catherine were married, the bells rang, and everybody smiled; and, as this took place within a twelvemonth from the first day of their meeting, it will not appear, after all the dreadful delays occasioned by the General's cruelty, that they were essentially hurt by it. (II.16.261)

"What probable circumstance could work upon a temper like the General's?" the narrator has asked her reader as the only remaining problem to be solved. We know it will be solved, she laments, because the physical shape of the book is betraying her secret: "The anxiety, which in this state of their attachment, must be the portion of Henry and Catherine, and of all who loved either, as to its final event, can hardly extend, I fear, to the bosom of my readers, who will see in the tell-tale compression of the pages before them, that we are all hastening together to perfect felicity. The means by which their early marriage was effected can be the only doubt" (II.16.259). This sentence in itself is both daring and joyous, as Austen cheekily bewails her inability to hold her readers' attention by suspense, and startles us with the assertion that Henry and Catherine are existing in some real place, quite apart from us, where grief is still their lot and other people who love them are anxiously wondering how the General's blessing is to be obtained while we, hard-hearted, contemplate it all with impassable superiority (for "all who loved either" are differentiated from "my readers").

Susan Wolfson notes that in *Northanger Abbey* "we can find ourselves in the company of a narrator whose pleased pretense to wry meta-narrative can itself seem an Austen-crafted character study."[22] She proposes that "the narrator's preferred mode of irony" could have a proper name: "'to quiz,' that is, 'to regard with amusement or scorn; to appraise mockingly … *Quizzers* are the agents and *quizzes* the objects of chic mockery.'" The term "quiz," which she proposes, will allow critics to name Austen's practice a "field of oscillation," which is "reading that sees through the narrator and past her words."

David Spurr proposes another term, which does not fully ironize the conclusion or its moral, and that is "frivolity." Although Spurr admits that Jane Austen herself tends to use the word pejoratively, as "emptiness" or "being incapable of attention to anything serious" (exemplified by Lydia and Wickham in *Pride and Prejudice*) in the end he defends Austen's version of frivolity as something "necessary to us."[23] This is because he has chosen a definition of frivolity, originating in eighteenth-century usage, that allows the reader to characterize Austen's own style as escaping from a utilitarian concept of language. Her own filiation from Johnson and Pope allows her to construct a language both morally serious and playful that exemplifies freedom from necessity. She claims for the "frivolous" genre of the novel a seriousness of artistic and moral purpose in her famous defence, when Isabella and Catherine immerse themselves in Gothic fiction:

> Yes, novels; for I will not adopt that ungenerous and impolitic custom, so common with novel-writers, of degrading, by their contemptuous censure, the very performances to the number of which they are themselves adding; joining with their greatest enemies in bestowing the harshest epithets on such works, and scarcely ever permitting them to be read by their own heroine, who, if she accidentally take up a novel, is sure to turn over its insipid pages with disgust. Alas! if the heroine of one novel be not patronised by the heroine of another, from whom can she expect protection and regard?

> I cannot approve of it. Let us leave it to the reviewers to abuse such effusions of fancy at their leisure … "It is only Cecilia, or Camilla, or Belinda"; or, in short, only some work in which the greatest powers of the mind are displayed, in which the most thorough knowledge of human nature, the happiest delineation of its varieties, the liveliest effusions of wit and humour, are conveyed to the world in the best-chosen language. Now, had the same young lady been engaged with a volume of the Spectator, instead of such a work, how proudly would she have produced the book, and told its name; though the chances must be against her being occupied by any part of that voluminous publication, of which either the matter or manner would not disgust a young person of taste: the substance of its papers so often consisting in the statement of improbable circumstances, unnatural characters, and topics of conversation which no longer concern anyone living; and their language, too, frequently so coarse as to give no very favourable idea of the age that could endure it. (*NA*, I.5.31)

"Idle" pursuits such as novel reading can hold the mirror up to nature, rather than being necessarily amoral or immoral.[24] Moreover, Austen's frivolous muse allows her to seem to subvert what she is at the same time earnestly supporting. Spurr reminds the reader of Mary Bennet's ill-timed disquisition on female loss of reputation to her sisters, who are in no need of the sermon: "There is something of the subversive in this absurd caricature of prudery, above all, at the same moment when the catastrophic events of the narrative seem to wish to persuade us of the fatal truth of the dangers posed to feminine virtue. Austen's brilliance of style resides in the maintaining of this fine tension where reason holds the drift, indeed the delirium, in check."[25]

Like the narrative mocking of Mr. Collins's sermonizing or Mary Bennet's preaching, the narrator's mock-dismay in *Northanger Abbey* over revealing the near-arrival of her happy ending and mistakenly proposing an immoral moral appears to subvert the serious purpose of her story, when it is necessary to it. At the end of the first chapter above, I discussed Austen's commending the way an acquaintance had of "speeding truth into the world": truth speeds when its feet are light, not leaden. For her, irony, quizzing, or frivolity amounts to a metaleptical means of expression that is almost like *hysteron proteron*, or later-first. An example of this figure of speech is found in Canto 2 of Dante's *Paradiso*. There Dante tells the reader he has ascended to the sphere of the Moon so quickly that it is the same as the time it takes an arrow "to strike, fly, and leave the bow" (2.23–6). The reversal of chronological order allows the reader to imagine unimaginable speed. So Austen rapidly inverts moral order to restore it.

Austen's conclusions often disturb her readers because she seems to be tossing them off, almost tossing them out, without regard for her readers' involvement in the moral lives and loves of the characters she has invented. Catherine's story rather hastily ends (that is the impression; she actually waits several months for her perplexity to be resolved) with Austen's usual method of panning out from the participants in the action to a wider, more general view of the drama that has just played out and a subtle sally, telling the moral of the story with tongue in cheek. No heroine speaks in her final chapter; nor does the hero. The flippancy of the ending is, however, not a sign of the ending's essential nothingness, or a deconstructive bomb unloosed upon the unsuspecting reader. Austen already has a method by the time she writes *Northanger Abbey*, and she is pursuing it.

In "Comic Resolution, Humorous Loose Ends in Austen's Novels," Margie Burns states,

> Outrageous comic wrap-ups are not new with Austen's novels. Romping endings with a cavalier disregard for painful realism date back to Euripides – the Ion and the Helen – to say nothing of Aristophanes, Plautus, and Shakespeare. What is new in Austen is that the outrageous unrealism does not feel unrealistic. For one thing, the rabbit-out-of-a-hat anomalies in Austen's endings are part of the warp and woof of the plots. For another, Austen's swift endings bear some resemblance to the mix of teeth-gritting and affection in extended family gatherings in real life. But mainly, the potential awkwardnesses in these endings are firmly subordinated by authorial control, hidden in plain sight by subtleties of tone. This, it may be added, is a consistent feature of the novels from first to last. There is no grand finale in this authorial pattern: Austen was not planning for her career to end.[26]

Austen is certainly daring in *Northanger Abbey*, since she is treading close to condoning the sin of disobeying a parent. On one hand, she whisks away the glamour of realism with which she has endowed her characters to tell us, it seems, that they are merely puppets, as Thackeray will do at the end of *Vanity Fair*. This type of removal of illusion, in the tradition of *Don Quixote*, seems to be a means of approaching realism or, perhaps more accurately, the position of fiction in the real world of the reader. However, Austen also assumes a pose of herself believing her characters all to be real people existing somewhere in the real world while the reader progresses blithely through the final pages, not feeling the pain of the real human beings because the readers themselves are in a fiction. For Austen, this frivolousness about her closure works as a double deconstruction, as she ironizes herself while ironizing her creations, and then draws the reader in to rescue her story. Tara Ghoshal Wallace has observed that Austen is doing more than inviting us to debunk romance conventions with her: "She mocks and undermines her own method – parodic discourse – so that both narrative and reader are kept off balance. In working toward her own concept of what constitutes novelistic discourse, Austen makes the reader a participant, now perhaps colluding with, now perhaps resisting the narrator's evaluation of her own novel. The reader thus becomes not only a partner in the unfolding of the narrative, but also an opponent who struggles with the narrator for control over the text."[27] Wallace's valuable insight is that Austen parodies parody in undermining Henry's authority as satirist with Catherine's sincerity and strong sense of what is right. In scenes such as the first dance, Beechen cliff, and elsewhere, Austen lands us back in Catherine's world of the unparodic, "a pre-parodic vision which does not reflexively admire mockery," though it often might still delight in it.[28] Though the narrator's satire does not spare the Morlands' insensibility to the real cause of Catherine's deep depression at the end of the novel, there is no question of whether Catherine wants Henry to approach her with mockery or simplicity and seriousness when he comes to Fullerton, for once not in possession of himself, nervous and fumbling.[29] If Henry is not serious about Catherine, there is no rescue from unhappiness in the near future for her, in spite of her parents' more stoic worldview.

A. Walton Litz says that the different parts of *Northanger Abbey* "never coalesce into a satisfactory whole," accusing Austen of "an abiding failure of narrative authority."[30] But at least as regards the closure of the novel, the narrator's authority is never more on display than when she appears to doubt it. She is glib, she is mock-horrified at the exposure of her own strategies, she throws in a *deus ex machina* and saves herself by informing us that Eleanor's "most charming young man in the world" is the original possessor of the laundry list Catherine found many chapters ago in her room at Northanger. Thus, his existence has been prepared for after the fact, and his sudden and unexpected accession to fortune and title (which the narrator could just as well have bestowed on Catherine if she had so chosen), instead of being the climax of the story, is merely an instrument that allows the General to adopt a more generous frame of mind in regard to his second son's marriage. In the universe of *Northanger Abbey*, it is more probable that such fortune should befall someone else rather than the ordinary young woman who is the subject of the story, so Catherine

Morland can achieve her heart's desire but remain an everywoman.

The narrator has either lost control or she is controlling things to her own satisfaction. Like Henry's, her "manner might sometimes surprise, but [her] meaning must always be just … The whole walk was delightful, and the conclusion must be delightful too" (I.14.115–16). The charm and gleeful, skipping pace of *Northanger Abbey*'s conclusion shows Austen attending to this requirement of an ending. Austen herself draws attention to a description of her real narrative strategy later in *Pride and Prejudice*, which she manifests in Mr. Darcy's (sometimes mistaken) power of understanding Elizabeth's speech: "You find *great* enjoyment in occasionally *professing opinions* which in *fact* are *not your own*" (II.8.195; my emphasis). Such speech already has a name, and it is Socratic irony. In *Northanger Abbey* Austen asks her readers if she is recommending parental tyranny or rewarding filial disobedience. The reader as interpreter is now challenged. Should parents be tyrants? Should children disobey? Austen exposes the mechanical workings of a comic plot: without both kinds of infraction against the bond between parents and children, there is no story to tell. Metalepsis and Socratic irony permit her to enlist the reader in the challenge of understanding the relationship between her fictional world and the real world.

And underneath all the arbitrariness and insubordination is the moving and prudent interaction between the Morlands and their daughter and soon-to-be son-in-law, steady, firm, fixed in their principles, keeping the fifth commandment, observing, with moderation, society's expectations, hoping against hope. And behind that, the immense secret, the little possible fault that the Morlands never forbid and therefore never allow to be a trespass, more secret even than the words upon the laundry list at Northanger: the contents of the letters that come and go, observed but not observed, between Catherine Morland and Henry Tilney.

CHAPTER FOUR

Forced Retrospection in *Sense and Sensibility*: Willoughby's Desire for "Something Like Forgiveness" on "More Reasonable Grounds"

Forced Retrospection as Narrative Strategy

One technique Austen consistently makes use of in her novels' closures is what I would call forced retrospection, or analepsis. In this common but little-discussed strategy, the author uses either the narrator's voice or a character's own reflections to draw the reader back to earlier parts of the narrative, often to reinterpret those events in the light of the later information. This technique invites rereading. Austen scholars and lay readers alike often comment on the rich experience of rereading Austen and the way in which the story reshapes itself in one's mind as one rereads. It is abundantly clear that she constructs her stories to invite that response. Even Mark Twain, that famous foe of Austen, began his famous comment (about exhuming and beating the author) with the words "*Every* time I read *Pride and*

Prejudice …"[1] Other critics have commented on how often Austen features confessional scenes in her novels, perhaps in *Sense and Sensibility* above all. I propose that there is a link between the narrative technique that requires readers to revisit past scenes, especially those in which the narrator has concealed something, and Austen's interest in confession: her own Christian habit of revisiting the events of the day in the evening Examen of Conscience combines both the actions of retrospection and confession. Moreover, Austen is inventing nothing new in intertwining these habits that develop interiority, for we find them in the confessional poetry of the biblical Psalmist, St. Augustine's *Confessions* and his meditations on music and the psalms, medieval romances,[2] and even Fielding's *Tom Jones*.[3] Narratologist Gérard Genette has discussed the necessity of repetition – revisiting a theme, character, type of scene, image – as a rhetorical trope to narrative itself.[4] In itself, this type of narrative antanaclasis, or repetition of a word or phrase with changing meaning the second or third time it appears, when extended over an entire story, forces retrospection.[5]

The end of *Sense and Sensibility* resolves the suspended love stories of Elinor and Marianne Dashwood, the two sisters whose suitors, having won their hearts, mysteriously disappear by the end of volume 1. The men both re-enter the narrative later in the novel: Edward Ferrars in a deliberate visit to the sisters' home in Devon, an act that underscores his real and continued devotion to Elinor; and John Willoughby for his confession to Elinor during Marianne's illness. However, both men (and Marianne's future husband, Colonel Brandon, who also disappears briefly) remain very much in the story as characters whose past behaviour Elinor and her sister reflect on and whose future actions are considered or projected. One could say that, like Achilles or Ivanhoe, these men are continually present, even though they are offstage.

One reason Austen's conclusions require retrospection is that she often spends a good deal of time on the disqualified suitor in the final chapters. While the reader does not care about what happens to John Thorpe in the end of *Northanger Abbey*, his disappointment and vengeful anger precipitate much of the final action, as the narrator emphasizes. The impudent Wickham has already married Elizabeth Bennet's sister Lydia, but once Darcy has married Elizabeth Bennet, would he ever be able to wash his hands of Wickham entirely? Emma Woodhouse's faux courtship with Frank Churchill has already been exposed as an imposture, but his long letter forms the focus of Emma and Mr. Knightley's dialogue after they become engaged. William Elliot's greed and wiliness no longer impose on Anne, who has been aware of Wentworth's jealousy for several chapters after his release from an implied obligation to Louisa Musgrove, but he will still inherit Kellynch. *Sense and Sensibility* and *Mansfield Park* feature the discarded suitors that readers are most disinclined to give up on, and many critics believe that the real heroes of their respective novels are Willoughby and Henry Crawford, whom Austen unfairly denies her heroine the opportunity to marry.[6] The personal charm the author attributes to both men is in large part responsible for this impression; moreover, their sexual adventures seem to recommend rather than disqualify them in some readers' minds. Both men have property, and neither one gambles (two strikes against the almost equally charming but more unpopular Wickham). Neither one attempts to impose with plausible excuses and lies upon a now-enlightened heroine (another strike against Wickham, and a strike against William Elliot and the female imposter-friends, Isabella Thorpe and Lucy Steele). Marianne's intense heartsickness over being jilted by Willoughby intensifies the sense that Austen ought to have granted her a reformed rather than guiltless husband.

However, the Tom Jones type had already begun to come under disapproving scrutiny by the time *Sense and Sensibility* came out, precisely because the reader cannot presume that such a male lead will remain constant in the unseen future. In *Self-Control*, Mary Brunton has her heroine, Laura, say to her acquaintance Julia on the subject of the desirability of Tom Jones as a husband: "I could not admire in a lover qualities which would be odious in a husband."[7] Laura has a Tom Jones–like suitor, Hargrave, whom she eventually rejects in favour of the virtuous Montague De Courcy. Austen came closest to Tom in her earlier scoundrels, and diverged from the type more widely in her later ones, but she rewarded none of them with the bride she allows the reader to see the caddish men would prefer. Mrs. Dashwood articulates the reason why: "'Happy with a man of libertine practices! With one who so injured the peace of the dearest of our friends, and the best of men! No – my Marianne has not a heart to be made happy with such a man! Her conscience would have felt all that the conscience of her husband ought to have felt'" (*SS*, III.11.396). What

Willoughby was when he seduced Eliza Williams, he still is. His remorse is not a guarantee of change; it is not contrition accompanied by a true desire to reform or make reparation.[8] Marianne's heart would have felt all the guilt and shame and sorrow Willoughby ought to have felt towards Eliza, but this is a counterfactual feeling. "Ought to have felt" is not "does feel." The phrase more than implies the opposite.

One strategy Austen repeats in concluding her stories is to illustrate the rejected man's qualities as potential husband one last time and, especially, to hint at the continuance of that unsuitability past the boundary of the last page. In *Sense and Sensibility*, Austen forces the reader to re-evaluate Willoughby's confession several times as we approach the finale and, in fact, suggests another retrospect a mere paragraph from the book's last words. We close *Sense and Sensibility* with a farewell look at Mrs. Dashwood, Elinor, and Marianne, but the paragraphs immediately preceding this final view are devoted to Colonel Brandon and then to Willoughby:

> Colonel Brandon was now as happy as all those who best loved him believed he deserved to be; – in Marianne he was consoled for every past affliction; ... Marianne could never love by halves; and her whole heart became, in time, as much devoted to her husband, as it had once been to Willoughby.
>
> Willoughby could not hear of her marriage without a pang; and his punishment was soon afterwards complete in the voluntary forgiveness of Mrs. Smith, who, by stating his marriage with a woman of character, as the source of her clemency, gave him reason for believing, that had he

> behaved with honour towards Marianne, he might at once have been happy and rich. (III.14.430)

The motion of Marianne's heart in this passage is both forward into the future and retrograde. That "her whole heart became, in time, as much devoted to her husband" is the secure prediction of the future, but it is followed by the return to the past: "as it had once been to Willoughby." That is the phrase Austen uses to bridge her transition to the topic of *Willoughby's* future, but it forces the reader to recall the whole history of Marianne and Willoughby's relationship. The same sentence both assures readers that Colonel Brandon is now paramount and reminds them that Willoughby once was. Marianne's inability to "love by halves" is an encomium that prevents us from censuring her for faithlessness and forgetfulness, for inconstancy.

But it is Willoughby's changing heart that interests Austen more, and she bids the reader remember his professions the last time he was onstage when she recounts his future state:

> That his repentance of misconduct, which thus brought its own punishment, was sincere, need not be doubted; nor that he long thought of Colonel Brandon with envy, and of Marianne with regret. But that he was for ever inconsolable – that he fled from society, or contracted an habitual gloom of temper, or died of a broken heart, must not be depended on – for he did neither. He lived to exert, and frequently to enjoy himself. His wife was not always out of humour, nor his home always uncomfortable! and in his breed of horses

> and dogs, and in sporting of every kind, he found no inconsiderable degree of domestic felicity. (II.14.430)

The narrator begins seriously enough but she ends up smiling a bit both at Willoughby and at our naive expectations of him. She assures us of something she did not in the chapter wherein he confronted Elinor: he is genuinely repentant. That is a great deal, though it comes too late. He views his loss of Marianne as his just punishment. His envy of Colonel Brandon introduces a more off-putting note, since envy is one of the seven deadly sins, and then comes the blow: if we had our hearts set on seeing him as forever lovelorn, a romantic hero desolated by melancholy or set on self-destruction because his heart is broken, we shall be disappointed. Mrs. Willoughby, unlike the feuding Fanny Dashwood and Lucy Ferrars, is not always unpleasant. Willoughby's home is even comfortable from time to time, the narrator assures the disappointed reader. And Willoughby comes full circle when we see him with his dogs and guns, the sportsman whose recreation was interrupted by Marianne's fall. He takes all his pleasant old pastimes up again. The annulation or circular motion of the narrative – ring structure, as it is known in rhetoric – confronts us with a lack of change. To look back does not prevent his circling back.

Austen's repeated use of negatives in this account is noteworthy: "need not be doubted," "must not be depended on," "he did neither," "not always out of humour, nor his home always uncomfortable," "no inconsiderable degree of domestic felicity." Austen decidedly vetoes the reader's potential projection of a moping and inconsolable Willoughby in her picture of the rather pleasant home he will enjoy. However, if we rephrase the paragraph into positive assertions, we can see why Austen does not use them:

> That his repentance of misconduct, which thus brought its own punishment, was sincere, the reader may believe; and that he long thought of Colonel Brandon with envy, and of Marianne with regret. But that he was for ever inconsolable – that he fled from society, or contracted an habitual gloom of temper, or died of a broken heart, must not be depended on – for he did something else. He lived to exert, and frequently to enjoy himself. His wife was sometimes in good humour, and his home sometimes comfortable! and in his breed of horses and dogs, and in sporting of every kind, he found a great degree of domestic felicity.

The shameful truth is that Willoughby is in general content without his beloved Marianne, but either to protect his delicate sense of self or the reader's more heroic conception of him, Austen proceeds more slyly.

The author is two sentences away from the end of the book and the narrator has not had done with Willoughby: "For Marianne, however – in spite of his incivility in surviving her loss – he always retained that decided regard which interested him in everything that befell her, and made her his secret standard of perfection in woman; and many a rising beauty would be slighted by him in after days as bearing no comparison with Mrs. Brandon" (III.14.430–1). The reader is left to imagine what his wife thinks of these depreciating statements, if she is near enough to hear them. Austen, however, is relentlessly devoted to the probable here, as she mocks her reader and Willoughby and Marianne's earlier romantic pretensions by terming Willoughby's curable heart an example of "incivility." The *litotes*, or understatement, encourages the reader to think of it as something worse than mere incivility. The word also recalls the scene in chapter 17 in which Edward notes of Elinor, "You have not been able to bring your sister over to your plan of general civility" (I.17.109), reminding the reader forcefully of the contrast between the two sisters' approaches to conduct. Austen adds to this the fact that Willoughby is constrained to call Marianne by her married name in his continued references to his paragon: that name steers the reader back to Colonel Brandon, for Marianne has willingly assumed the title "Mrs. Brandon" and, moreover, has been even more "untrue": she would never hold Willoughby up as her ideal anymore. It is also noteworthy that Austen's last fillip at Willoughby concerns the shallowness of his devotion: his comparisons to other women all focus on external beauty.

Counterfactual Narrative at the Close

What Willoughby does not do, contrary to expectations, is the note on which Austen ends her development of his character. And Austen often resorts to the counterfactual in the confession scene itself. Counterfactual narrative is a tool that aids her in driving home the lack of rectitude in Willoughby's behaviour, as she reveals that Mrs. Smith would have forgiven him his misconduct towards Eliza if he had remained true to Marianne and married *her*. Happiness and wealth combined were within his grasp, but he had to act without knowing he could have both. Once he made his choice, he forfeited happiness. However, it is important to remember what Marianne said to elicit Mrs. Dashwood's exclamation that *her Marianne* could not be happy with such a husband. Willoughby might have proposed but, if she knew the truth, would Marianne have accepted? "I never could have been happy with him, after knowing, as sooner or later I must have known, all this. – I should have had no confidence, no esteem. Nothing could have done it away to my feelings" (III.11.396). Here Marianne projects a counterfactual future: a future in which she has married Willoughby and only then discovered his cruel treatment of Eliza Williams. That future is one in which Willoughby might have been happy, but Marianne, linked indissolubly to a heartless seducer, would always have been filled with vicarious shame and dishonour.

When the narrator distinguishes true happiness from the assurance of financial comfort in the above statement, she undercuts the value of Willoughby's comfortable existence, which she is about to describe. In this subtle way, Austen distinguishes the kind of marriage he enjoys from true "connubial felicity," as Elizabeth Bennet terms it. The same hand that takes away the histrionic romantic hero gives us a mixed character, truly repentant, not inconsolably unhappy, but never "happy" in the way the virtuous Brandons will be.

This section of the conclusion makes the reader look back on several previous scenes – most importantly, Willoughby's appearance before Elinor at Cleveland in volume 3, chapter 8, the scene in which he professed his continued emotional tie to Marianne and evidenced his disregard for his wife. Austen uses the mode of confession at important junctures in her plots in all six novels, and *Sense and Sensibility* is no exception. In fact, it features people confessing more than in any of the other five novels. Willoughby's confession is the longest of these and is the only one ever undertaken by a villain.[9] Unique and dramatic, this confession deserves the attention of every careful reader of the novel. Many of the men in *Sense and Sensibility* have been called flat characters, as Ivor Morris pointed out many years ago,[10] and Willoughby, like Edward, makes an early appearance, gains the love of his lady, and then disappears for most of the rest of the novel. He hardly has a chance to prove he is multidimensional. The controversial confession scene, however, is proof that, as E.M. Forster claimed of Lady Bertram in *Aspects of the Novel*, Austen can at any time take a flat character and make it leap into rounded life as it begins to become aware of its own moral being.[11] Willoughby's confession and the moral realizations in the Dashwood family that follow in rapid succession from his failure's impact upon Marianne are in many ways the climax of the novel, after which the tidying up of the romances in the final chapter may well feel anticlimactic. Far from being an injection of moral confusion, as Mary Poovey argues, or a way of confirming Willoughby's thorough villainy, as Charles Durning Carroll asserts, this scene allows Austen in a tour de force to investigate the difference between sincere and staged emotion, between reasoned and emotive judgment, and allows us to see that, for Willoughby as for Elinor, conscience performs a judicial function.[12] This is significant because it means Austen understands conscience not as right reason, but as divine spark; in fact, confession implies a mutually recognized moral law and the need for forgiveness. Willoughby recognizes that he needs moral cleansing, but Austen shows that, at the same time, he refuses to expose his inner wounds completely. In the end, she portrays him as professing a fatalism that ostensibly justifies his actions, and, she also shows he is himself uncomfortable with maintaining this pose in front of Elinor. The forgiveness he hopes to receive from her on more reasonable grounds is actually a mélange of things. He wishes to engage reason, yes, but also, more obviously, emotion, to restore himself in her graces. Unlike Marianne, who later will say that she needs reconciliation with God as well as her family after courting death, Willoughby sees himself as offending not against a divine law, but a moral code. It is a moral code that still matters to him, nonetheless, because it binds him to people he respects and values as he respects and values no others: the Dashwoods.

Elinor is the recipient in this scene in which Austen challenges her reader to a kind of discernment of which even the heroine finds herself incapable, as Mary Poovey has discussed in *The Proper Lady and the Woman Writer*.[13] Elinor may not be fully capable of discerning and judging during this scene, and she certainly does revisit her immediate reaction to the disclosures Willoughby makes. Austen makes Elinor gradually judge and rejudge, just as she makes Elizabeth Bennet judge and rejudge Darcy's letter, and just as she makes Anne Elliot gradually judge and rejudge her terminating her engagement to Wentworth at Lady Russell's behest. This kind of revisitation of a decision or event emphasizes that Willoughby's confession scene is absolutely essential to our understanding of the development of the novel's ideas, and, since Austen harks back to it in the conclusion, it acquires a growing importance after the fact.

The centrality of the confession to the conclusion of the novel derives from its exposition of Willoughby's motivations, hidden until this moment, its testing of Elinor's powers of judgment, and its very important revelation to Marianne of both the sincerity of his passion – for what it's worth – and the inferiority of his moral compass. In this confession, the interior of the self is at least partially on display, a fact both satisfying and dramatically disappointing to the reader who had invested some hope in the striking appearance of Willoughby and his attentions to Marianne. The confession is in many ways the climax of the novel's theme of being versus seeming, but the reader needs Austen's final mention of Willoughby in the last chapter to understand it fully.

Retrospection is essential to gauging the role of emotional appeal or charm in judging this character. Willoughby's excuses and passionate conviction are compelling, although his sincerity and honesty in this scene are very questionable. As C. Durning Carroll has said in his study of the scene, "Willoughby's apology, though long and apparently sincere, will not alter his reputation as a libertine." If that is the audience's reaction to the scene Austen has created, then we must ask, why did Austen include it, and, moreover, what does she imagine to be Willoughby's goal? That is precisely Carroll's question:

> The curious thing about this scene is that, although Marianne was the only person harmed, Willoughby chooses to apologize to Elinor. Surprisingly, Willoughby wishes to speak just to her. His insistence on apologizing to Elinor is an implicit acknowledgement that any forgiveness from Marianne is illegitimate. Yet if the only wronged party has forgiven Willoughby before the apology begins, then the ostensible aim of the apology has disappeared, and the true reason for this apology *cannot* be forgiveness. Several pages after Willoughby has finished his explanation Elinor concludes, "The whole of his behaviour, … from the beginning to the end of the affair has been grounded on selfishness" … If indeed Willoughby is judged as utterly selfish even after a sincere and heartfelt apology, then what is the real purpose of his apology?[14]

Carroll is right that Willoughby's purpose is far from overt. It can only be one of two things: the purpose he professes to Elinor, that is, to secure a better opinion of him from the Dashwoods, or one that seems to surface as the conversation continues, that is, to secure Marianne for himself in some way. The latter goal is wicked, not only because he is a married man, but also because he still has not done anything to make up for his abandonment of Colonel Brandon's ward. However, that does not make the aim improbable. On the other hand, the former goal, of restoring his reputation with the Dashwoods, can be seen as laudable, and it is to that probability that I first wish to turn our attention. Whether Willoughby's reputation as a libertine is altered or not, Austen alerts the reader to something significant in this vital scene, and this justifies Willoughby's continued persistence to the end of the book as a figure to be understood as well as judged. A founder of Russian formalism, Boris Tomashevski, once distinguished between *fable* or *fabula* and *sujet:* the first is the import and the shape of the tale, the second its chronological ordering, which is often related out of sequence.[15] Willoughby is essential to the *fabula* (the thematic and artistic development) of the novel, not just the *sujet* (the chronology of events), and thus the conclusion returns to him and requires the reader to remember and compare his earlier appearances.

Willoughby's confession to Elinor is one of the most dramatic moments in a novel that chooses merely to narrate a seduction, a duel of honour, and its proposal scenes: it never shows these more stage-worthy events. Does Austen bring Willoughby all this way from London to Cleveland to stage a remorseful soliloquy? Why should he merit so much of the audience's time when Edward and Colonel Brandon do not? Once we begin comparing this scene to other pivotal conversations in the novel, we realize that Austen gives preference to conversations that involve confession (one might think of Marianne, Lucy Steele, and Colonel Brandon with Elinor),[16] though almost all these confessions are partial and tend to involve others in blame – that is, they tend to contain accusations as well. Both of the longest conversations – Colonel Brandon's with Elinor explaining Eliza Williams's story, and Willoughby's here – point the reader to the centrality of Willoughby and perhaps partially account for the regret so many readers feel at his abandonment by his author. Austen clearly considers him a pivotal actor in her drama. Willoughby thus is not merely a plot device for Austen – the seducer whose abandonment showcases Marianne's indulgence in sensibility – but a character whose motivations and actions we must understand to understand the novel. What the confession scene reveals above all is his wish to be thought good by the Dashwoods, and his many exposures and concealments in this conversation all seem geared rhetorically towards this end.

Willoughby's Attempt to Rescue His Self-Image, Not His Soul

It is not unusual for someone who is bad to wish to be thought good; Shakespeare's Richard III, Milton's Satan, and Spenser's Duessa and Archimago from *The Faerie Queene* are prime examples well known to the eighteenth-century reader. For these three Renaissance authors, the evil person may have two motives for wishing to be thought good: to deceive others, or to deceive themselves about the tenor of their life. Both ends presume the same basic premise: that to be good is better than to be evil. To be thought evil is an evil in and of itself. Willoughby's conversation with Elinor reveals his underlying motivation to be thought good.

Willoughby describes his moral judgment of himself several times during the course of his conversation with Elinor. At first, when he speaks of his resolution to propose to Marianne, after being needlessly negligent about doing so for too long, he is approving of himself and happy with everyone: "'I had left her only the evening before, so fully, so firmly resolved within my self on doing right! A few hours were to have engaged her to me for ever; and I remember how happy, how gay were my spirits, as I walked from the cottage to Allenham, satisfied with myself, delighted with every body!'" (III.8.367). Austen could scarcely pick more baldly moral language: "so fully, so firmly resolved within my self on doing right!" The alliteration of the "f" underscores the resolution but also Willoughby's self-dramatization to Elinor. The words are scarcely those of a lover. Willoughby is not, in that evening before the separation, overwhelmed by the passion of love. By his own description, what has come over him is a resolution to do right, to treat a woman as she deserves and as he has led her to expect him to behave. His emotional reaction to the resolution is gaiety, lightness of heart. But the emotion does not precede or determine the action.

However, the visit that actually occurs after his interview with Mrs. Smith is a different matter:

> "Why did you call, Mr. Willoughby?" said Elinor, reproachfully; "a note would have answered every purpose. Why was it necessary to call?"
>
> "It was necessary to my own pride. I could not bear to leave the country in a manner that might lead you, or the rest of the neighbourhood, to suspect any part of what had really passed between Mrs. Smith and myself, and I resolved, therefore, on calling at the cottage, in my way to

> Honiton. The sight of your dear sister, however, was really dreadful; and, to heighten the matter, I found her alone. You were all gone, I do not know where." (III.8.367)

Willoughby wishes to appear good to the Dashwoods because of his own image of himself. This picture he cannot bear to have sullied in the minds of those he seems genuinely to care for. Certainly, he recognizes that his behaviour is socially unacceptable and, even more, that knowledge of it would damage his status irrevocably in the eyes of those he esteems. Immediately, however, he finds his own motives clashing with the real effect of his actions. He is distressed by the emotional turmoil he causes, but another sense is operating, which is even more important: "'In this, our last interview of friendship, I approached her with a sense of guilt that almost took from me the power of dissembling.'" Willoughby describes this "sense of guilt" in a memorable way: it "almost took from [him] the power of dissembling." He understands his ability to present a false face to others as a "power." What is he dissembling? Innocence, good conscience, reliability, trustworthiness – all the virtues opposed to what he is really doing, which is lying. Faithless both to Eliza Williams and to Marianne, he nevertheless wants Marianne to believe him faithful. To what end? Willoughby has no hope any longer of attaining Marianne's hand, and he does not seem to have considered seducing her in the way he seduced Eliza. What Willoughby wants is for Marianne to believe him to be good.[17] His first motive for wishing this, as he describes it, is pride.

Why does Austen take pains to designate pride as the characteristic Willoughby himself confesses to in this scene? She is revealing the way a person thinks who is able to throw aside any scruples. "We perceive that the conscience (conscientia) is itself … thrown aside and driven from its place by some who have no shame or modesty in their faults," St. Jerome once said.[18] We have yet to determine whether or not shame or modesty have any place in Willoughby's confession, but because pride goads him to make the final visit to the Dashwoods, his behaviour there does not seem to have been guided by conscience, as his intended proposal was. Were he to lose the power to dissemble at this point, it is clear that humiliation would ensue. Nevertheless, something is happening to him, though he perhaps does not perceive it until later. Reflecting on his last meeting with Marianne, he says to Elinor: "'I do not know what I told her,' … 'Less than was due to the past beyond a doubt, and in all likelihood much more than was justified by the future. I cannot think of it. It won't do'" (III.8.367). Even at this point, Willoughby fears full revelation of his ability to lie to Marianne. His expressions make it clear that the recollection of his false reassurances to her is painful and that he still cannot face the fact that he did not live up to his obligation towards her. Of the two phrases, "Less than was due to the past" is far more sinister than "Much more than was justified by the future." This means that, aside from lying, Willoughby is now aware of another defect in his conduct: "Oh, God! what a hard-hearted rascal I was!" (III.8.367).

What Willoughby now looks back at with shame is that he was able to undergo the pretense and divide himself from Marianne with less regret than he ought to have done. His final visit, born of pride rather than a manly resolve to confess, is evidence of his self-absorption, just as so many of his other acts are. Now, at Cleveland, he knows that. Before, even in the misery of facing Marianne at Barton, he did not. It takes one more step to open up the possibility of further self-knowledge in Willoughby – the arrival of Mrs. Dashwood at the scene at Barton: "Then came your dear mother to torture me farther, with all her kindness and confidence. Thank Heaven! it did torture me. I was miserable. Miss Dashwood, you cannot have an idea of the comfort it gives me to look back on my own misery. I owe such a grudge to myself for the stupid, rascally folly of my own heart, that all my past sufferings under it are only triumph and exultation to me now" (III.8.367–8).

Austen seems to have composed Willoughby's choice of words here with particular care and thought. Yet, what Willoughby has to say is so complex and so very odd. Austen has Willoughby speak with warmth of Mrs. Dashwood, whose welcoming sweetness and confidence in him *tortures* him – a strong word, but not unexpected coming from the hyperbolic Willoughby. And for this feeling of misery he thanks "Heaven." Why bring God into the experience at this point? What does his misery prove to him? What follows offers an interesting answer. First, Willoughby derives comfort at present from the knowledge that he felt badly back at Barton about Mrs. Dashwood's confidence in him. The reader deduces that this present comfort arises because he detects in himself some native goodness that rebels against his deceptiveness and anything else that is unworthy and ignoble in his behaviour; he senses that he does not deserve Mrs. Dashwood's trust. But this is not what Willoughby says, though Austen may mean us to think it. What he says is, "I owe such a grudge to myself for the stupid, rascally folly of my own heart, that all my past sufferings under it are only triumph and exultation to me now."

Willoughby enjoys the sensation of having felt the emotions proper to sincere guilt. Austen is describing something quite complex here. He did feel the emotions a moral man should feel in comparing what he ought to have done to what he did. He does feel even now that he deserved the tormented feelings that afflicted him. However, he describes the torment of those moments as "past sufferings" that are directly linked to the "stupid, rascally folly" of his own heart. His language is filled with terms denoting suffering and torture, but folly and rascality hardly are commensurate language. These are terms that disappoint: where is his remorse over Eliza? His sense of having abandoned Marianne to intense emotional suffering and the mockery of others? Nowhere. Willoughby feels only the justice of the self-inflicted pain. Or does he? "All my past sufferings under it [the stupid, rascally folly of my own heart] are only triumph and exaltation to me now," says he. Willoughby still does not see evil in the dark picture of himself, only foolishness and a kind of base mischievousness. More, he exults in the knowledge of his past suffering. Again, why? Is he a repentant sinner or a self-congratulating suffering romantic? Austen almost certainly intends this moment to be highly ambiguous, and to leave it to the reader to see that Willoughby could very easily be interpreting himself as some kind of Wertherian hero, rushing about to make his dramatic declarations because impelled by deep emotion. The resolution of doing right that preceded his intended proposal to Marianne seems lost among other more dominant impulses at this point. Willoughby remains at least to a certain extent a captive of his own dearly loved image of himself. His conscience is not dead, but its state reminds one of Good Deeds in the medieval play *Everyman* – weakly lying prostrate in a corner, neglected and forgotten, though not completely gone. William Lyons's description of the Old Testament view of conscience is helpful here: "for King David, wrongdoing was followed by an emotional, visceral response: 'his heart smote him' (Samuel 24:6)."[19] Willoughby in dismay before Mrs. Dashwood in Barton cottage is in this condition. Willoughby before Elinor? Perhaps not. His exclamation about his current "triumph" and "exaltation" casts shadows all about his change of heart. Let us look further.

Elinor's challenge in this scene is to discern correctly – to make full charitable allowance for repentance, but not to be gulled. As Sarah Emsley points out,

> In loving one's neighbor, there is an inherent tension between respect and affirmation; that is, it is difficult to draw the line between being polite and sympathetic to someone, and being complicit with that person's behavior. The danger is that one can enable the other person to continue with destructive actions … While sympathy can be a great virtue, allowing one to share in and ideally to alleviate the sufferings of another, it must be tempered by judgment so one does not affirm good and evil equally.[20]

Durning Carroll agrees with Mary Poovey that "Elinor's emotions – her sensibility – and not her reason, tell her that Willoughby remains morally wrong."[21] However, what Austen represents in this fraught scene is something less simple than a tug of war between emotion and reason. For Austen is trying to depict, perhaps to define, what sense it is in Elinor that knows Willoughby is in part deceptive and his presentation sophistically persuasive when her sympathy sways her to his cause. At that time, to show sympathy and compassion as capable of error was to cast doubt on Rousseau, Shaftesbury, and Hume and to question the tenets of some Enlightenment philosophies as well as Romanticism. If Elinor errs, the error is not great; Elinor, when called to forgive "on more reasonable grounds" – or to ask Marianne to do so – is of course also being asked to perform a Christian act. In addition, candour, that Austenian virtue, requires her to impute to him a better frame of mind than she imagined he possessed at the time he abandoned Marianne. Candour is on Austen's mind here; after all, it is the allegorical character the narrator tells us Marianne assumes in the last words she speaks in the entire novel (III.13.422). Nonetheless, the Dashwood women, all mindful of their emotional attachment to him, agree that Willoughby's true weakness, selfishness, makes it unthinkable for Marianne to be united to him, and the reader assumes it will be a key part of his eventual destiny, which the narrator will predict for us on the last page of the novel.

Neither sympathy nor antipathy can direct the Dashwood family's reactions to Willoughby in the end – Willoughby's intrusion is proof he still has no care for right conduct or the effect of his dramatic gestures on others' well-being. Getting something for himself – even if it is just the Dashwoods' good opinion – ranks paramount with him as an objective, and the narrator implicitly calls on the reader to continue judging him negatively as he retains his devotion to Marianne well into his marriage. While one may infer that his love and even respect for Marianne lie behind this gallantry, the narrator allows this glimpse into the future for more than one reason. The reader need not like Sophia Grey to understand that it is wrong for him to exhibit disloyalty to her publicly, shaming the wife he chose and perhaps even unintentionally inviting others to impute guilt to the Mrs. Brandon he considers so beautiful.

But Austen would not have devoted so much time to his confession if she had not wanted her readers to see something else: that Willoughby might have acted differently had his intelligence and attraction to the good not been in the bad school of self-indulgence, and that he even might have come around to Mrs. Smith's principles if he had been with the Dashwoods longer. He was required by his author, however, to make a moral choice when he was not prepared for sacrifice and selflessness. For Austen, timing plays a large role in the choices of her characters. This is why she makes the planned proposal and the summons from Mrs. Smith coincide. However, this coincidence is not the consequentialism that Robert Hopkins hints Austen espouses in *Persuasion*. Willoughby has the entire novel to right his wrongs, and every time he has the opportunity to do so, he forgoes it. The simple and unromantic sense of duty that keeps Edward Ferrars by Lucy Steele when his heart is Elinor's does not even at this late date speak to Willoughby of any binding responsibility towards the virtuous Marianne or the less-than-virtuous (by his account) Eliza Williams. Willoughby lacks Edward's level of self-knowledge, and even if Edward's public constancy to Lucy is undermined by his devotion to Elinor, at least it assures the reader he will not easily let his heart lead him to be unfaithful.

Austen portrays this unstable ambiguity in Willoughby's sense of self perhaps most fully in his statement that it would be "a kind of comfort to [him] to know [he] knew how she [Marianne] looked to those who saw her last in this world" (III.8.371). If readers are inclined to assess Willoughby by the genuineness of his emotions, Austen challenges the reader here. Willoughby imagines the intimacy of presence at the deathbed of his beloved Marianne; it appears to be a thought that has actually occurred to him, that he ought to be there at her side and should be one of the last to look upon her face. As far as Elinor or the reader can tell, he is moved by the thought. The pathos of the scene would be appealing were Willoughby an author or cinematographer interested in creating emotion in his audience and not a potentially bereaved lover. Marianne, as it happens, is not going to die, and she will not provide him or anyone else with the picturesque spectacle he imagines. The "kind of comfort" provided by his knowing that he knew how she looked at the last is hard to conceive. On the one hand, both natural curiosity and personal attachment probably prompted Jane Austen's own inquiry into the appearance of her sister-in-law's corpse when Edward Knight's wife, Elizabeth, died after childbirth: "I suppose you see the corpse?" she wrote to Cassandra, "How does it appear?"[22] But Willoughby's self-congratulation here is of a piece with his understanding of his behaviour as spectacle, an exhibition for others. Knowing what Marianne looked like in death elevates him in his own eyes, as viewer of the spectacle of her beauty in unconsciousness and pain. It is all the more offensive when we realize Austen has him equating this vision to her appearance when she had fainted at the assembly where he snubbed her:

> "Such an evening! I ran away from you all as soon as I could, but not before I had seen Marianne's sweet face as white as death. *That* was the last, last look I ever had of her; – the last manner in which she appeared to me. It was a horrid sight! Yet when I thought of her to-day as really dying, it was a kind of comfort to me to imagine that I knew exactly how she would appear to those who saw her last in this world. She was before me, constantly before me, as I travelled, in the same look and hue."
>
> A short pause of mutual thoughtfulness succeeded. (III.8.371; emphasis in original)

Willoughby's fault exhibited throughout the novel and in his speech to Elinor is a disregard for how his actions and words will truly affect others, in tandem with an intense desire to be perceived in a performance. Here Marianne's shock and grief are not sufferings to be compassionated but to be consumed. He admits he fancied to himself, after leaving Barton, that Marianne was experiencing a kind of mirror of his own disengagement: not missing him, considering their courtship an idle and passing fancy, even perhaps planning to get married soon herself. His characterization of Eliza also smacks of this inability to recognize otherness, as he scornfully exclaims that in the view of outsiders "because [*he*] was a libertine, *she* must be a saint" (III.8.365).

However, Willoughby recalls thinking that the Dashwoods' image of him is already destroyed, so it does not matter in what way he expresses his break with Marianne, claiming that his wife had dictated the last letter to him:

> "And after all, what did it signify to my character in the opinion of Marianne and her friends, in what language my answer was couched? It must have been only to one end. My business was to declare myself a scoundrel, and whether I did it with a bow or a bluster was of little importance. 'I am ruined for ever in their opinion,' said I to myself; 'I am shut out for ever from their society; they already think me an unprincipled fellow, this letter will only make them think me a blackguard one.' Such were my reasonings as, in a sort of desperate carelessness, I copied my wife's words, and parted with the last relics of Marianne. Her three notes – unluckily they were all in my pocket-book, or I should have denied their existence, and hoarded them for ever; I was forced to put them up, and could not even kiss them." (III.8.372)

Breakfasting with his wife-to-be, Willoughby still hoards Marianne's desperate letters and her lock of hair in his pocket-book. Pressured by Sophia, Willoughby surrenders these mementoes to preserve the wealth his marriage will bring him. To maintain a façade in front of his fiancée, he must resist his impulse to kiss Marianne's hair and notes. However, he finds it necessary to tell Elinor of this impulse after she has warned him, "'Relate only what in your conscience you think necessary for me to hear'" (III.8.369). Willoughby has not listened much to his conscience; it is no wonder he has a hard time distinguishing between necessary detail and self-congratulatory reminiscences.

Elinor's request for brevity sheds light on her as well; she understands Willoughby's conduct in their interview simply as an attempt to exculpate himself and to open a door for further communication with Marianne. She is not entirely wrong, but Willoughby wants something more, which he repeatedly declares – he is not even hinting: he wants a place in the affections of a family whose principles and ways have the potential to elevate him. Willoughby, through his relation of his own conduct, tries to make himself a human being who still matters to Elinor, Marianne, and yes, to Mrs. Dashwood, too. Disdaining the society of his wife, he rushes to assure himself a place in the Dashwoods' hearts, although he cannot meet them ever again. He is refashioning their memory of him, consciously and unconsciously, throughout the conversation. He reveals things deliberately and also without meaning to. He even reveals that he constantly hid from them in London while Marianne longed every day to hear from him, to see him, as John Wiltshire notes.[23] Elinor, overwhelmed by his passionate speech and attractive physical presence, related by Austen almost as a seduction, will need distance and time to order rightly her impressions and her judgments of what he has revealed.

Austen turns to forced retrospection again when she portrays Mrs. Dashwood's later exclamation as the family sits revolving in their minds the import of the confession (as Elinor relates it). The need to reinterpret brings the reader face to face with a question of the nature of sympathy, so important for the period and for the questions of conscience that arise repeatedly in the novel. Austen indicates that persons who are close to each other do experience sympathy, but it is not necessarily romantic sympathy. United with a man whose conscience is not developed and strong, Marianne would have suffered pangs of conscience for her husband, deeply repining at the injury to Colonel Brandon and Eliza. That admission reveals why Austen stubbornly refused to unite Marianne with Willoughby, or even Fanny Price with Henry Crawford: a reformed rake does not make the best husband in Austen's world because his conscience is defective, and it is something with which his wife cannot supply him, contrary to the established tradition.[24] In fact, Austen imagines the better half of the couple taking on an insistently painful burden of guilt rather than providing redemption. If the husband does not exhibit his own change of heart, if he himself does not manifest unsullied contrition, what prize is the woman who loves him getting? She is taking on herself a kind of moral suffering justly due only to the guilty. The husband will always be her inferior because he cannot see, even in his admiration for her innocence, that he ought to endeavour to deserve her. He is content to say that he does not deserve her.

Why does Austen have Willoughby confess to Elinor near the end of *Sense and Sensibility*? We see that Willoughby is a kind of nexus of a great deal of the action, and that his misconduct does not just affect one young couple who seemed to be on the path to a romantic marriage. It validates Brandon's decision to challenge him to a duel, as he is next to unrepentant about Eliza. It validates Mrs. Smith's decision to cut him off, as he chooses money over right conduct. Yet it also reveals he is a human being, not a monster – his tender and guilty recollections of Mrs. Dashwood's trust and kindness are real indications that he still has a heart and a conscience. Carroll has justly pointed out the problem with assuming that Austen's moral system is threatened by the emotional power of Willoughby's speech: "Mary Poovey comments on this moment as representative of a kind of 'moral anarchy.' Her thesis is that the intense emotion of Willoughby's apology scene is an essential part of Austen's perspective on morality: 'Austen attempts to bend the imaginative engagement [emotion] elicits in the reader to the service of moral education' ... Elinor's emotional vacillation, however, shows the problems with assuming Willoughby to be without redeeming qualities."[25]

Austen does not depict Elinor as suddenly excusing seduction and fornication, deception, fortune-seeking, or selfishness. She, rather, understands the difficult truth that Willoughby is not all bad although he has done many bad things; nonetheless, he is still lost to them as an acquaintance. Willoughby is not a flat character, and in this chapter I have shown the extent to which the complex admixture of promising intellect, self-indulgent wealth, strong but fleeting feelings, great personal charm, and romantic performance of histrionic behaviour can affect both Austen's heroine and the reader. Elinor's accusation of cruelty can remain true even when we admit that Willoughby's fear of being thought "contemptible" shows he is not entirely lost. "Some kind of apology," "some kind of explanation," is what Willoughby offers; "something like forgiveness" "on more reasonable grounds" is what he wants and gets – the only thing he can now get from the Dashwood family. It is not the spontaneous, full-hearted forgiveness he wants, but it is *like* it. It is not the swaying of the Dashwoods' emotions but the recognition of the emotions' constituent part in the make-up of a moral person. Willoughby veers between right feeling and wrong, between sincere and dramatized feeling. Fear predominated over justice in his choices, and thus he fails the test of manliness Mr. Knightley proposes in *Emma*: "There is one thing, Emma, which *a man can always do*, if *he* chuses, and that is, his duty" (I.18.157; my emphasis). As Mrs. Smith reminded him, Willoughby failed in his duty towards Eliza. Why? Because it "could not be" (III.8.366). Willoughby failed in his duty towards Mrs. Smith. Why? Because it "could not be." Willoughby failed in his duty toward Marianne. Why? Because *"I cannot think of it – it won't do"* (III.8.367; my emphasis).

Austen's use of Willoughby as part of her *fabula* is apparent in the importance of his confession to the closure of *Sense and Sensibility*.[26] The scene happened six chapters earlier, but he returns on the last page of the book, the envier of Colonel Brandon's happy marriage to Marianne. Given prominence through Austen's persistent return to him, Willoughby remains in our memories as well as Marianne's, but his punishment contrasts with the happy ending in which Marianne unexpectedly finds herself.[27] She forgets Willoughby and marries Colonel Brandon not because, as some Bergsonian critics maintained in the past, Willoughby is the sexually vibrant potential lover Marianne is denied by her author as punishment, but because the repentant Marianne receives a greater reward than she ever imagined in her system. Willoughby, on the other hand, remains in that liminal territory he occupied in his confession, always interested in and attracted to the superior Marianne, a good; but fixated on a woman he did not deserve and who is married to another, an evil.

Willoughby doesn't *just* want "something like forgiveness," it turns out: he wants Marianne, a Marianne who is blind to his failings and under the sway of his charm once again: he wants from her a "more spontaneous, more natural, more gentle, less dignified, forgiveness" (III.8.373–4). That is, Willoughby wants a Marianne under the rule of her passions, which he still sees as more authentic and the source of his erstwhile power: "'You tell me that she has forgiven me already. Let me be able to fancy that a better knowledge of my heart, and of my present feelings, will draw from her a more spontaneous, more natural, more gentle, less dignified, forgiveness. Tell her of my misery and my penitence – tell her that my heart was never inconstant to her, and if you will, that at this moment she is dearer to me than ever'" (III.8.373–4).

As Willoughby projects in the future such a fervent and emotion-driven Marianne, Austen is already planning to reveal his own placid and pedestrian domestic existence. She perfectly shows that he is still standing at a crossroads, punished but not sufficiently penitent. His penalty is to be forgiven when he has already tied himself to what he thought was his redemption – it turns out to be his imprisonment. Looking back at this confession six chapters later, the reader is surprised by Willoughby's ordinariness. When he is not speaking himself, all dash and passion and penitence and impatience, he is just another English sportsman enjoying the hunt, not quarreling much with his wife, sipping his port, going to London for the Season and examining the year's newest debutantes. The reader may think that Edward Ferrars is a crashing bore, especially in contrast to the more exciting Willoughby, but, though Willoughby persists almost to the bitter end as a subject for the narrator's attention, he is diminished. In his case, to be deprived of dialogue is to be deprived of everything that made him a potential hero.

CHAPTER FIVE

"The Happiest, Wisest, Most Reasonable End": Silence, Spatial Dislocation, Secrets, and the Sublime in *Pride and Prejudice*

Elizabeth Bennet: "Beyond Her Own Knowledge"

Of the many "lasts" Austen features towards the end of her novels, there is always a last conversation between the heroine and her husband-to-be.[1] Elizabeth Bennet and Mr. Darcy's conversation in the penultimate chapter of *Pride and Prejudice* is the last time Austen features the two speaking to each other before they fall silent in the final chapter. This conversation, in volume 3, chapter 18, lacks a physical and temporal setting, floating between Elizabeth's reception of her parents' consent and her writing to Aunt Gardiner to disclose her engagement to Mr. Darcy.[2] Although it is rather clear that the conversation must happen two days after the proposal, Austen is beginning to unmoor her characters from time and even, in this case, from specific geography or domestic space.[3] This unmooring is a significant movement in the novel that helps create the inimitable atmosphere readers of the novel seem to agree characterizes the best conclusion in Austen's oeuvre. And yet much of what passes between Elizabeth and Darcy in the final chapters passes in silence. I would argue that in this novel Austen agrees with Shakespeare's declaration that silence is, or can be, the "perfectest heralt of joy" (*Much Ado About Nothing,* II.i.306). Austen carefully deploys silence as well as spatial and temporal dislocation to evoke the sublime and to help create the tone of profound joyousness that we associate with the end of Elizabeth Bennet's story.

Critics have noted that Elizabeth and Mr. Darcy are already falling silent in the proposal scene in chapter 16, two chapters earlier – or rather, they are conversing out of earshot. Both Mary Lascelles and John Wiltshire, among others, comment on Austen's reticence in this scene, although the exchange between Elizabeth and Darcy that follows her acceptance of his proposal runs to almost six pages of uninterrupted dialogue. Lascelles thinks Austen's reserve "instinctive" (and, sadly, "limiting [Austen's] province"), seemingly regretting that "the dialogue gives place to narration and reported talk," that we "hear only the story-teller's voice – until those private moments are past; and when the lovers become audible again, they are still walking").[4] Wiltshire notes that the dialogue after the proposal "takes place as they walk together, unconscious of time passing … The reader is kept at a distance."[5] The lovers are half in focus, half out of focus, and as Austen prepares to send them off on their own, she does indeed permit them to wander in a timeless, unpeopled, and unspecified landscape: "They walked on, without knowing in what direction. There was too much to be thought, and felt, and said, for attention to any other objects" (III.16.407). When time returns, it only dominates briefly: "After walking several miles in a leisurely manner, and too busy to know anything about it, they found at last, on examining their watches, that it was time to be at home" (III.16.411). When they arrive at home, clearly late, Jane asks, "My dear Lizzy, where can you have been walking to?" a question repeated by everyone else as soon as they sit down to table. "She had only to say in reply, that they had wandered about, till she was beyond her own knowledge" (III.17.413). Elizabeth's blushes communicate nothing to the assembled family; her secret is safe, and she and Darcy remain in their own private world a little while longer, a place "beyond her own knowledge."

Austen does not use this phrase lightly. Since Lizzy is walking in her own countryside and she has lived there all her life, the narrator surely cannot mean the reader to understand merely that she went to a location she had not seen before; that kind of information is purposeless, and Austen is always purposeful. The phrase Elizabeth uses seems not to describe a geographical location near Longbourn or Meryton, but a state of mind, another world. Juliet McMaster has talked about the "geography of a mind" in *Emma*: though conceding that Austen is not habitually an allegorist, McMaster proves that she clearly makes allegorical connections between landscape or the weather and the intellectual, imaginative landscape within.[6] With no geography, no map, Elizabeth may well be beyond the familiar world that she knows in her first walk with the man she has now promised to marry, the person she once took joy in disprizing but whom she has grown to esteem and love. She is experiencing the newness of her new life; she is on a threshold leading into uncharted territory. This is one source of her agitation: she "rather *knew* that she was happy, than *felt* herself to be so" (III.17.413; emphasis in original). This extraordinary phrase even dislocates the passions from their realm: How does one know happiness without feeling it?

Austen is describing an experience of novelty that we would do well to examine. Christopher Miller has written of Austen's "aesthetics and ethics of surprise"; although one could argue the point, he finds in Joseph Addison's definition of "wit" a replacement for the *utile* in Horace's famous dictum in his *Ars Poetica* that the useful should be mixed with the sweet. He believes Austen, too, is interested in the combination of delight and surprise. Miller's discussion mostly focuses on *Northanger Abbey*, but one could say that surprise as an effect of wit is an inarguable element in *Pride and Prejudice*. I would go further and add that this surprise, this effect of wonder, seems to be something Austen is trying to evoke even in the silence of her most witty lovers.[7] Miller himself connects surprise to the ancient concern with "wonder": "it is the quiet inner movements of feeling and thought – the pleasurable carriage ride, the burst of sun, the apt metaphor, the dropped pen – by which Austen excites, in the best sense of the term, our wonder."[8] Miller notes that Henry Tilney's wit evokes this same wonder in Catherine Morland. Whereas wit requires verbal expression to provoke this reaction, Austen reduces the role of verbal wit in the second half of *Pride and Prejudice*, as many readers have noted, sometimes with disappointment. However, Austen has more than one tool with which to elicit wonder in her characters and her readers. The prevalence of the word "wonder" in the novel would alone tell us that it is something she is concerned to treat in the story,[9] but its being featured in the revelation of Elizabeth's engagement to Mr. Bennet confirms its prominence: "This is an evening of wonders indeed!" (III.18.418).

Philosopher Eva Brann has described a sense of wonder as a type of dislocation from oneself. She traces the definition back to its roots in the classical tradition:

> When things are going on in life that seem impossible in thought – that is the moment at which something flashes out, for some people …, that has the name "wonder." Wonder is that sense of fascinated estrangement from yourself and your world that makes you think. Both … Plato and Aristotle think that wonder is the origin of that peculiarly searching kind of thought called philosophy. Plato has Socrates say: "This is indeed the special feeling the philosopher has – wondering" … Aristotle says: "It was because of wondering that people first began to philosophize" … Wonder is the sense, which comes in a flash but won't go away, that things are not as straightforward as they seem, that the ordinary way, or explanation and argument leaves you with unbearable contradictions and impossibilities.[10]

Austen is interested in describing this kind of experience of wonder in Elizabeth and Darcy (though in chapter 17 she also describes both Mr. and Mrs. Bennet as undergoing wonder). Although she may indeed be asking the reader to philosophize, it seems one of her main goals is to suspend the ticking clock and to provide a sense akin to the romantic sublime, which did not always require Alps and oceans for its evocation. The unknown and the invisible are also things that provoke the effect; Edmund Burke even adds privation to this list, and, perhaps most importantly for this study, silence.[11] These are all types of open spaces that have a power decorated, described, filled spaces do not. Austen places her heroine in such a space. For Austen, that open space is nonetheless not a void. It is full to the brim.[12]

Elizabeth and Darcy's unconsciousness of time and space is an effect of their great joy and their detachment from a kind of tyranny of mortality, a promise to the reader that they will always exist as they are now.[13] Their ignorance of their surroundings, which they see as little as we do, manifests their total absorption in this crucial decision of their lives, this momentous event for their hearts. Austen links the experience of timelessness that she is infusing into the closure of her narrative with the experience of being blissfully in love. As Darcy says when Elizabeth plies him for information about his falling in love with her, it was no particular, datable occasion: "I cannot fix on the hour, or the spot, or the look, or the words, which laid the foundation. It is too long ago. I was in the middle before I knew that I *had* begun" (III.17.421). And of course, Elizabeth has just said the same thing to Jane about the beginning of her love for Darcy: "It has been coming on so gradually, that I hardly know when it began" – although she then playfully adds,

"But I believe I must date it from my first seeing his beautiful grounds at Pemberley" (III.17.414). Jane's rejection of this particular date and her demand for seriousness means we are back in the undatable gradualness Elizabeth first asserted. Austen gives us a "solemn assurance of attachment," not a date (III.17.415).[14] Perhaps she eschews love scenes in order to offer in their place a description of experiencing pathlessness, timelessness, something that verges on the inexpressible. To her as a writer, tackling a mimesis of that experience could very well be more interesting than the verbal acceptance of a proposal.

Anne Toner has said of Austen's use of apophasis, the rhetorical term for saying one will not say something, that "to declare that something is indescribable is essentially apophatic: in denying expression, that which is denied is expressed. The denial intensifies the object described and thus proves descriptive. The declaration that feelings are beyond expression becomes, paradoxically then, the most affective and efficient way of expressing them."[15] But, although we cannot hear them, Elizabeth and Mr. Darcy are not silent. The freedom with which the two discuss their proposal and their obligations contrasts strikingly with the grave and taciturn visits Darcy has been making to Longbourn with Bingley and with the castigating observations Elizabeth has made to herself about him in the past.[16] They are revealing secrets. The fact that they themselves had two secrets – Darcy's, that he loved her, and Lizzy's, that she hated him – is the thing that makes the first proposal scene at Hunsford so explosive, for they reveal the terribly painful truth to each other rudely and suddenly. The secretive nature of the truth has allowed both of them to count on the other's feeling precisely the opposite of what they had really been feeling. That experience of the new also had provoked wonder in both participants, a wonder leading to a grappling with the other's point of view. Later, the social impediments to open communication and the natural hesitancy arising from the previous rejection as well as the *real* modesty of true love (which Darcy lacked at the first proposal) all conspire to prevent Darcy and Lizzy from understanding each other's silences during Darcy's visits to Longbourn with Mr. Bingley.

Elizabeth thus imagines she has taken a bold step when she divulges to him in their first walk that she has heard of his charitable actions on behalf of Lydia. The narrator tells the reader immediately beforehand, "Elizabeth was secretly forming a desperate resolution," but she adds something Elizabeth cannot know: "and perhaps he might be doing the same" (III.16.405).[17] And then when Kitty parts from them to call on Maria Lucas, Lizzy "went boldly on with him alone. Now was the moment for her resolution to be executed, and, while her courage was high, she immediately" spoke (III.16.405). This all sounds like a heroic spy mission, not like the prelude to a love scene. Until the two can break the silence and speak, however, their secret thoughts *are* potentially dangerous, and Elizabeth also *should* not know what she is about to bring up, the secret of Darcy's role in Lydia's marriage. Silence partakes of the sublime because it is fearful: it may contain a threat or a danger. As their previous experiences have shown, shared silence is not always an experience of intimacy or mutual knowledge. Silence is fraught. Thus, Austen shows there are different silences her heroine shares with her intended; they shift and progress.

It is not during this walk, but on the third walk (the second is only narrated), in the full assurance of Darcy's affections, that Elizabeth discusses secrets and secret-breaking with Darcy. She faults herself for benefiting from the breaking of one of his, which is of course one key to the whole progress of their relationship – it is Darcy's entrusting her with a secret that begins her gradual movement towards him, and it is her and Jane's decision to keep his secret that leads to Lydia's being allowed to go to Brighton, thus bringing on the crisis that enables Darcy to intervene as a (secret) demonstration of his devotion to Elizabeth. This last secret of Darcy's involvement in Lydia's rescue serves as a pretext for talk, which will lead to a silence of understanding beyond words.

"You Need Not Distress Yourself. The Moral Will Be Perfectly Fair"

This third walk is without a setting: Elizabeth and Darcy either wander about without any sense of space or time or have found some secluded spot at Longbourn – Austen does not tell the reader – and "Elizabeth's spirits soon ris[e] to playfulness again" (III.18.421). Their conversation previews the couple's future relationship, as Austen allows Elizabeth to indulge in some teasing – mostly directed at Lady Catherine, during which Darcy shows himself perfectly willing to be an unflappable straight man to her wit, with his own glint or two of dry humour. Although this is the scene that most explicitly brings up a potential moral to their story, it is really a comic scene as much as a romantic one. Its topics are secrets and silence, but it showcases verbal dexterity in both characters and reveals Austen's usual concern with the "moral" of her stories. It also reveals something about Austen's concerns as a writer that when the two are not silent at this point in their relationship, they talk about silence.

After Elizabeth directs Darcy to exaggerate all her virtues, which are now under his protection, she requires him to explain his silence upon his first returning to Longbourn.

> "I shall begin directly, by asking you what made you so unwilling to come to the point at last? What made you so shy of me when you first called, and afterwards dined here? Why, especially when you called, did you look as if you did not care about me?"
>
> "Because you were grave and silent, and gave me no encouragement."
>
> "But I was embarrassed."
>
> "And so was I."
>
> "You might have talked to me more when you came to dinner."
>
> "A man who had felt less, might." (III.18.422)

Darcy wins at the repartee in which they engage here: he has the best reason for his silence, a silence that brought some hours of painful anxiety to both of them. They endured it in a solitude the current conversation assures the reader they will not need to suffer again the future. As noted above,

Austen seems to ally herself with Shakespeare's assessment that deep feeling cannot be expressed in words, and that garrulous declarations of love are shallow or false: "I were but little happy if I could say how much" (*Much Ado About Nothing*, II.i.306–7); "What, gone without a word? / Ay, so true love should do; it cannot speak, / For truth hath better deeds than words to grace it" (*Two Gentlemen of Verona*, II.ii.16–18); "Love, and be silent" (*King Lear*, I.i.62). Darcy's defence of his silence satisfies Elizabeth – who would not be flattered by such a declaration of deep feeling? – but his termination of this subject raises another, equally important to Austen's design of her conclusion – that is, the issue of whether or not she is teaching bad morality by having her heroine's happy ending depend on a dishonest action.

Elizabeth launches into this subject by teasing Darcy, suggesting that this time he was incapable of bringing himself to propose on his own, and that she has incurred moral guilt by taking the reins, as it were, and encouraging him to speak. Notably, the problem is not that she as the woman should not be prompting a proposal; Austen does not focus on gender in this instance. Instead, Elizabeth's concern here, and part of what instigates her bravado, is the question of whether she may legitimately reach for happiness by means of the immoral act of a broken promise.

> "How unlucky that you should have a reasonable answer to give, and that I should be so reasonable as to admit it! But I wonder how long you *would* have gone on, if you had been left to yourself. I wonder when you *would* have spoken, if I had not asked you! My resolution of thanking you for your

> kindness to Lydia had certainly great effect. *Too much,* I am afraid; for what becomes of the moral, if our comfort springs from a breach of promise? for I ought not to have mentioned the subject. This will never do." (III.18.422; emphasis in original)

Talking about their story *as* a story, speaking very much like the narrator in *Northanger Abbey* who jokingly sighed over the amoral tendency of her work, Lizzy tut-tuts over the immorality she has woven into their narrative.[18] Austen laughingly evokes a large number of writers whose heroines suffer because they cannot violate a secret, though their own happiness would be secured thereby (including her own Elinor Dashwood). Of course, Lydia is the one who did not keep the secret, so Elizabeth has already been partially exonerated by her creator, and yet it must be admitted that she plied Lydia, and then her aunt, for details. "This will never do" because the happy ending is being secured through an immoral act, the use of ill-gotten gains, instead of by an act of virtue – a direct fling at poetic justice. Elizabeth, however, is too happy to care, really. This is banter, not philosophical discussion on her part. Nonetheless, Darcy drily replies, "'You need not distress yourself. The moral will be perfectly fair. Lady Catherine's unjustifiable endeavours to separate us were the means of removing all my doubts. I am not indebted for my present happiness to your eager desire of expressing your gratitude. I was not in a humour to wait for any opening of your's. My aunt's intelligence had given me hope, and I was determined at once to know every thing'" (III.18.423). As usual, Darcy makes an effort to remove sources of anxiety from Elizabeth, even if he knows she is joking. He proclaims, in favour of our author's moral purpose, that Elizabeth's declaration had nothing to do with his proposal. He reveals his own moral progress and his consistency as a character at the same time as Austen slyly inserts a phrase that circles the reader through a forced retrospection back to the first thing he said about her in the novel, "*I am* in *no humour* at present to *give consequence* to young ladies who are slighted by other men" (I.3.12; my emphasis).

"I was not in a humour to wait for any opening of your's" is a phrase that might justly chill the faint-hearted. However, Darcy's pompous language (and Austen probably means for this reference to be unnoticeable to him) shows how far he has come from his initial scornful detachment. Austen gives no stage directions to illustrate the way he says this, but it is impossible to read the second sentence in the same way as the first. This time he means, "I was not in the mood to wait any longer to find out if you would marry me," a far cry from "I am not in the mood to honour a wallflower with my attention." Austen's echo of his earlier locution is a way of bringing closure to their story, repetition closing a circle and nonetheless confirming moral change.[19] In the Middle Ages, the name for this narrative strategy was "annulation," or *annulatio*. J. Hillis Miller calls it "repetition," but, like the trope known as antanaclasis – the repeated words or types of scenes in a sentence or stanza – Austen's use of structural repetition encompasses more than simple reiteration. The term, which derives from the Latin word for "ring," describes a method of connecting the various episodes in a story by repeating a type of scene or a phrase, often with progressively different details. It is a way of advancing the plot but keeping the story unified. Austen uses annulation to do something she is very good at, changing a character while keeping him or her the same. The phrase about not being in humour is recognizably Darcy-esque: how different from Mr. Knightley's stumbling and humorously indecipherable, "Stay, yes, why should I hesitate? – I have gone too far already for concealment" (*E*, III.23.468) or Captain Wentworth's desperate, "I must speak to you by such means as are within my reach" (*P*, II.11.257).

Moreover, Darcy's rescue of the moral of the story happens in a kind of counterfactual narrative. Austen uses counterfactual statements throughout her novels, but she especially features them at the conclusion, where what might have been is on several characters' minds, either because Austen thinks it is a probable thing for people to consider when they are resolving complications in their lives, or because she is inviting the reader to consider her authorial choices. Perhaps it is both. Elizabeth will never have any idea of how Darcy would have broached the topic if she had not made it easy for him. She is clearly speculating about how he would have made the leap from silence to speech. However that might have happened if she had not spoken, the real irresolution of the previous visits (unlike his pretended fears of rejection in the proposal at Hunsford Parsonage) has helped pave the way for the assurance he now feels, based on his better knowledge of Elizabeth and the confirmation Lady Catherine unintentionally provided. "I was not in a humour to wait for any opening of your's": perhaps this is true, but no matter what Mr. Darcy's humour, the fact is that he did wait for that opening. He rates his own resolution to propose as morally unimpeachable because it is based on the undoubtedly plain-spoken account his aunt has given of her outrageous conversation with Elizabeth, not on Lydia's betrayal of a secret. The phrase "Lady Catherine's unjustifiable endeavours to separate us were the means of removing all my doubts" shows that Darcy considers that removal the source of their happy ending, attained in a way to satisfy the most exacting novelistic ethicists. "The moral will be perfectly fair" – that is, the moral will be both just and beautiful, both meanings packed into Darcy's polyvalent term "fair."

In this metatextual moment, Elizabeth and Darcy comment on the narrative ploys Austen has used to bring them happiness. Although Elizabeth feels her agency is compromised, Mr. Darcy does not. Austen's heroines often have to think about the injustice they might be committing in accepting their suitors – Catherine, about Henry's disobedience to his father; Elinor, about Edward's disobedience to his mother; Emma, about Harriet's disappointment and her father's fear of abandonment; and Fanny, about reaping her own happiness out of Edmund's sorrow. *Pride and Prejudice* unites the lovers' joyous silences with the most explicit discussion about the justice of their attainment of that joy. Austen shows the reader that she can appear to flout a moral convention of the novel and rescue her moral at the same time. It is proof of her ingenuity that she uses the moment to advance the intimacy of her main couple rather than merely indulge in writerly self-commentary.

The two conversations between Lizzy and Darcy that bring Austen's portrayal of them to a close are among Austen's most intimate lovers' dialogues; in these pages, Mr. Darcy first calls Elizabeth by her first name, "dearest, loveliest Elizabeth," as Wiltshire notes.[20] Enjoying the privilege of family relationship, Mr. Knightley always calls Emma "Emma" (though never "my dearest" until the end), and Edmund Bertram has always called Fanny "Fanny," and often "my dear Fanny," from their very first conversation on (he *does* venture to call her "My very dear Fanny" in the uncompleted note he writes to go with the gold chain he has bought her and even "my dearest Fanny" when narrating his last interview with Mary Crawford). But Mr. Darcy has never called Elizabeth by her first name before (in fact, outside of her immediate family, who generally call her "Lizzy," few characters address her using her first name: only Caroline Bingley and Sir William Lucas call her "Miss Eliza," and only Aunt Gardiner and Charlotte call her "Eliza"); it is a liberty, and as soon as he may take it, he does. In the second reported interview, he is using her Christian name as if he has done it all his life:

> "Lady Catherine has been of infinite use, which ought to make her happy, for she loves to be of use. But tell me, what did you come down to Netherfield for? Was it merely to ride to Longbourn and be embarrassed? or had you intended any more serious consequence?"
>
> "My real purpose was to see *you,* and to judge, if I could, whether I might ever hope to make you love me. My avowed one, or what I avowed to myself, was to see whether your

> sister were still partial to Bingley, and if she were, to make the confession to him which I have since made."
>
> "Shall you ever have courage to announce to Lady Catherine what is to befall her?"
>
> "I am more likely to want more time than courage, Elizabeth. But it ought to be done, and if you will give me a sheet of paper, it shall be done directly."
>
> "And if I had not a letter to write myself, I might sit by you and admire the eveness of your writing, as another young lady once did. But I have an aunt, too, who must not be longer neglected." (III.18.423)

Aside from using her Christian name, Mr. Darcy demonstrates a kind of perfect ease in repartee with Elizabeth. He does not quail at the assault on his courage or get on his high horse about her fanciful description of his real purpose in coming to her home with Mr. Bingley: "to ride to Longbourn and be embarrassed" (she could hardly invent a more unlikely aim).[21]

And yet Darcy admits to disguising his real purpose even from himself, so how could Elizabeth or the reader know it if he himself did not acknowledge it? He pretended *in his own mind* that he was just coming to help Bingley along and to make amends for his interference in his friend's relationship with Jane; but in truth, Bingley was a means to an end. He really wanted to see Elizabeth and "make" her love him. Darcy's purpose is so secret he even tries to keep it from his conscious self. Like Mr. Knightley in *Emma*, Mr. Darcy arrives to find that he does not need to make an effort to achieve this goal. The deed is already done. However, Darcy would have had a hard time finding a pretext for his visit if Mr. Bingley had not provided such a convenient disguise. He might have needed to write another letter, even less appropriate than his first.[22] Instead, he will write to Lady Catherine to inform her of their engagement, and Elizabeth will write to her Aunt Gardiner. This is the next step after securing the permission of her parents, and once again, as in *Northanger Abbey*, Austen makes drawing the older generation into the process of forming the new family a significant element in closing her narrative.

Elizabeth and Darcy will write their letters by themselves, without hanging over one another's desk and admiring each other's writing or dictating personal addenda. Another instance of annulation in this conversation, uniting the end to the beginning, is Austen's inclusion of a reference to Caroline Bingley's frantic flirting with Darcy at Netherfield. Now it is Elizabeth who may sit by him if she chooses, but she is so sure of him she does not so choose, and she makes sure he knows it. Recalling Caroline's vain attempts to fascinate Darcy provides an opportunity to the reader to call to mind earlier sections of the narrative and to project into the future. Elizabeth's kind of flirting will replace Caroline's, as the reader always wanted (and, clearly, Darcy did too), the privileged teasing with loaded allusions that intimate knowledge provides. Darcy will not have to suffer from a barrage of calculated female flattery (of the fulsome kind Austen shows the Musgrove girls bestowing on Captain Wentworth in *Persuasion*). Lizzy does not care if Darcy knows she is laughing at Caroline's ridiculous blandishments, nor does he pretend ignorance or attempt to defend the sister of his friend, who has always aroused his impatience and at times as sharp a reproof as courtesy allowed. Whereas at the beginning of the novel he tolerated Caroline and even allied himself with her against the Bennet family, now he and Elizabeth are united against her. Caroline, like Lady Catherine, is going to be a reliable source of humour Elizabeth can tease him with. He has no objection.

As I have argued elsewhere, Caroline Bingley is a strange sort of rival to Elizabeth. Whereas, from the very first, Caroline seems instinctively alert to the threat Elizabeth poses to her pretensions and becomes increasingly hostile to her as she perceives Darcy's interest growing, Elizabeth always seems unaware of the possibility of herself being a romantic threat. Austen has reminded her readers of Caroline before when she was absent, notably when Elizabeth thinks with glee about her disappointed hopes should Darcy wed his cousin Anne de Bourgh. It is Austen who keeps Caroline in the forefront of Elizabeth's speculations about Darcy, and Austen who now once again reminds the reader, even as Elizabeth reminds her intended, that she has noticed the way other women treat him and does not intend to follow their example.[23] Austen has used Caroline to attract Elizabeth's attention to Darcy instead of making romantic attraction the main force. Elizabeth can pay careful attention to him without being motivated by infatuation. She does not like Darcy in volume 1, but she does like watching him dislike Caroline, as do we. Perhaps Austen means the reader to see from the time of Jane's illness at Netherfield that the one thing Lizzy cannot help but approve of in Mr. Darcy is his dislikes (except, initially, his dislike for Wickham). At Rosings, if Caroline is not there to be jealous of Anne de Bourgh, Elizabeth is there to imagine her being so, and that is almost as good. And now, near the end of the novel, here is Caroline again, as Elizabeth laughingly reminds Mr. Darcy of a fate, which could have been his for the asking, but which she has *always* known he would abhor. Elizabeth is on the verge of sharing novelistic imaginings with her creator; she is thinking about the way the story is ending.

Caroline's defeat is necessary to the novel's end. The defeat is both romantic and social for, in becoming Mrs. Darcy, Lizzy takes the man she wanted and rises above her on the social ladder. But it is also no defeat at all, since Mr. Darcy always had better taste than to contemplate uniting himself to a person he clearly thought was fawning towards him and mean spirited to others. There was never a competition where he would be the prize. Still, Austen makes sure to grant Caroline a place in the novel's closing chapter: "Miss Bingley was very deeply mortified by Darcy's marriage; but as she thought it advisable to retain the right of visiting at Pemberley, she dropt all her resentment; was fonder than ever of Georgiana, almost as attentive to Darcy as heretofore, and paid off every arrear of civility to Elizabeth" (III.19.430). Elizabeth thinks of other ways Mr. Darcy's story at least might have ended, and laughs. Whereas counterfactual propositions about the narrative will upset many readers of *Mansfield Park*, no one who reads *Pride and Prejudice* is unhappy that Caroline Bingley and Lady Catherine have suffered defeat.

To "Teach the Admiring Multitude What Connubial Felicity Really Was"

"Her uncle and aunt had already lost three days of happiness" before Elizabeth replies to her aunt's letter (III.18.423–4); and in imitation of this deferral, one more element in *Pride and Prejudice*'s closure must be dealt with before I consider the function of this letter in the novel's conclusion. The reader might be surprised to realize that the purpose of the story has been announced far in advance of its actual ending. However, in the conversation examined above, Darcy and Elizabeth are both aware of what it is. They are more than aware of it: they choose to have agency in creating it. When Lizzy reveals her engagement to Jane, and in disbelief her sister asks if she can be happy with Darcy, Elizabeth says with aplomb, "There can be no doubt of that. It is settled between us already that we are to be the happiest couple in the world" (III.17.414). In this way, Austen lets the reader know at least one topic of conversation from the proposal scene. Lizzy, however, had determined what their marriage should mean nine chapters earlier.

It is significant that the phrase that contains the heading for the present section – "But no such happy marriage could now teach the admiring multitude what connubial felicity really was" (III.8.344) – can be read as free indirect discourse, or interior monologue, from Elizabeth herself.[24] The sentence is remarkable, coming as it does when Elizabeth is beginning to love Darcy and, because of Lydia's disgrace, beginning to despair of having him. But it is jaunty, perhaps even cocky, and it foreshadows their actual happy marriage in a way that undercuts Elizabeth's frustration and grief. Is it Elizabeth mocking herself or Austen gently teasing her? On the one hand, the sentence imagines a large audience to her excellent love, in the manner of a John Donne, who never seems to think of experiencing true love without also becoming a figure of admiration and emulation to the entire population of lovers in the world. Elizabeth is already a kind of modern bride, enjoying the pedestal afforded the central figure of the wedding and also enjoying the envy of her friends. This is marriage as elevation above the multitude. Being chosen is a kind of election in a political or religious sense, and Elizabeth is definitely thinking in these terms.

She has already formed a picture of her happiness with Darcy *after* marriage that has to be expressed in Darcy-esque latinate language, unlike Charlotte's more everyday and humdrum "happiness in marriage," which is resolutely Norman and Germanic and, coincidentally, like the ancient Germanic religions, relies on hap or *wyrd*: it "is entirely a matter of chance" (1.6.25). "Connubial felicity" is a different matter entirely. These words constitute half the joke of the sentence because they are so elevated, so overly formal. Yet the scholarly or preacherly quality of the words also elevates their marriage; Elizabeth and Darcy will experience not just "happiness in marriage" but "connubial felicity," and one can hear what a rare, precious, and noble thing that is because Elizabeth imagines it in Latin (Com + nubere = to marry with; felicitas = happiness). And it was to have been "real," not a sham, so the showmanship of the sentence is tempered by this claim of authenticity.

Although this sentence by no means ends the novel, it is one of several views into the future that Austen provides the reader in her most admired depiction of a couple suited to each other, for whom she predicts the happiest kind of marriage. It harks back to Elizabeth's lines about amazing the whole room with their speech: "'We are each of an unsocial, taciturn disposition, unwilling to speak, unless we expect to say something that will amaze the whole room, and be handed down to posterity with all the eclat of a proverb" (I.18.103). And it also calls to mind Bingley's criticism of Darcy's speech: "'That will not do for a compliment to Darcy, Caroline,' cried her brother, 'because he does *not* write with ease. He studies too much for words of four syllables. Do not you, Darcy?'" (I.10.53). Because *Pride and Prejudice* features a main couple who are always making the kind of pronouncements Elizabeth describes here, and drawing attention to their own verbal virtuosity in the way Bingley describes Darcy doing, the reader is constantly challenged to assess magisterial summations and the way they are articulated. And it so happens that "connubial" and "felicity" are both "words of four syllables."

Elizabeth's first conscious imagination of herself and Darcy as a married couple is as spectacle for the admiring multitude. But the words do not convey the uncomfortable tinge of potential voyeurism John Donne's imagining of himself as a spectacle of love does. The grandiose imagination is a self-mockery; the very inflation is already a sign of Elizabeth's deflation as she reminds herself of her real situation. The admiring multitude has already dispersed before it has gathered, because "rational expectation" tells Elizabeth that

Darcy's characteristic pride will prevent him from desiring a union with her and that the situation must – "while he was mortal" – give him a secret laugh over his narrow escape: "What a triumph for him, as she often thought, could he know that the proposals which she had proudly spurned only four months ago, would now have been gladly and gratefully received! He was as generous, she doubted not, as the most generous of his sex. But while he was mortal, there must be a triumph" (III.8.344). As it turns out, Darcy is *not* mortal, since he feels no such triumph, as the reader suspects and Elizabeth soon learns. Because Elizabeth has already described the secret triumph of the spurned Darcy as a normal expectation, and Darcy defeats that expectation, he becomes an even more desirable spouse, and the promise of happiness in their marriage becomes even more credible. Though their relationship started out with sparring, such competition and one-upmanship are vanishing by the time Elizabeth visits Pemberley. Perhaps more importantly, a real threat in the novel, the husband who lords it over his wife, embodied in Mr. Bennet and Mr. Collins, is defused before the couple even takes their vows. However, Elizabeth's meditation on the loss to the world of their exemplary marriage is yet another example of the way silence and secrecy can weigh upon and damage a person. When Austen returns to the topic of "connubial felicity," such misunderstandings of each other's "generous" or "trifling" attitude will be done away with.

This sense of security about Darcy's good character and his renunciation of competition with Elizabeth is one of the factors in *Pride and Prejudice*'s success. The curse upon Eve in the book of Genesis, which Elizabeth seems in the process of suffering from here – "thy desire shall be to thy husband, and he shall rule over thee" – is overcome. It is interesting that Austen describes Elizabeth's increasing desire for Darcy in tandem with her conviction that he wishes to dominate or defeat her. The language of victory and defeat in the novel in regard to marriage is something one finds later in *Emma* and in *Persuasion* as well. Austen describes in both these later novels two strong wills coming into collision as well as union.[25] But Darcy is the best kind of alpha male, as Joan Klingel Ray has described him, because he has no inclination to dominate or defeat his wife-to-be.[26]

Austen's psychological depth is on display as she narrates Elizabeth's realization that she and Darcy are suited to each other – and her conviction they will never meet again. As long as she could scorn or was desired, she felt elevated above the person who had the highest social standing in her circle, Darcy. Now she has tumbled off her own pedestal through vicarious guilt and shame, and, as Emma, Fanny Price, and Anne Elliot will later, Elizabeth paints a portrait to herself of her beloved's reactions to current events that are no more flattering to him than to herself.[27] She assumes he will enjoy his revenge, but he is anxious only to please her and protect her family. This reverie is part of Austen's continued progress towards the equality of the two. While revelations of the extent of Darcy's generosity of hand and heart will continue in the last section of the novel, at this point we are aware that Elizabeth's new-found reverence for his character is already coupled with a desire for his devotion.

> From such a connection she could not wonder that he should shrink. The wish of procuring her regard, which she had assured herself of his feeling in Derbyshire, could not in rational expectation survive such a blow as this. She was humbled, she was grieved; she repented, though she hardly knew of what. She became jealous of his esteem, when she could no longer hope to be benefited by it. She wanted to hear of him, when there seemed the least chance of gaining intelligence. She was convinced that she could have been happy with him, when it was no longer likely they should meet.
>
> ... She began now to comprehend that he was exactly the man who, in disposition and talents, would most suit her. His understanding and temper, though unlike her own, would have answered all her wishes. It was an union that must have been to the advantage of both; by her ease and liveliness, his mind might have been softened, his manners improved, and from his judgment, information, and knowledge of the world, she must have received benefit of greater importance. But no such happy marriage could now teach the admiring multitude what connubial felicity really was. An union of a different tendency, and precluding the possibility of the other, was soon to be formed in their family.
>
> How Wickham and Lydia were to be supported in tolerable independence, she could not imagine. But how little of permanent happiness could belong to a couple who were only brought together because their passions were stronger than their virtue, she could easily conjecture. (III.8.344)

Without ever having been Darcy's fiancée, Elizabeth is suffering from all the self-doubt the end of a relationship brings upon a young person. Although she, like the rest of her family, desires the marriage of Lydia and Wickham, she knows that the union has little chance of permanent happiness, and the narrator's conclusion confirms this prediction. She also thinks she knows that Darcy can now have no serious interest in her. His high opinion of her was something she was able to depend upon and, eventually, to value, and now she believes herself to be deprived of it. Part of the happiness of the conclusion is the surprise Austen is preparing for Elizabeth here: she will achieve the felicity she so recently thought was forever unattainable.

Few things in the world give an individual a more powerful sense of being valued above all others than being loved. Moreover, marriage gives consequence, a fact understood by people today perhaps as much as those of Austen's time. Being noticed and valued by a member of the opposite sex does the same. A popular Austen meme on the internet says, "Mr. Knightley is in the mood to give consequence to young ladies slighted by other men." The joke is on Mr. Darcy, who once was not so inclined, and the joke aligns him with Mr. Elton, of all people. And yet, the author of *The Female Instructor* (1811) says in a chapter entitled "Advice to the Fair Sex," "Be assured a woman's power, as well as happiness, has no other foundation than her husband's esteem and love; which, consequently, it is her undoubted interest, by every possible means, to preserve and increase."[28] Perhaps young ladies were to deduce from this that men's power, as well as happiness, had other foundations, but Mr. Darcy might disagree, since he was obliged to reconstruct his entire image of himself through the force of a lady's disapprobation, and he explicitly locates his happiness in Elizabeth's acceptance of his suit.[29] Although he is a fictional character, and much has been made of his being the ultimate wish fulfillment for both author and reader, research by historian Amanda Vickery has shown that eighteenth-century men in general wanted to marry and establish a family.[30] Austen emphasizes that Darcy associates happiness with acquiring Lizzy's assent: "the happiness which this reply produced was such as he had probably never felt before" (III.16.406); "I am not indebted for my present happiness to your eager desire of expressing your gratitude" (III.18.423). And, of course, in the decision she reports to Jane, Elizabeth was not alone in plotting her and Darcy's status as the happiest couple in the world.

Reporting his plan for happiness to Lady Catherine must have been a delicate affair, but Austen does not allow the reader to see the letter Darcy now writes (as an aside, if Austen imagines they are out walking in the penultimate chapter, his request for a sheet of paper is strange). Others have noted the number of letters that fly from writer to recipient in the final chapters, often focusing on the question of whether *Pride and Prejudice* was originally an epistolary novel. The letters as they now stand, whatever their original aim, form an important part of Austen's strategy for closure. *Northanger Abbey* has the famous letter from Isabella Thorpe in chapter 11 of volume 2, but even more important are the letters between Catherine and Henry that pass unimpeded by parental intervention. In *Sense and Sensibility*, Elinor and Edward peruse Lucy Steele's letter, which, with her usual imbalance of formality and slanginess, informs Edward he is released from their engagement because she has already married his brother Robert. In *Pride and Prejudice*, Elizabeth and her Aunt Gardiner exchange some of the happiest correspondence in English literature, but Darcy also promises to pick up his pen to write to Lady Catherine to inform her of their engagement, and Mr. Bennet writes to Mr. Collins to advise him to side with the nephew over the aunt because "he has more to give" (III.18.424). Lydia's congratulations and request for help is the last epistle in the novel, reiterating Austen's usual strategy of only letting the fools and villains speak in the final chapter. In *Mansfield Park*, Edmund's letter to Fanny with its shocking close, "There is no end of the evil let loose upon us" (III.15.513) two chapters before the conclusion announces the end of her exile to Portsmouth and a powerful conviction that she will be bringing good back to Mansfield. *Emma*'s extremely long dénouement features Mr. Knightley and Emma in a tête-à-tête in volume 3, chapter 15, over Frank's extremely long letter of apology from chapter 14, in which he apologizes for nothing (and Frank himself will get to have the longest conversation with Emma before she marries Mr. Knightley), but there are still five more chapters to go, and a letter from John Knightley to be read together in chapter 17. And in *Persuasion*, the most famous letter in all of Austen's oeuvre informs Anne Elliot that Wentworth is "half agony, half hope." The letters, like Willoughby's confession, invite the reader's retrospect over the entire action of the character in the plot. They also allow the heroine an opportunity for exercising her interpretive skills – or rather, the reader is challenged to read the letters as Elinor, Fanny, Emma, or Anne would read them, or, in the case of Catherine, to imagine their entire contents. Perhaps those unseen letters in *Northanger Abbey* are the most interesting of all.

The letters as hermeneutic challenges allow readers, along with the heroine – and, in the case of Frank's letter, Mr. Knightley – to exercise their knowledge. The language of these missives is often far from straightforward. Edmund and Wentworth's poignant notes, brief and full of emotion, make use of the least elliptical or equivocal language. Lucy Steele tries to be clever as she assumes the moral high ground in a transparent attempt at self-justification; Frank Churchill succeeds in being clever but does not even bother to justify himself. Only Elizabeth Bennet and her Aunt Gardiner communicate joy, but they do so through ellipsis and other strategies that encode their letters, making them models of intimate communication.

"Slyness Seems the Fashion": Dexterous Revelations

As Mrs. Gardiner says in her letter to Lizzy after Lydia's marriage, "Slyness seems the fashion" (III.10.360). Her own letter is an example of it, as is Elizabeth's joyful, if tardy, reply. Slyness affords the reader the pleasure of humour, whether that reader be Lizzy, Aunt Gardiner, or the actual reader of the novel. It also allows us and the characters access to truth in a roundabout manner and therefore provides an additional source of pleasure, the intellectual act of interpretation and discovery. The word "sly" itself indicates, and traces itself etymologically to, a form of dexterity. *Pride and Prejudice* as a novel revels in word play, and of course the heroine and hero enjoy their mastery of language as much as their creator enjoys hers. Aunt Gardiner's use of the term "slyness," however, implies something more than mere verbal virtuosity. It also suggests duplicity or at least astuteness at the service of an ulterior motive – and, in fact, one of Austen's few other uses of the word in the novel is related to Mr. Collins's secretive wooing of Charlotte Lucas "with admirable slyness" (I.22.136).[31]

In her letter, Mrs. Gardiner is referring to what she supposes to be Lizzy's disguising of the real state of her relationship with Mr. Darcy. Yet, Aunt Gardiner does not reprimand Elizabeth for being less than fully open with her; instead, she herself engages in the form of communication she believes Elizabeth is using, the dexterous revelation that is not a revelation, the assertion that is not an assertion. By constructing this intimate language of slyness, of teasing, and assigning it to Aunt Gardiner, one of the most reliable judges in her cast of characters, Austen shows she is interested in more than the "beauty of truth and sincerity" that Mr. Knightley endorses in *Emma*. In *Pride and Prejudice*, Austen is clearly thinking about the nature of slyness and its uses. Moreover, she is thinking about it as a moralist and as a British Protestant necessarily concerned with the ethics of plain speech. She masterfully constructs a vocabulary of slyness (and a framework in which she can include meaningful silences) to engage the deductive powers of both the recipient of Mrs. Gardiner's letter and the reader of the work. If we examine the interchanges between Elizabeth and her aunt towards the end of the novel, we see the way in which slyness can, in part by engaging the intellect, manifest and strengthen the capacity to love.

Austen is interested in sly or cunning speech from the outset of her career; it may almost be said to be her hallmark. Mary Lascelles has claimed that "the simplicity of her novels, together with that other quality, slyness or shrewdness, which gives this simplicity its value, seems to belong to another tradition … The essayists of the eighteenth century had been kindly masters to the young Jane Austen; the turn of wit, the phrasing, of their lighter moods had come easily to her." This point is valuable to the present argument inasmuch as Aunt Gardiner herself is a voice from an older generation, an age difference Austen carefully delineates in her characters in the narrative. Lascelles, however, also asserts that "this tone of sly simplicity is not audible … in Jane Austen's later [post-juvenilia] writing."[32] I would argue that this eighteenth-century love of wit and gnomic expression is certainly traceable in aspects of all the novels, and of course in *Pride and Prejudice*, Austen creates in Mrs. Gardiner a remarkable adept at the plain style who is capable of introducing hidden meanings in an otherwise very straightforward narrative of events.

Letters in particular provide a forum for sly communication where the voice must perform the clever speech in the absence of the speaker. The language of letters is generally more formal and even formulaic than that of personal speech, but Austen gives her characters personal voices even in epistolary communications. Norman Page argues that, for Austen, since "a letter offers a much more sustained revelation of an individual manner than dialogue normally provides, it can also offer a magnified view of an idiosyncratic style."[33] James Sherry connects the letters of the novel with greater straightforwardness: "Like Elizabeth," he asserts, "we have trusted ourselves too implicitly to qualities like liveliness, openness, and apparent good nature, without really questioning their ultimate value. Darcy's letter is thus the herald of a new sobriety and detachment."[34] Sherry associates the second half of the novel with the sober and unaffected language he describes here. When Elizabeth asks her aunt to "tell [her] in an honourable manner" what caused Darcy's presence at Lydia's marriage (III.9.354), we detect a desire for simplicity and forthrightness in keeping with the character of the eighteenth century, a period that eschewed paradox and baroque imagery. Christopher Gillie argues for the influence of Gilpin's aesthetic on Austen's mode of expression, citing the *Three Essays*: "'The true philosophic stile … exhibits objects clearly, and distinctly, without soliciting attention to itself … The stile of some writers resembles a bright light placed between the eye, and the thing to be looked at. The light shews itself; and hides the object.' Here we have the reason for Jane Austen's own studied plainness of expression."[35] Sherry's assessment unsurprisingly presumes that the movement towards frankness is a moral advance. Lizzy's warning to her aunt, "I shall certainly be reduced to tricks and stratagems to find it [the truth about Darcy's involvement] out," prompts the reader to expect clarity and to feel a certain, albeit comic, trepidation about Elizabeth's moral danger (III.9.354). Aunt Gardiner's letter is very informative, but it is far from simple, and its dexterous revelations play to an audience with special knowledge. One can hardly say her mode of expression is dishonourable, but the letter is not written in the "true philosophic stile." Moreover, as early as the "Three Sisters" and *Lady Susan*, Austen employs letters to convey more than the literal meaning of the missives – that is, to foreground the cleverness and interpretive depth of any writer. In the case of the early short works, the slyness is often negative, as amusing as Lady Susan's voice may be. However, Mrs. Gardiner's intention in her letter is to reveal truth, to encourage truth, and to demonstrate affection. The slyness here does not have deception as its end; its purpose is to be transparent to the right reader.

Aunt Gardiner's slyness consists of a kind of indirect speech that refers obliquely to knowledge and incidents she is quite sure (sometimes incorrectly so) Lizzy is fully mistress of: "'I must confess myself surprised by your application; I did not expect it from *you* … I had not imagined such enquiries to be necessary on *your* side'" (III.10.355; emphasis in original). By emphasizing her addressee in these lines, Mrs. Gardiner gives Lizzy to understand that she sees her niece as being in a special position, a position that grants her superior knowledge of the ongoing events. One can deduce that Mrs. Gardiner believes Elizabeth and Darcy are already secretly engaged and corresponding. Elizabeth can imagine no less, though her imagination is simply prodded to take that leap by her aunt's elliptical expressions.

Thus, when Aunt Gardiner adds, "if you do not choose to understand me, forgive my impertinence," Elizabeth is meant to decipher what is perhaps the most interesting sentence in the letter: how can her aunt's comments be taken as impertinent *unless* Lizzy understands what she means by them? Obviously, she may feign ignorance, but Aunt Gardiner does not believe for a moment that Elizabeth is "innocent and ignorant." She would not use these terms without any explanation of their context unless she were sure that Elizabeth could read without effort the main assertion of the letter: you are in love with and loved by Mr. Darcy. You are a "party concerned," as Mr. Gardiner seems to have put it. Explicitness, Mrs. Gardiner says here, is for the "innocent and ignorant." Witty ellipses are for the implicated and informed. The truth Aunt Gardiner is concerned to express, or at least to encourage Elizabeth to express, is the truth of her closeness to Darcy. The pleasure Elizabeth experiences when she interprets this truth would be unmitigated if she did not doubt the force of Darcy's affection. Her newfound humility makes her doubt what Aunt Gardiner encourages the reader of the novel to believe most firmly. Here, then, the epistolary language of Elizabeth's clever aunt affords the greatest enjoyment to the delighted reader, who does not share Lizzy's doubts.

What is the writer's intention in being sly if she means to convey truth? Why reveal truth in a way that could be misconstrued? It cannot always be to provide enjoyment to the reader. The circuitousness of slyness may provide pain to the person intelligent enough to read it properly. Caroline Bingley's letters to Jane, for instance, are sly. They do reveal truth to Jane in a way Caroline's previous conduct has not, but they do not amuse Jane as a reader. Miss Bingley wishes

Jane to extrapolate the meaning behind her comments, just as Mary Crawford wishes Fanny Price to understand her sly hints in her letters in *Mansfield Park*. In those cases, the pain is partly caused by an arrogant or impertinent pretense of intimacy and mutual knowledge that slyness creates. In other words, Caroline's communications with Jane are more barbed because they engage in this pretense; her ability to communicate in this way is a sign of her verbal dexterity, not of affection. For Caroline, that dexterity is a weapon, but it has been a weapon for Elizabeth and Darcy too.

Closely associated with her use of wit, Austen's employment of slyness seems most allied to her depiction of intelligence, rather than virtue, in a character (notwithstanding the slyness of Mr. Collins). I would argue, however, that slyness united to virtuous affection produces an effect that slyness united to selfishness or malice does not: those letters that combine the former allow Austen to depict for us a sense of the overwhelming exuberance and joy that only the best characters can know. It also permits a sense of familiarity and retains decorum in a written relation that, without it, would be too formal to be called intimate. Slyness, then, though the less admirable characters can exhibit it, is a quality that the more admirable characters use most properly to articulate affection or love in a way that engages the intellect as well as the heart. Thus, Sherry's understanding that *Pride and Prejudice* investigates the "impossibility of maintaining values like simple openness [and] candour … in a world dominated by their opposites," helpful as it is, neglects Austen's own concern in *Pride and Prejudice* with the potential positive qualities of those opposites.[36]

Dorothy Van Ghent speaks of the quality of "emotional intelligence" in which Austen, like Henry James, locates the moral life.[37] That Elizabeth has this quality is undeniable. While the novel in its entirety reveals her immaturity as a reader of character, it also highlights her native warmth and her lovability. Where did she get her warmth, her wit, her tact? Certainly not from her mother, who finds it difficult to be indirect; she can manage a "that gentleman" from time to time if she wants to slight Mr. Darcy, but she is so straightforward as to be rude for the most part, and Joan Klingel Ray has argued that some of Elizabeth's verbal peccadilloes are reflections of her mother.[38] Elizabeth's father has taught her wit but not playfulness. His game is to communicate with Elizabeth and Jane over the heads of the rest of the family: he can establish intimacy by this means, but perhaps does not do much to increase the girls' capacity to love. Lizzy is a willing learner of his type of communication through slyness that allows one to feel superior to others, but she avoids his extremes. Though Page asserts, "linguistically, Elizabeth is undoubtedly her father's child," he also concedes that her language is "free" from "his cynicism and even callousness"; however, he gives no explanation for that freedom.[39] For intelligent communication united with warmth and virtue, we have to look to Elizabeth's aunt and uncle. The Gardiners have long been acknowledged to be Lizzy's exemplars for married felicity. It is important to remember that the last sentence of the novel is devoted to them and their relationship with the young Darcys: "With the Gardiners, they were always on the most intimate terms. Darcy, as well as Elizabeth, really loved them; and they were both ever sensible of the warmest gratitude towards the persons who, by bringing her into Derbyshire, had been the means of uniting them" (III.19.431). The straightforwardness of this final pronouncement by the narrator may blind us to the importance Austen assigns to this couple. They are older adults worthy of the respect of the scintillating Elizabeth and the exigent Darcy, and they are explicitly credited with the union of the hero and heroine. The collection of superlatives and closure on the theme of union provide a key to the language of "emotional intelligence" in the novel.

The Gardiners best exemplify what Sherry calls the "dialectic of social participation ... For it is only [in *Pride and Prejudice*] that [Austen] fully explored the necessary tension between the impulse, indeed the responsibility, to be open, engaged, and responsive members of a community, and the need for reserve, distance and privacy lest social intercourse become vulgarized and degraded by familiarity."[40] To take this observation further, Austen is negotiating the two extremes of openness and reserve on a "microcosmic" level even in familial relationships, just as she does between friends and rivals and in social groups – and, one could say, even between the narrator and the reader. Aunt Gardiner's playful tone with her niece provides the reader with an example of a missive explicitly meant to negotiate a path between presumption and deference even with a family member – a path towards intimacy, not distance. She wants to draw Elizabeth to acknowledge facts with her and to be happy with her, to laugh with her in her delight at the discovery of Darcy's devotion to her niece. Jan Fergus has pointed out that "laughing at" is not simply a matter of a superior laugher and an inferior butt. Hobbes and some other analysts of laughter seem to ignore the more complicated strategies of "'laughter with' or indeed laughter at oneself – strategies that create communal feeling instead of establishing dominance ... At ... times [Austen] uses laughter to produce community."[41] Aunt Gardiner's brand of laughter does exactly this. When she relates the events having to do with Darcy's intervention in Lydia's fiasco, she not only shows an affectionate older person's amusement at and indulgence of the younger man's exaggerated sense of his own responsibility, but she adds, "If he *had another* motive, I am sure it would never disgrace him" (III.18.322; emphasis in original). Not only does she draw in the theme of Darcy's anxiety about his own reputation for honourable behaviour once again, a reference that invites the reader to engage in retrospective on his earlier words and actions, but she also nudges Elizabeth to produce in her the same knowing smile with which she no doubt writes the line. The italicized words are inexpressive in that they state nothing directly, but they are nevertheless laden with meaning.

It is worthy of note, too, that Aunt Gardiner's line about slyness seeming to be the fashion is not directed solely at her niece. It is preceded by this observation about Darcy: "I thought him very sly; – he hardly ever mentioned your name" (III.10.360). Once again, slyness is associated with hidden motives and unexpressed intentions. Mrs. Gardiner does not believe she is meant to misconstrue the message conveyed by Darcy's deliberate omission. Though once again she does imagine more than actually exists in terms of the formalization of the growing relationship between Darcy and Elizabeth, she detects unerringly the true state of their affections and purposes.

Elizabeth echoes her aunt's playful slyness in the letter she writes after talking to Darcy. In fact, her words about Caroline and her letter to her aunt are the last words we hear in her voice. But the bravura performance of joy comes in the letter, words to the substitute mother who has taught her a language different than the abrasive satire of her father or the equally abrasive abuse, boasting, and whining of her mother.

> "I would have thanked you before, my dear aunt, as I ought to have done, for your long, kind, satisfactory detail of particulars; but, to say the truth, I was too cross to write. You supposed more than really existed. But *now* suppose as much as you chuse; give a loose to your fancy, indulge your imagination in every possible flight which the subject will afford, and unless you believe me actually married, you cannot greatly err. You must write again very soon, and praise him a great deal more than you did in your last. I thank you, again and again, for not going to the Lakes. How could I be so silly as to wish it! Your idea of the ponies is delightful. We will go round the Park every day. I am the happiest creature in the world. Perhaps other people have said so before, but not one with such justice. I am happier even than Jane: she only smiles, I laugh. Mr. Darcy sends you all the love in the world that he can spare from me. You are all to come to Pemberley at Christmas. – Yours, etc." (III.18.424)

The central truth Elizabeth is communicating is something she never says explicitly, that she has just become engaged to Mr. Darcy. "Every possible flight which the subject will afford" is a phrase that is completely opaque to anyone who does not know Elizabeth's situation, although, as we go on, it is not hard for anyone to guess that she is a young lady in love. Anyone opening up the letter before Mrs. Gardiner, however, would not know who was meant by "him" in the sentence, "You must write again very soon, and praise him a great deal more than you did in your last." Lizzy names *him* finally near the end, but until then he is just *the one who ought to be praised more*. No one but Mrs. Gardiner and perhaps her husband would know what the "idea of the ponies" was, though it clearly has something to do with a park – but what park? Ponies, park, happiness – the middle sentences are disjointed, referring Aunt Gardiner back to her own letter and the reader's mind to the visit to Pemberley in the first chapter of the last volume. Only in the last two sentences is communication more clear and specific. Elizabeth is enjoying confiding her secret to her complicit aunt, and she especially loves that Aunt Gardiner is in the know.

Lizzy's letter is also playful in its use of sound effect. "Particular," "praise," "ponies," and the "park" have already introduced the plosive consonant "p"; Elizabeth's announcement of her superlative happiness continues it: "I am the ha*p*-*p*iest creature in the world. *P*erha*p*s other *p*eo*p*le have said so before, but not one with such justice. I am ha*pp*ier even than Jane: she only smiles, I laugh." "S*p*are" and "*P*emberley" finish the pattern. One reason that Lizzy's response sparkles so much is because Austen is using this plosive consonant to punctuate it. Usually such sounds can indicate the vigor of scorn, but here the power is the explosion of laughter: Together with the fizzing of the s's throughout, the letter fizzes and pops like champagne or a Christmas cracker.

An earlier letter in the novel, Lydia's to Mrs. Forster, spoke of laughing, but it is heedless laughter of enjoyment at giving a shock: "'You will laugh when you know where I am gone, and I cannot help laughing myself at your surprise to-morrow morning, as soon as I am missed. I am going to Gretna Green, and if you cannot guess with who, I shall think you a simpleton, for there is but one man in the world I love, and he is an angel'" (III.5.321). Elizabeth's is, in contrast, the laughter of pure joy. She is not going to Gretna Green (or, misled, carted to London); she is going to Pemberley, not a place of concealment, but a home. Another difference is clear: while Lydia says she loves Wickham, the letter nowhere says he cares for her; in contrast, Elizabeth closes by assuring her aunt that Mr. Darcy loves her very much, so much that he can spare some love for Aunt Gardiner: "Mr. Darcy sends you all the love in the world that he can spare from me." That is a prodigious love indeed.

It is hard to see how earlier critics found fault with such final expressions as heavy-handed, bourgeois moralizing. Rather, Austen seems to be trying to transfer to all her readers the "heartfelt delight" that suffuses Darcy's features after Elizabeth accepts him, to laugh with Elizabeth, to imagine that first Christmas at Pemberley with all the Gardiners present, to "give a loose to [our] fancy." For though Elizabeth is writing to her aunt, she is speaking to the second person, and the reader can easily become her audience.

Aunt Gardiner is a "party concerned" and will understand sly communications, but so are the readers. We are among the implicated, for we understand every reference and also thank her aunt for not going to the Lakes. We have never supposed more than really existed, for we have been in on much of Darcy's secret from the moment he said he was "meditating on the very great pleasure which a pair of fine eyes in the face of a pretty woman can bestow" (I.6.30). Part of the perfection of this letter, the last time we hear Elizabeth's voice quoted, is its preoccupation with delight, a delight to be crowned by the last feast of the year, Christmas: "she looked forward with delight to the time when they should be removed … to all the comfort and elegance of their family party at Pemberley" (III.18.426). What other author has done so much to describe the experience of happiness so fully at the end of a novel?

These final letters lead us to that happy day "on which Mrs. Bennet got rid of her two most deserving daughters" (III.19.427), but they also give us a foretaste of what that new community centred in Pemberley will be like. In her letter, Aunt Gardiner provides a model of respectful but affectionate language manifesting her closeness to her niece and providing a bridge to their relationship's future as Lizzy changes her state in life. She expresses both implicitly and explicitly not only her approval of Darcy but her warm affection for him, and, in accusing him of slyness – the same accusation she levels against Elizabeth – she essentially attributes to him love and intelligence. In speaking as she does, she reveals her own status as the proto-Elizabeth: her sly language engages the reader and reveals her capacity for love. Austen looks to her to prompt, in the letter written in response, Elizabeth's most effervescent expressions of joy and to set the tone of knowing delight with which the novel ends. In the close of *Pride and Prejudice*, Austen deploys both silence and speech to portray happiness as the end that she fashioned Elizabeth Bennet to attain.

CHAPTER SIX

"As Nearly for Ever as Possible": Apophasis in *Mansfield Park*

"A Juster Appointment Hereafter": Counterfactual Narrative and Apophasis

Apophasis – the unsaid that appears in spite of or because of being unsaid – is a technique Austen uses in abundance, together with ellipsis, as she approaches the end of *Mansfield Park*. These techniques allow her to venture into the world of what cannot be said and to evoke in the reader a sense of the telos of all the novel's characters that lies beyond the scope of her narrative to narrate. Why is apophasis a technique Austen would have been drawn to? She uses this strategy widely, not just in knitting her threads together in the conclusion to this novel. Indeed, Douglas Glover has argued that the entire novel proceeds via apophasis, revealing its preoccupation with holiness and the angelic virtues by means of what it refuses to say explicitly: "[Austen's] strategy is apophatic; she is more intent on describing the here and now and, through Fanny, critiquing its ethical superficiality than talking about faith, grace, and other divine interventions. With typical Austenian irony, she leaves it to her villain, Henry Crawford, to recognize Fanny's figurative divinity."[1] Whether Fanny is as divine as Henry thinks she is or not, Austen is positioning the reader throughout the last two volumes to sympathize with the Crawfords, because otherwise they, as our main appreciators of Fanny and Edmund, must be wrong about the path to virtue and happiness they believe has beckoned to them. The conclusion will prove not only that Mary and Henry have been right but also that they have gravely miscalculated their own ability to pursue that path.

Apophasis serves Austen's purpose in the conclusion because it allows her to lead the reader to contemplate what has been missing from the very beginning, from the story of the Ward sisters' privileging of wealth and status over family bonds and Christian charity. Something has been wrong, something has been lacking, since before Edmund and Fanny and the Crawfords were even born. This great thing need not be said, because we all understand it, and Austen knows her closure is more effective the more she withholds the direct statement, the more she says without saying. The fulfilment of Fanny's love for Edmund will proceed the same way, and this explains why the heroine of this novel, very much like the heroines of all Austen's other novels, becomes beloved without angling for it or having to prove herself to the man she loves. Apophasis is the rhetorical power that Fanny Price exercises in imitation of her creator.

Anne Toner explains the power of apophasis in Austen's rhetoric:

> Austen endorses moments of inexpressibility in human experience, but encourages inner scrutiny to accompany them. While free indirect discourse contradicts the inexpressible, it also enforces it, as expression remains private and internal, and also removed, in the indirect form, from direct presentation of speech or thought. The comic contradictions of the early fiction are transformed into a complex narrative strategy that voices and leaves unvoiced at one and the same time. Apophasis, with its paradoxical claim for expressing that which is not expressed, provided Austen ... with a structure to speak of silence and yet intimate something beyond.[2]

Toner's point applies not just to Austen's early works, but even more particularly to the mature works, the Chawton novels.

Near the close of *Mansfield Park,* the reactions to Maria Rushworth's affair with Henry Crawford sort the characters into their prescribed fates. The four main characters, above all, are preoccupied with what might have been, and Fanny's silent attendance to Edmund's narrative of his last meeting with Mary Crawford forms, in a way, the culmination of the action. This is the last conversation of the two cousins Austen chooses to portray. In it we have Mary Crawford, in Edmund's narrative, also thinking about what might have been, which is not precisely apophasis, but rather counterfactual musing. In this analepsis, or flashback, which Edmund is using to explain to Fanny the end of his relationship with Mary, he does not proceed by saying he will not say something – apophasis – until the very end, when he says he will not return to this material again, when he actually does so, repeatedly. By telling the story of his misguided love to his not very sympathetic cousin over and over again and assuring her he will not repeat it, Edmund invites comment, yet he receives only Fanny's silence. Her silence in part tells the reader that she knows he cannot stop repeating the same narrative until he reaches the point of what cannot be said. Edmund risibly attempts to make the story interesting to Fanny by what he imagines will garner her sympathies – that is, Mary's laments over losing her as a sister-in-law:

> "I was like a man stunned. She went on, began to talk of you; yes, then she began to talk of you, regretting, as well she might, the loss of such a —. There she spoke very rationally. But she has always done justice to you. 'He has thrown away,' said she, 'such a woman as he will never see again. She would have fixed him; she would have made him happy for ever.' My dearest Fanny, I am giving you, I hope, more pleasure than pain by this retrospect of what might have been – but what never can be now. You do not wish me to be silent? If you do, give me but a look, a word, and I have done."
>
> No look or word was given. (III.16.526–7)

Here, the conditional "would have … would have" means "did not … did not." The conditional mood itself, one might say, is an apophatic way of speaking. More interestingly, however, Edmund is unable to say one word here, substituting an ellipsis: "the loss of such a —." It is the word that would have re-ordered all their relationships as the proposed novelistic narrative of Henry and Mary Crawford would have wished. It would be the final affirmation that Fanny is a "sister." But Edmund cannot make Fanny Mary's sister even in his report of what Mary said. The word will not come out. What "might have been" can only now be seen as a "retrospect," and even the retrospect has to omit the actual bonds that might have been. Here Austen is careful about the chronology of wishes and suppositions. These belong to the whole range of characters outside of Fanny, and they now belong in the past. They constitute a future that looked appealing to everyone but Fanny herself, and the novel is going somewhere else in the future.[3]

Edmund's speech proceeds as Fanny, through *her* ellipsis, her silence, invites him to continue. In this, their last conversation in the novel, he is balancing out the good and the evil, the kind and the unkind, in Mary Crawford's last words about Fanny. Yet even here, Edmund cannot speak explicitly about what he believes to be the intervention of Divine Providence:

> "Thank God," said he. "We were all disposed to wonder, but it seems to have been the merciful appointment of Providence that the heart which knew no guile should not suffer. She spoke of you with high praise and warm affection; yet, even here, there was alloy, a dash of evil; for in the midst of it she could exclaim, 'Why would not she have him? It is

> all her fault. Simple girl! I shall never forgive her. Had she accepted him as she ought, they might now have been on the point of marriage, and Henry would have been too happy and too busy to want any other object. He would have taken no pains to be on terms with Mrs. Rushworth again. It would have all ended in a regular standing flirtation, in yearly meetings at Sotherton and Everingham.' Could you have believed it possible? But the charm is broken. My eyes are opened." (III.16.527).

Edmund's mention of Providence in this speech, which is the only mention of the divine power in the novel, is, unbeknownst to him, counterfactual. Providence did not spare Fanny; her love for Edmund did. Or does Austen mean us to see the statement as factual after all? His exclamation, "Thank God," is one of only three mentions of God in *Mansfield Park*. Although that expression hardly can be said to be noteworthy, given how common an interjection it can be, Edmund's following it with "Providence" makes it clear he is really thinking of the Almighty. He imagines that God has spared Fanny suffering because she is guileless. This statement shows Edmund's own Christianity is still immature, since it leaves no room for the Cross. Moreover, the action of the whole novel demonstrates that Edmund is wrong. God has not singled Fanny out for a life without suffering; she has been suffering for all the years since her arrival in Mansfield, and her most intense suffering is associated with Edmund, not Henry. But Austen hints at, without affirming absolutely, another possibility: Providence might have had a role at a much earlier date, shielding Fanny from Henry by allowing Edmund to become planted in her heart. The narrator is ambiguous about whether Fanny would ever have married Henry, but one thing she is always clear about: Edmund's prior claims, as the novelist portrays their effects on her heroine, have meant no other young man who has entered the scene has a chance of engaging Fanny's affections. That is the special providence of her author, at least, if it is not the Providence of God. Edmund fears he is making Fanny unhappy by his recitation, but the reader knows she can bear it with equanimity because she alone desired this outcome, though not the means by which it occurred. Austen allows the reader to weigh the different possibilities by the enforced retrospective of the whole passage but also through Edmund's incomplete and perhaps mistaken observations. Fanny herself confirms nothing here.

Edmund draws attention to Mary Crawford's lament over Henry's loss of Fanny and underscores the pain the outburst reveals Mary is experiencing through the word that cannot be said and that now must always remain counterfactual. In voicing "this retrospect of what might have been," Edmund both announces Austen's narrative strategy and describes his own. And if Fanny's name had been Sophia Western, or Pamela, if Fanny had been courted by a Henry Crawford in a novel by Henry Fielding or Samuel Richardson, the retrospect *is* what would have been. Henry, after all, was anxious to keep Fanny, even while he was sleeping with Maria: "He was entangled by his own vanity, with as little excuse of love as possible, and without the smallest inconstancy of mind towards her cousin. To keep Fanny and the Bertrams from a knowledge of what was passing became his first object" (III.17.541). But Henry apparently does not succeed in silencing Mrs. Rushworth senior or her maid, and just a few weeks' dalliance does not satisfy Maria. Maria degenerates into a Lydia Bennet or a Mrs. Clay, blinded by her own desire to the real danger to herself of her conduct, for sexual liaisons always have social consequences for the woman involved. Maria believes she has put another woman out of Henry's mind by having relations with him, the potency of her real envy of Fanny blinding her to the realities of her situation. The history of the real world is filled with the sad and often tragic stories that could prove the counterfactuality of her presumption. Austen declares that Henry is never inconstant of mind to Fanny, but her understanding of the human being, as discussed in chapter 1, is far more complex than a mind in an unmeaning physical container. She knows what she is not saying in this declaration.

Henry Crawford is cut from the same cloth as the eighteenth-century rogue heroes designed to be improved and rewarded by the heroines, complete with a heart that remains constant to the heroine while another part of the anatomy is otherwise roaming. Female authors in general were not as fond of the type as were male authors. Mary Brunton, for example, provided a prototype of the virtuous heroine wooed by the licentious but sincere cad-hero who does not end up married to her. Austen had read Brunton's *Self-Control* at least once if not twice before she wrote *Mansfield Park*, and she refers to it when speaking of *Mansfield Park* in a letter. In Brunton's book, the first love of the heroine, Laura, is a handsome scoundrel, Colonel Hargrave, whose initial proposals to her are indecent ones, but who soon resolves to marry her honourably. When she rejects him and imposes a two-year period of waiting that he may prove his sincere reform, he impregnates a married woman who has pursued him. A near cousin to Henry Crawford, Colonel Hargrave is a "hero" of sensibility. Having lost Laura, Hargrave has her kidnapped and transported to a cabin in Canada, from which Laura makes a desperate escape over a waterfall while tied to a canoe. Hargrave, convinced she has died, commits suicide in a frenzy of self-reproach and despair at her loss.[4] He is not alive to contemplate what might have been, unlike Henry Crawford, for he has already suffered his punishment.

Jane Austen's judgment on *Self-Control* is now practically the only thing preserving the novel from oblivion: "I am looking over Self Control again, & my opinion is confirmed of its' [*sic*] being an excellently-meant, elegantly-written Work, without anything of Nature or Probability in it. I declare I do not know whether Laura's passage down the American River, is not the most natural, possible, every-day thing she ever does."[5] While writing *Emma* a year later, she brings up Brunton again in a letter to her niece Anna, making a clearly – and comically – desperate resolution to improve *Mansfield Park* after it has been criticized: "I will redeem my credit with him [the critic], by writing a close imitation of 'Self-Control' as soon as I can; – I will improve upon it; – my Heroine shall not merely be wafted down an American river in a boat by herself, she shall cross the Atlantic in the same way, and never stop till she reaches Gravesend.'"[6] Not done with Brunton, Austen parodies the best-selling *Self-Control* once again in her own "Plan of a Novel," which she says is *not* to be called *Emma*.[7] Here is narrative contrary to fact with a vengeance, since Emma does not go to exotic foreign countries like Canada or "Kamschatka"; she only goes to Box Hill and wishes she had not. Austen will not provide her with an American waterfall. Clearly, in spite of her stated resolution to imitate Brunton and excel her, Austen is not in the least tempted to alter *Mansfield Park*, and well might she show a little reluctance to change an ending whose superiority over her predecessors' resides in its rhetorical genius, and its subtlety, not in the sensational incidents of a pot-boiler. What these statements about Brunton's novel show is that Austen stands by her conclusion of *Mansfield Park* and does not believe it can be improved.

Thus, what Austen does in the ending of *Mansfield Park* is deliberate, and one could argue that her examination of her characters as they recede from the reader's view is masterful. If it perplexes those who want a more conventional ending, such readers have not been reading this book carefully. Austen has prepared for the conclusion over and over throughout the novel, setting the reader up to believe or hope for counterfactual possibilities much as most of the characters do. She uses several rhetorical techniques to create one of the challenging cruces in her final chapter – that is, her description of Henry's life after the novel's action closes. The negative expressions she used in describing Willoughby's unexpectedly comfortable life in *Sense and Sensibility* give way to something even more ambiguous. Here is apophasis again, with Austen brilliantly exploring its powers. That strategy's most famous practitioner was Cicero, the Roman orator and statesman:

> Cicero gives us a definition of this Figure, and furnishes us at the same time with instances of it in the following passage: "Omission [or apophasis]," says he, "is when we say we pass over, or do not know, or will not mention, that which we declare with the utmost force. As in this manner: I might speak concerning your youth, which you have spent in the most abandoned profligacy, if I apprehended this was a proper season, but I now purposely wave [*sic*] it. I pass by the report of the Tribunes, who declared that you was [*sic*] defective in your military duty. The affair about the satisfaction concerning the injuries you had done to Labeo does not belong to the matter at hand: I say nothing of these things; I return to the subject of our present debate."[8]

Apophasis is often an attack (though it can clearly be used to convey compliments in a sly way as well). It works on the listener's imagination by naming the things it says it will not describe, making the audience participate in the judgment by daring them not to imagine something.

Austen employs a difficult apophasis as a skilled rhetorician when she describes Henry's fate in a paragraph that offers one of the harshest judgments that she invites the reader to pass on a character in her novels. Hilary Dannenberg has pointed to this passage as an example of counterfactual narrative by which the author invites the reader's interaction with the text.[9] But this is not the only thing Austen is doing. She does not just offer a possibility that she is not going to confirm: she also tells by not telling. The counterfactual narrative she employs several times in the novel causes perhaps the greatest interpretive problems for the reader in evaluating Henry here. But in addition to informing us about Henry's future, she demands that we think of something she has just said we need not think about:

> That punishment, the public punishment of disgrace, should in a just measure attend *his* share of the offence is, we know, not one of the barriers which society gives to virtue. In this world the penalty is less equal than could be wished; but without presuming to look forward to a juster appointment hereafter, we may fairly consider a man of sense like Henry Crawford, to be providing for himself no small portion of vexation and regret: vexation that must rise sometimes to self-reproach, and regret to wretchedness, in having so requited hospitality, so injured family peace, so forfeited his best, most estimable, and endeared acquaintance, and so lost the woman whom he had rationally as well as passionately loved. (III.17.542; emphasis in original)

This passage contains an extraordinary number of rhetorical gambits engaging the reader's moral outrage, moderating it, and elevating it again; requiring the reader to imagine Henry Crawford's future without Fanny, just as Austen wishes the reader to imagine Willoughby's future without Marianne. Far from providing the comforts of hunting and a sometimes not disagreeable wife, the narrator gives us a list of losses that needs to be pondered carefully, if we are, as Wayne Booth puts it, to desire the desire the author wishes to instill in us.[10]

In the first sentence, Austen announces that Crawford will not be punished, and she draws on the poetic force of alliteration to make that announcement: "That punishment, the public punishment of disgrace, should in a just measure attend *his* share of the offence is, we know, not one of the barriers which society gives to virtue." The powerful plosive "p" that begins the paragraph is our first sign of the narrator's scorn, and it is followed by plenty of hissing "s's" that increase the negative effect of the sentence. What kind of punishment will he not receive? At first Austen makes it any punishment but then immediately modifies that impression with her appositive phrase, "the public punishment of disgrace." None of her cads receive this kind of punishment, and here Austen tells us why: although it would be just that such punishment fell on men's heads as much as it does on women's, society does not raise the barrier of potential lifelong disgrace before men to impede them on their path to vice. Austen chooses a tortuous phrase to convey this simple fact, a fact she says "we know." Society seems to be something that is not "we," for we deplore this injustice, the narrator and the reader, between us. Thus we know, were we governing the world, society would justly see Henry Crawford as disgraced. It doesn't, but we know he should be.

As the author, Austen is fashioning the final chapter to draw us more closely within this "we" that includes the narrator and us as readers. We are knowers; we are aware of the injustice in the world. And we value that justice the world does not give, like the narrator who is telling us she will not give it to her character.[11] Austen would have sympathized with her fellow author's sentiments when, in *Self-Control*, Mary Brunton has the heroine, Laura, argue with her father over accepting Hargrave, who has had affairs, and they both know it. Although at this point in the novel, she is passionately in love with Hargrave, unlike Fanny Price with Henry, Laura is dumbfounded by her father's conventional defence of the young man:

> "Tell me then, were Colonel Hargrave your son, and were I what I cannot name, could any passion excuse, any circumstances induce you to sanction the connexion for which you now plead?"
>
> "My dear love," said Montreville, "the cases are widely different. The world's opinion affixes just disgrace to the vices in your sex, which in ours it views with more indulgent eyes."[12]

Laura responds that, having taken on herself the name of a Christian, she has become bound not to allow the world to form and guide her principles or her practice. She declares the tempter more vile than the tempted. And then she invokes the marriage ceremony's promises to love, honour, and obey: How could she, she exclaims, perform any of these actions towards a profligate? Her father, terming these sins "the follies usual to men of his rank," tries to convince her that Hargrave has purified his life and that she should emulate Heaven, which "forgives the sins that are forsaken."[13]

This conversation is probably one model Austen had in mind for her contretemps between Sir Thomas and Fanny over Henry Crawford's proposal, though it is very interesting to see what elements she seems to have changed to suit her heroine's situation and the tone of her own work. It illustrates for the modern reader how contemporary authors approached the issue of the promiscuous novelistic hero, a type of hero Brunton, like Austen, refused to saddle her heroine with, as she imagined life after marriage to such a creature, habituated to selfish sexual predation. Laura's father's persuasion escalates to commands and to accusations of ingratitude, which Laura, like Fanny Price, withstands. Austen further complicates the obligation of filial duty through having Fanny not formally adopted – a daughter but not quite a daughter. Her actual assumption of that position will depend on her marriage. Sir Thomas, however, uses her dependence and his fatherhood that is not fatherhood as a weapon. Brunton and Austen both imagine a father, or father-like figure, ordering his daughter to marry a man she considers immoral and unreliable, someone who will make her miserable though he can offer her rank and consequence. Sir Thomas is forgivable because he does not know until too late – no one does – how very bad Henry Crawford is. Laura's selfish father, Montreville, on the other hand, earns his descent into peevish madness and death. Austen's Sir Thomas repents and lives, and Henry lives and repents. Or at least regrets.

"In this world," Austen says of the Crawford-Rushworth affair, "the penalty is less equal than could be wished." More subtly than Brunton, Austen signals that there is more than one world to take account of.[14] If we think this is an exaggeration, we should remember that Austen repeats the reminder in the penultimate paragraph of the novel: "With so much true merit and true love, and no want of fortune and friends, the happiness of the married cousins must appear as secure as earthly happiness can be" (III.17.547). The narrator's ellipsis asks to be filled in: as much of earthly happiness as can be garnered by these securities was theirs. But she does not end with the phrase "and they lived happily ever after." She ends by saying their happiness is as secure as earthly happiness – not the other kind – can be. Such a phrase would not have been opaque to Austen's readers, accustomed to reminders that earthly happiness is passing. Perhaps this solemn recognition, so very close to our last farewell, is one reason *Mansfield Park* does not fill the reader with that glow of happiness, the sparkling security, of *Pride and Prejudice*. Austen is asking us to do something other than to bask in the glow.

She also wants the reader to go further than to sympathize with her besieged heroine and thus to take her part in defending a woman's right to choose a virtuous husband instead of a rich one.[15] The reader is asked to wish that the penalty facing a rake were indeed more equal as a universal law. In *Self-Control*, Montreville's bald-faced attempt to convince Laura that male virtue is secured by marriage to a virtuous lady, no matter how conversant in amorous intrigues the man has been up till that union, is, of course, intended to arouse the outrage of the reader against a man blinded to moral and psychological truths by the habitual prejudices in his own sex's favour that Austen will mention in *Persuasion*. In *Mansfield Park*, in the second sentence in the paragraph on Henry Crawford's fate, Austen's narrator makes the desire for equal punishment universal by strategically couching it in the passive: "than could be wished." She does not say, "than I wish" or "than we all wish," or "than we women could wish." Austen chooses as a first phrase in this momentous sentence an expression that is both moderate – she uses the conditional "could" – and sweeping.

The sentence is momentous because of the apophatic second clause: "but without presuming to look forward to a juster appointment hereafter" (III.17.542). Austen allows the reader to imagine the damnation of Henry Crawford while excusing herself from presuming so far as to enter into the metaphysical realm. She says she will not do it and in the same breath conjures up the idea of "a juster appointment hereafter." Apophasis in this case is performing its task as irony. Readers might be tempted to submit to the denotative value of the sentence: let us not look into the judgments of God; let us restrict ourselves to the earthly and the probable. Austen will enumerate those probabilities, far more bitter than those awaiting John Willoughby, in a moment. But as she does with Marianne in *Sense and Sensibility*, she allows the reader to note that her world of the probable and the verisimilar is a world not governed by divine justice, which *nonetheless exists*. The casual and almost offhand way in which she delivers Henry over imaginatively to this appointment, which will be "juster," is breathtaking, not because Henry does not deserve to be judged and punished, but because that world where such things happen to us all is not Austen's concern. "Know then thyself, presume not God to scan," Alexander Pope had intoned, "the proper study of mankind is man."[16]

Austen, as has often been noted, tends to subscribe to the belief that the realm of her fiction is the visible world, not the invisible one. But Ian Watt has called her a "moral realist," a term that has never been sufficiently defined.[17] I suggest that Watt's term implies a necessary imbrication of the metaphysical world into Austen's world of the probable, the here and now. For if Austen is a realist who believes the moral structure of the universe is real as well, she expects her readers (and, in her day, such an expectation would have been normal) to believe that it exists even when human society abandons it as a norm. The reference to "hereafter" ineluctably calls up the world after death, its usage for this purpose dating at least as far back as the early 1700s.[18] Austen cannot mean that Henry will encounter a juster punishment later in this life, because the punishment she is about to describe as his real penalty is potentially lifelong and entirely self-inflicted. Instead, Austen suggests her story's terminus lies outside the bounds of the book, and out of her hands. Just like the many instances where she suggests depth by obscuring from our view scenes she tells us are taking place, here Austen makes Henry Crawford more real, and confirms the gravity of his actions, by not presuming to take his eventual fate out of the hands of God, before whom we can be pretty sure no fictional character has ever been arraigned.

The narrator describes the punishment Henry receives in this world in two clauses describing intensifying emotion and increasing losses as the potential self-inflicted penalty that precludes the need to look into the metaphysical realm. However, Austen's narrative is not absolutely affirmative: "we *may* fairly consider a man of sense like Henry Crawford, to be providing for himself no small portion of vexation and regret" (my emphasis). After withdrawing from the reader the prospect of Henry Crawford before the throne of the divine Judge, and therefore conjuring up its very possibility, the narrator suggests but does not assert absolutely that Henry might be feeling vexed and regretful. It is worth noting, however, that the suggestion about these milder emotions changes to a "must" in the next clause as she evokes stronger reactions. The last phrases are assertions, not suggestions, and the picture is one of a far more self-conscious Henry Crawford than we have encountered in the novel to this point. The reader can imagine him vexed at the outcome of his affair with Fanny's cousin. But Austen says it "must rise sometimes to self-reproach." Self-reproach is a new thing for Henry, yet in the ending of the novel Austen leaves the reader to imagine it rather than portraying it. She instead continues her variation on the rhetorical figure of *gradatio*, or climbing stairs that take us from one point to the next until "regret" rises to "wretchedness." Yet that "we may fairly consider" remains as the main action the narrator says we are all imaginatively performing, which is different than thinking "Henry Crawford did such and such."

Austen is being very specific, very technical. Wretchedness is not contrition, but it is something better than insensibility about one's faults. Readers may find it almost impossible to believe that the almost conscienceless Henry is in this state, but the narrator asserts it would follow, something "we may fairly consider." She makes use of *gradatio* again as she moves from Henry's probable recognition that he has betrayed the hospitality of the Bertrams, who welcomed him into their home and fed and entertained him.

A traitor to his hosts (one of the most primitive and ancient of taboos), he has made use of their eldest daughter for his own pleasure and discarded her to her fate. This alone seems enough to condemn him, but the list continues. By this act he injured family peace: the reputation, security, and calm of the family are all attacked by the affair – in fact, Austen has already said that the shock over Maria's actions has caused the illness of her brother Tom to worsen to the grave state that almost meant his death. Of course, Henry has introduced a breach into the family too in abandoning Maria, now an adulteress in a world that expects the family to set her aside. Her sister, Julia, and her cousin Fanny could not be married respectably if she remained at home; even Mary Crawford flies her uncle's house in London when he allows his mistress to live there. This isolation from other unmarried women is the necessary consequence for such women in this society, and Maria's situation is unrelieved even by such a marriage as Lydia achieves, mending her reputation with Darcy's help in *Pride and Prejudice*. Maria's absence from the Bertram household seems unregretted on the one hand: no one misses her company, and she alienated Julia, the only sibling she ever seemed close to. But Austen nevertheless has Henry eventually seem to lament both divorces, the division of Maria from her husband and from her family. He regrets it so much that he is – we may fairly consider – miserable. But the final clause in the sentence, reserved for the most important item in the gradated list, is the loss of Fanny, the woman he loved. In the end, the wretchedness is over the loss of his friends who were, with all their faults, worthy of more esteem than anyone else he knew, and of

Fanny, whom he had loved with his reason and his passions. Interestingly, though, the part of the human being so central to Austen's favorite sermon writer, Thomas Sherlock, the heart, appears nowhere in this description of Henry's love.

Henry has a large following among Austen's readers, but his charm always seems calculated, his kindnesses self-aggrandizing, and his heart, as Mary Musgrove says of the more deserving Captain Benwick in *Persuasion*, "not worth having." It is possible – indeed, perhaps necessary – to stand apart from the chorus of voices protesting that Henry really loved Fanny, because Austen suspends affirming it to this brief and rhetorically ambiguous summary at the very end of the novel; before that, there is no real assurance from the narrator that Henry loved Fanny with sincerity. The delay of the revelation and its obscuring of Henry's actions, Austen's refusal to endorse all his assertions about the sincerity of his emotional state, are all deliberate on her part. She does not want to violate the primarily non-dramatic nature of the final chapter for him (or for Edmund and Fanny, either). The truth is that she could, however, and chooses not to. I believe she consigns Henry to his misery in this way because she is allowing the reader the freedom to believe him penitent or not, and because it is probable that, once aware of Fanny's superiority, he should continue to believe in it, especially when he has lived for a while with Maria's temperament and conduct. Unfortunately, his habits, like Willoughby's, also make it reasonable to assume he would not have practised self-denial when a beautiful woman offered herself to him, especially one whose devotion he wanted to reignite.

Why does Jane Austen do this? Did she not know she was making the worst kind of mistake devotees of the lively Elizabeth Bennet could imagine, creating a different kind of heroine? Couldn't she have redeemed Henry and saved Fanny from dull, if far more handsome, Edmund? Even her sister, Cassandra, wanted this ending for the novel and argued with Jane about letting Fanny and Henry marry.[19] Austen's bland, unglossed recording of her family's and acquaintances' reactions to *Mansfield Park*, which still exists today, shows she was interested in her audience's response, but not that she intended to make her next book any less difficult, though she once more turned to a witty heroine after inventing Fanny Price. It is significant that she resisted even familial pressure to change Fanny or the trajectory of her story. Austen deliberately chooses this novel's ending, then she stubbornly insists on it and will not budge. The novel ends exactly the way she wants it to.

I believe the clue to what interested Austen in constructing this novel and crafting its conclusion as she did lies in the nod to God the Judge in this paragraph on Henry's regrets. Whereas Henry has dreamed of guiding Fanny's life and governing everyone's reactions to her in the manner of a demigod, even wishing for governance of the winds, as Colleen Sheehan points out, Austen seems to create a dramatization of authorial limits in declining so great a power.[20] Like Fanny Price, who shrinks from becoming Henry Crawford's substitute conscience, Austen believes in the moral universe, but she does not think her place is to make her characters always align with it, or to punish them when they don't. She observes the characters whom she has made as probable as she can. But she goes so far and no further. She does not venture to examine the bitter but fruitless wilfulness of a woman who has trespassed: she never mentions Maria's potential repentance, for instance. Instead she says, after observing the relative mildness of Mr. Rushworth's punishment for stupidity, that Maria "must withdraw with infinitely stronger feelings to a retirement and reproach which could allow no second spring of hope or character" (III.17.537). Interestingly, though Austen has not portrayed Maria in the least as a thorough-going victim, she reserves her vague image of divine retribution to the seducer and not the woman whom society has reprehended. Henry's affair with Maria was a "take-in" the likes of which he and his sister never imagined any bad marriage to be. Austen represents Henry as perhaps the most aware of his own responsibility for his loss, for he was "taken in" by his own habits, thinking it possible to avoid retribution. At the same time, the narrator confirms the man's greater crime and leaves it up to God to sort out if it can ever be forgiven. For her part, the only outcome is that such a man can never attain the hand of one virtuous woman who loves another, albeit imperfect, man. As Henry Tilney points out in *Northanger Abbey*, in both dancing and marriage, "man has the advantage of choice, woman only the power of refusal" (I.10.74). It is a power with which Austen can change the conventions of the novel's plot. With that smaller power she is content.

Mary Crawford, Time, and Prophecy

For Austen, the ending of *Mansfield Park* would of necessity have to do with the constancy implied in the word "forever." As Joyce Tarpley has pointed out, the word "constancy" appears more often in *Mansfield Park* than in any other of Austen's novels.[21] Likewise, the sustaining of love through time, of values through time, is a major interest she pursues throughout the action of the novel and in the interior reflections of the major characters. Eternity appears more than once as the context within which the actions of her characters unfold while they progress on the line of time. What is the source of this ideal of everlastingness, the stability opposed to the continual change that Fanny notes in her discussion with Mary Crawford in the shrubbery at Dr. Grant's, and that the narrator returns to in her closure?

> [Sir Thomas] had pondered with genuine satisfaction on the more than possibility of the two young friends finding their natural consolation in each other for all that had occurred of disappointment to either; and the joyful consent which met Edmund's application, the high sense of having realised a great acquisition in the promise of Fanny for a daughter, formed just such a contrast with his early opinion on the subject when the poor little girl's coming had been first agitated, as time is for ever producing between the plans and decisions of mortals, for their own instruction, and their neighbours' entertainment. (III.17.546)

The narrator pinpoints time, but the final sentence introduces apophasis once again. Time "for ever" produces this contrast between plans and what actually happens. Moreover, the plans and decisions are made by "mortals," a designation by which the narrator introduces once again what is immortal into her text. The presence of time as a personified character might indicate Austen is tiptoeing around the issue of immortality, but she herself takes a panoramic view of the comic presumptions of those who live in this transitory life and who think to decree what will unfold. She invites the reader to take this view as well. The narrator takes delight in the frustration of the narrative designs of those who do not dwell in eternity.

Tarpley discusses the Bakhtinian concept of a "superaddressee" who will comprehend what the speaker utters even if that speaker is misunderstood by all other readers; "accordingly, Austen submits herself to a framework for truth that transcends her own creation, perhaps seeking thereby to counter too great a reliance on the narrative for truth."[22] However, the narrative does allow the characters to think about this extratextual reference point. I suggest that Mary Crawford hints at the existence of that apophatic judge in regard to Henry's love for Fanny. Mary also seems to understand the limitation of a fairy tale narrative's "happily ever after," and this understanding, perhaps fittingly, prevents her from attaining it. The truth Austen is conveying through the narrative ending of *Mansfield Park* has to do with the value of constancy, the objects of constancy, and constancy's metaphysical grounding as well as its final cause.

Austen allows a better ending for Mary than for Henry, though she never affirms Mary's love for Edmund as explicitly as she does Henry's for Fanny. Mary has hardly admitted to herself the strength of her own attachment, and if she were to shrug it off, it would be no sin. She has not really offended greatly against the law of God and man in her own relationship with Edmund Bertram. However, it remains true that she does not regard those laws as laws. As laws of time are insignificant to her (which the episode with the horseback riding lesson no less than her refusal to be "dictated to by a watch" evinces), Mary, like Fanny but for different reasons, has a complex experience of time. Time to her is tedious, intractable, expandable, negligible – and often the theme of her humour.

To examine how Austen meditates on time and eternity through Mary, we need to turn to an episode that illuminates Mary's estimate of the durability of human affections. She makes a joke at Fanny's expense when Edmund explains that Fanny rejected Henry because the newness of an idea is always a mark against it; she loves what is familiar and comfortable. Edmund tells Fanny, "Miss Crawford made us laugh by her plans of encouragement for her brother. She meant to urge him to persevere in the hope of being loved in time, and of having his addresses most kindly received at the end of about ten years' happy marriage." Fanny smiles at this; but notably, it is a false smile, for "all her feelings were in revolt" (III.4.409). She smiles only because she knows it is "called for." The joke consists in Fanny's being married before actually accepting Henry's addresses, a temporal impossibility.

Fanny also smiles a little when Mary assures her in the next chapter that Henry will love her "as nearly for ever as possible": "If any man ever loved a woman for ever, I think Henry will do as much for you" (III.5.419). Mary has many faults, but overestimating her brother is not one of them. She tries to express as positively as she can what she thinks the extent of Henry's love could be, and to her it seems a very long time. She really thinks she is reassuring Fanny and encouraging her to accept Henry. Fanny again smiles, not because she is happy to hear these assurances but because she is sceptical: it is an Elizabeth Bennet sort of smile. This is not a response to what the other sees as a joke but to what she sees as a joke. Fanny's two smiles may be fruitfully compared, as she thinks of herself being loved against her will, which is bad enough, but also as loved temporarily, which is perhaps even worse. She smiles because Mary sees these as inducements to marriage. "As nearly for ever as possible" is for Fanny an insulting and unattractive vision of her own worth and of human love in general.

The joke is that Mary, like Henry, Edmund, and Sir Thomas, thinks a pathetically short amount of time is a long time. Mary also confides in Fanny in *their* last meeting in the novel that her friend, Janet, married after thinking about it for three days. Readers might consider why it is that all of Mary Crawford's friends are like characters in the juvenilia. Janet Fraser is like a character out of "The Three Sisters" or, better, this letter writer from the story called "A Collection of Letters" that Austen wrote as a teen:

> WHY should this last disappointment hang so heavily on my Spirits? Why should I feel it more, why should it wound me deeper than those I have experienced before? Can it be that I have a greater affection for Willoughby than I had for his amiable predecessors? Or is it that our feelings become more acute from being often wounded? I must suppose, my dear Belle, that this is the Case, since I am not conscious of being more sincerely attached to Willoughby than I was to Neville, Fitzowen, or either of the Crawfords, for all of whom I once felt the most lasting affection that ever warmed a Woman's heart. Tell me then, dear Belle, why I still sigh when I think of the faithless Edward, or why I weep when I behold his Bride, for too surely this is the case.[23]

Such a person, writing about lasting affection for a string of amours, is only an object of hilarity for the young Jane Austen.[24] But to return to Mary: she describes Janet as a "beautiful young woman of twenty-five" and asks, how can she be "expected to be … steady?" She adds that Janet Fraser and her husband are as "unhappy as most other married people," lamenting in a gossipy way, "Poor Janet has been sadly taken in … and yet there was no want of foresight … She took three days to consider of his proposals; and during those three days asked the advice of every body … and especially applied to my late dear aunt" (*MP*, III.4.417).

Sir Thomas also is impressed by the durability of Henry Crawford's love for Fanny, though the reader can easily trace its inception in November to his betrayal of it in the following May.[25] In fact, Henry doesn't pull his chair forward to talk more intently with Fanny until mid-December; he becomes determined to marry her in early January; and Sir Thomas considers him remarkably constant when he tries to argue Fanny into accepting his proposal about two weeks later.[26]

Fanny sees time differently. One of her objections to all the pressure being put on her to marry Henry Crawford is an outcry against the normal expectation that young women should not fall in love until they were assured of the man's serious intentions: "Was I to be – to be in love with him the moment he said he was in love with me? … And – and we think very differently of the nature of women, if they can imagine a woman so very soon capable of returning an affection as this seems to imply" (III.4.405).[27] How long do people love each other? And how long does it take for them to love each other, really? Fanny poses the same question as her author will in *Persuasion* – what are people like who see others as easily taken up and discarded, as opposed to those who love "longest when existence or when hope is gone" (II.11.256)? Fanny, like Anne Elliot, thinks women cannot transfer affections quickly, if ever. Austen allows both her heroines to be right, although she proves almost everyone else wrong.

Mary has already indicated that "for ever" is not in her vocabulary: she says to Henry when he announces his intention to propose to Fanny, "I know that a wife you *loved* would be the happiest of women, and that even when you ceased to love, she would yet find in you the liberality and good-breeding of a gentleman" (II.12.343). Mary does not think an "if" is the proper word here: her word is "when."

She believes love is temporary, but also that Henry would never embarrass Fanny or put her on short funds once he started looking further afield for amorous diversion, a pretty clear picture of what Admiral Crawford has done, in addition to his adultery, to make his wife hate the name Crawford. Though Henry protests, Mary does not change her views on human love.

It is one of Austen's final ironies that Mary lives to prove the truth of Fanny's beliefs. Although D.A. Miller says she is "forcibly reduced" in the final chapter's evaluation of her,[28] he has to admit that the final narrative about her does not reduce her at all. This is the passage in question: "Mary, though perfectly resolved against ever attaching herself to a younger brother again, was long in finding among the dashing representatives, or idle heir-apparents, who were at the command of her beauty, and her 20,000*l*, any one who could satisfy the better taste she had acquired at Mansfield, whose character and manners could authorise a hope of the domestic happiness she had there learned to estimate, or put Edmund Bertram sufficiently out of her head" (III.17.543). The narrator prophesies a long spinsterhood for Mary Crawford, entirely of her own choosing, as she searches for another domestically minded young man. This prophecy raises Mary in the reader's esteem, even though it reflects a panorama of failure, because she, against her will, loves Edmund longer than he loves her. Her resentment and resolution against younger brothers remind us of the resentment of a Captain Wentworth: it is futile, because her heart and head still place someone first, but that person is in the unreachable past. And unlike Captain Wentworth with Anne Elliot, Mary can never see Edmund again, even should she want to, because of her brother's trespass. Still, it is important that Austen says "head" instead of "heart" at the end of this description. And it is "as nearly for ever as possible" – but perhaps not forever. Mary may live to get over Edmund Bertram, and thus readers should not lament that he lost her, for it is Fanny who could not get over him, unless in some counterfactual universe she were morally compelled by the fact of his marriage to another. Otherwise, for Fanny, forever is not only possible, it is certain.

The Whole Delightful Astonishing Truth

Perhaps the biggest scandal of *Mansfield Park* is the hasty romance of Edmund and Fanny in the final pages. However, Fanny has loved Edmund from volume 1 on, with no hope of a return and with a constant sense that she is ungrateful, presumptuous, and irrational because she persists in that love. While Edmund must be the problem, then, critics do not confine their displeasure merely to the improbability of Edmund's falling in love with Fanny. The criticism is full of outraged second guessing of Austen's resolution: Joseph Duffy argued that Jane Austen had no business telling her readers what her fiction means: she allows herself "a tactless display of sympathy and prejudice towards her characters, and it takes over completely in the concluding chapter when the novelist intrudes upon her created world, assumes a maddeningly pontifical air, and informs the reader of what might have been if only certain individuals had known how to behave."[29] Duffy is provoked to anger by Austen's use of metalepsis, apophasis, and counterfactual narrative techniques. Yet she has employed them deliberately throughout the creation of the novel. This opinion closely follows the famous condemnation by Marvin Mudrick, who further claimed that Austen willingly "destroys every character" to advance her thesis of severe morality.[30] Although Lionel Trilling defended the novel's difficulty and irony, many more recent critics take offence at Austen's project in similar tones. Nonetheless, Paula Byrne finds the ending "sexy" and realistic, and Thomas Edwards finds it subtle and profoundly interested in its characters' will to control and even *become* others, to incorporate them into the character's performance.[31] Edwards seems the most responsive to Austen's subtle characterization and reformation of novelistic convention. He understands Austen is not the one doing the compelling in her plot; the Crawfords and Sir Thomas, among others, are the ones who love that kind of power.

The arguments nonetheless seem to run like this: Edmund's infatuation with Mary Crawford is an inexcusable flaw in a twenty-one-year-old hero; except that Mary Crawford is more universally admired than Fanny Price, that self-righteous prig. Edmund should have loved and married Fanny, except she was his cousin, which makes it incest.[32] Edmund should have overlooked Mary's casual attitude towards adultery because that has nothing to do with being able to contract a constant, stable marriage. Mary should not have fallen in love with Edmund because he is so boring. Henry Crawford fell in love with Fanny because she was the only single girl around, but of course Fanny should have fallen in love with him because he meant to reform, and fictional heroines are always guaranteed this outcome.[33] The titles demonstrating the popular readership's dissatisfaction with Austen's resolution of her novel include *Henry and Fanny: An Alternate Ending to Mansfield Park* by Sherwood Smith; *Revisit Mansfield Park: How Fanny Married Henry* by Sarah Ozcandarli; *Mansfield Park: The Crawfords' Redemption – An Improved End to the Classic Story* by Kirsten bij't Vuur; *A Contrary Wind: A Variation on Mansfield Park* by Lona Manning; *Mansfield Park Revisited* by Joan Aiken. The list goes on. Of course, the existence of continuations does not always imply dissatisfaction with the original novel, since continuations of and variations on *Pride and Prejudice* dominate the market.[34] But the tenor of all of these alternative takes on *Mansfield Park* is that readers ought to buy the revised books because there they will find fixed the arbitrarily moralizing ending provided by Jane Austen in the original. But in the universe ruled by Jane Austen, one kind of hubris is always punished, and that is the desire to take the course of the drama out of the hands of the author. It is a mistake to second guess *her*, although she invites fanciful guessing at characters' futures continually in the chapters leading up to the end of this novel. To take the bait is to reveal oneself to be susceptible to the overweening pride that Henry displays in wishing to govern the winds and delay the return of Sir Thomas from Antigua, and that Mary exhibits in creating a plot wherein the worthless oldest son dies, leaving the second son to inherit land and title. Jane Austen brings up such Crawfordian counterfactual possibilities only to explode them. The endings of each volume, the climaxes of each published portion of the novel, are slaps on the hand of the greedy Crawfords, who think they know better than Austen herself. Readers who want a marriage that unites the Crawford, Price, and Bertram families get only an affair, no matter how much Cassandra Austen might have pleaded their cause. Austen is clear up to the very end which two characters belong together.

Juliet McMaster counters the popular notion that Austen ruined her own novel by making the Crawfords backslide and by marrying off Edmund and Fanny. Her argument is that Fanny has indeed suffered from unrequited love for the entire novel, but, ironically, and unbeknownst to both, Edmund has always loved her. McMaster observes:

> Readers have I think missed one of the major subsurface movements of the novel:
>
> Edmund's unconscious courtship of Fanny, which is concurrent with his deliberate courtship of Mary. The reader is constantly informed of how his love for Mary and his love for Fanny grow together. The three are always "in a cluster together," they seem "naturally to unite." The more Edmund's ardour kindles for Mary, the more fervent become his feelings for Fanny. He speaks of them as "the two dearest objects I have on earth." When he confesses his love for Mary to Fanny, he calls her "Dearest Fanny!" and "[presses] her hand to his lips, with almost as much warmth as if it had been Miss Crawford's."[35]

McMaster exposes one of the most important secrets of *Mansfield Park*: Edmund has always loved Fanny best. He is like the heroine of *Emma*, the novel Austen is about to write: he has always had an ideal woman, as Emma has always had an ideal man; he just did not realize it. Edmund has always considered Fanny's mind superior to Mary's, and he deludes himself into thinking that Mary's values are the same as Fanny's. He likes the dark-eyed physical form better, but throughout his infatuation, the girl he is in love with in his imagination is for all intents and purposes a double of Fanny with a more playful disposition. He is always baffled or making excuses when Mary says or does things Fanny would not do. He continually confuses two terms the novel insistently separates: temper and principles.

Moreover, for those unconvinced by his transfer of allegiance from dark to light eyes, Austen has no trouble imagining physical contact between the hero and heroine. Edmund touches Fanny more than any other hero of an Austen novel ever touches the heroine. As McMaster notes, unlike any of Austen's other heroes, he kisses her hand, on the eve of her first ball (Mr. Knightley only begins to kiss Emma's, then desists). Moreover, Edmund gives Fanny gifts of an inordinate value, considering they are from a brotherly cousin to a sisterly cousin: he has just given her the gold chain he ordered after William brought her a cross. Edmund's idea of a gift that he ought to give to Fanny – on an occasion that is not very significant – is nothing like the workbaskets his older and wealthier brother Tom gives her every year. Earlier, Edmund has secured a horse for Fanny (the cost of which – the modern equivalent of around £10,000 – also explains in part why Willoughby's gift of a horse to Marianne was inappropriate).[36] Gifts were not supposed to pass between young people who were unengaged. Fanny and Edmund may be family, but that does not justify a *gold* chain, especially when it is not even Christmas yet (just December 21st).[37] Moreover, we never hear of Edmund giving any gift to his sisters.

Edmund usually also sets Fanny apart by the superlatives he uses when he speaks of and to her. From their first interactions when Fanny arrives at Mansfield Park, Edmund consistently calls her his "dear" or "dearest." These words are accompanied by physical gestures of affection and closeness that he uses with no one else. When Edmund is reporting to Fanny on Mrs. Grant's and Mary Crawford's surprise at her refusal of Henry, he urges her to think of Mary's anger as sisterly disappointment, but he is not content with just words: "'My dearest Fanny,' cried Edmund, pressing her arm closer to him." This is followed by "My dear, dear Fanny" (III.17.407, 409). Similarly, in *Emma*, Mr. Knightley, right before his proposal, also presses Emma's arm closer to him when cursing Frank Churchill. Edmund's gesture could, of course, imply vicarious affection, in that he may be drawing her close because Mary is on his mind and he might wish to draw her close in the same way. But later, Edmund holds Fanny tightly to his heart when he first enters the Prices' house in Portsmouth after the debacle of Maria's flight with Crawford. There are no such embraces between any other Austen hero and heroine. And yet Austen has made the reader so accustomed to Edmund's affectionate treatment of Fanny that the reader consistently overlooks these demonstrations of more than brotherly warmth.

Why does Edmund fall in love with Fanny so quickly? For now, let us rely on the narrator's information: "Having once set out, and felt that he had done so on this road to happiness, there was nothing on the side of prudence to stop him or make his progress slow; no doubts of her deserving, no fears of opposition of taste, no need of drawing new hopes of happiness from dissimilarity of temper" (III.17.544–5). Once Edmund even has an inkling it might be preferable to fall in love with another kind of woman rather than find someone *like* Mary, there is no barrier to the headlong progress his affections are able to make: Fanny is meritorious, suited to him in her shared taste and by temperament (notwithstanding his earlier arguments for opposites attracting and improving each other), and already has, as he thinks, a "warm and sisterly regard for him." All the things that made him hesitate over proposing to Mary Crawford are absent. If he had been surer of Mary, the reader can well believe he would have proposed to her before his father's return at the end of the first volume. But, of course, he never proposed. And after Henry and Maria's adultery, he never could. Thus, unlike Mary, he does not need to wait to find someone who is as worthy as her, "such another woman":

> Edmund had greatly the advantage of her [Mary] in this respect. He had not to wait and wish with vacant affections for an object worthy to succeed her in them. Scarcely had he done regretting Mary Crawford, and observing to Fanny how impossible it was that he should ever meet with such another woman, before it began to strike him whether a very different kind of woman might not do just as well, or a great

> deal better: whether Fanny herself were not growing as dear, as important to him in all her smiles and all her ways, as Mary Crawford had ever been; and whether it might not be a possible, an hopeful undertaking to persuade her that her warm and sisterly regard for him would be foundation enough for wedded love.
>
> I purposely abstain from dates on this occasion, that every one may be at liberty to fix their own, aware that the cure of unconquerable passions, and the transfer of unchanging attachments, must vary much as to time in different people. I only entreat everybody to believe that exactly at the time when it was quite natural that it should be so, and not a week earlier, Edmund did cease to care about Miss Crawford, and became as anxious to marry Fanny as Fanny herself could desire. (III.17.543–4)

Edmund, in fact, has always loved Fanny better than anyone in his own family:

> With such a regard for her, indeed, as his had long been, a regard founded on the most endearing claims of innocence and helplessness, and completed by every recommendation of growing worth, what could be more natural than the change? Loving, guiding, protecting her, as he had been doing ever since her being ten years old, her mind in so great a degree formed by his care, and her comfort depending on his kindness, an object to him of such close and peculiar interest, dearer by all his own importance with her than any one else at Mansfield, what was there now to add, but that he should learn to prefer soft light eyes to sparkling

> dark ones. – And being always with her, and always talking confidentially, and his feelings exactly in that favourable state which a recent disappointment gives, those soft light eyes could not be very long in obtaining the pre-eminence. (III.17.544)

Readers dwell on the last sentence and, rhetorically, it has greater power than what is hidden in the middle: according to the rules of rhetoric, what comes last has most emphasis, what comes first has the second most, and the middle parts can sort it out among themselves. This psychological truth, or truth about our memory and our attention as readers and listeners, is what gave birth to the present book in the first place. However, in this case, the truth is hidden in the middle, like a nut in a shell: Fanny was "dearer by all his own importance with her than any one else at Mansfield." That Fanny is dearer to him than Maria or Julia does not surprise us. But she is also dearer than Tom, even though they have lately become truly brothers, and is dearer even than his mother and father. Fanny is dearest. It may be because, as Austen says, Edmund is important to her, but the fact remains: Fanny *is* dearest. Edmund never calls Mary Crawford dearest; he never is in a position to, but he has said it to Fanny over and over again from their first encounters: dear, dearer, dearest.[38] And even before the narrator does so, in her metalepsis in the final chapter, he too calls her "My Fanny": "She was ready to sink as she entered the parlour [of her parents' house]. He was alone, and met her instantly; and she found herself pressed to his heart with only these words, just articulate, 'My Fanny, my only sister; my only comfort now!' She could say nothing; nor for some minutes could he say more" (III.15.514–15).

Austen suspends the logical deduction Edmund should be making at this point: he should ask himself why he turns to Fanny and no one else for comfort when his heart is broken and his mind oppressed by his family's shame. Why can he discard Maria and Julia when they make shameful choices, and then cannot do anything but fly to Fanny for aid? It is not because she is his sister. She has always been different from and more to him than his sisters. As Mr. Knightley will later comment of his apparently fraternal relationship with Emma Woodhouse, "Brother and sister! No, indeed" (*E*, III.2.358). In the apophatic silence that envelops Fanny and Edmund as they share an embrace, Austen occludes the truth of Edmund's heart. It is a kind of secret from himself very like the one she prepares for Emma Woodhouse. It is right that the ending of the novel, so devoted to Edmund's *desengaño* and not Fanny's, should open up his unknown interior self to his previously blinded eyes. But what the readers see taking place before them should give them an inkling of what is to come.

Apophasis and the Next Generation

At the end of *Mansfield Park*, Edmund and Fanny move into their new home at Mansfield parsonage:

> With so much true merit and true love, and no want of fortune and friends, the happiness of the married cousins

> must appear as secure as earthly happiness can be. Equally formed for domestic life, and attached to country pleasures, their home was the home of affection and comfort; and to complete the picture of good, the acquisition of Mansfield living, by the death of Dr. Grant, occurred just after they had been married long enough to begin to want an increase of income, and feel their distance from the paternal abode an inconvenience.
>
> On that event they removed to Mansfield; and the Parsonage there, which, under each of its two former owners, Fanny had never been able to approach but with some painful sensation of restraint or alarm, soon grew as dear to her heart, and as thoroughly perfect in her eyes, as everything else within the view and patronage of Mansfield Park had long been. (III.17.547–8)

The "event" referred to is the death of Dr. Grant, but the reader might pause here and ask the question Austen continually asks in the final chapter – at what time is it appropriate for a person to A, B, or C? In this case, Dr. Grant's death fortuitously happens "just after they had been married long enough to begin to want an increase of income, and feel their distance from the paternal abode an inconvenience." There *is* no set time in which a couple is married just long enough to need more money and more closeness to the "paternal abode," but there is an event that occasions these needs, and that is the arrival of a child. For people with modest wishes like Fanny and Edmund, Austen would not suggest the need for greater income, unless there are more people to clothe and convey. Like Sheila Kindred and

Richard Jenkyns, I believe this passage indicates that Fanny is pregnant or has had a baby by the end of her novel.[39] The suggestion of a growing family may be covert, yet it is also out in the open.[40] The narrator clearly states there is "no want of fortune or friends." Edmund and Fanny are not poor. They do not need more space or income unless a Bertram baby has arrived.

All the novels demonstrate at some time or another that the hero and heroine, if faced with the difficult task of parenting, will be able to exert their patience and set a good example, though Austen stops her story's *sujet* at the altar or just before it. In one sense, for the sake of a comic plot, our heroines and heroes must be lovers on the brink of marriage. We meet them, as Austen herself said to her niece about child, as opposed to adolescent, characters, at the most interesting and emotional point of their lives. Their decisions and blunders as they make their way towards marriage demand our interest, before the banality of everyday life and its other challenges require other virtues of them than the ones that attract and secure affection. The comic drama and the comic novel rely on marriage as a catalyst for our interest, and the moment the main couple fall into each other's arms is all the gratification some readers seek. But in another sense, Austen is always engaging her main couples with children in some way or another, pointing to what is perhaps in her mind the central task of humanity, to educate and raise moral and lovable individuals with the capacity for both self-restraint and warm affection. This is a task *Mansfield Park* asks readers to have in the forefront of their minds as they judge the Bertrams and the Crawfords as parents, from the opening of the first volume to the conclusion of the last.[41]

A large part of *Mansfield Park* is devoted to the question of upbringing, and Austen has displayed all too clearly the defects of the Bertrams as parents, with their odd ménage-à-trois in which Aunt Norris is not a rival in love but a rival in authority, filling the vacuum left by Lady Bertram's emotional absence. It is a theme to which Austen returns in the final pages of the novel, as Sir Thomas's irrational and uncharitable plan for the education of his daughters (and Fanny) turns out to have the opposite effect of what he intended – as time whimsically always produces such reverses.

This belief in the power of time to overthrow human plans is one reason Austen's novels seem to invite us to prophesy the future, which must always remain in an ellipsis at the close of any novel, including her own. Closure is necessary to the narrative, but there is always a sense that more could be told. Austen uses apophasis to open the novel's last chapter, saying what she will not say: "Let other pens dwell on guilt and misery. I quit such odious subjects as soon as I can, impatient to restore everybody, not greatly in fault themselves, to tolerable comfort, and to have done with all the rest" (*MP*, III.17.540). She delineates the magic circle of her comedy, but she tells us "guilt" and "misery" do indeed exist. Readers are made uncomfortable by the ending of the novel because we are told what we are not being told. Some might think, confronted with the exclusions and the exiles at the end of *Mansfield Park*, if only she had kept up the charade more thoroughly. If only she had pretended scoundrels could easily be reformed by erotic desire or at least had Maria Bertram commit suicide, à la Madame Bovary or Anna Karenina. Austen resigns these concerns and these kinds of characters to others. She is not envious of their themes or their powers. Perhaps the hint that children are coming, and will have better parenting from the kinder branch of the Bertram family, is Austen's way of placating those wishing for more mercy or more dramatic justice. A marriage between like-minded people shows itself to be more fruitful and freer of self-inflicted wounds than the destructive liaison between the frustrated and peevish Maria and the indolent yet always busy Henry Crawford.

Austen has shown throughout the novel that not all suffering in a love relationship is meritorious – or, indeed, proof of love at all. A Denis de Rougemont *avant la lettre*, she knowingly counteracts the elevation of hopeless and tragic love, which is so often the theme of love narratives in the past. In *Love in the Western World*, de Rougemont claims that the Western concept of love, originating in part with the troubadours, is a narcissistic passion "where the lover's self-magnification is emphasized more than the relationship towards the beloved. The love which is developed in Romance literature is a love through obstacles, even of obstacles. If there were no obstacles, there would be no love."[42] This is the kind of love Henry Crawford always participates in, whether the object be Maria or Fanny, and it is partly what compels Mary Crawford to return again and again to Edmund as long as she can. Fanny's realization of that kind of love's rootedness in self provides her with much of her moral suffering in the novel, as she battles jealousy and self-interest while watching Mary and Edmund grow ever closer. Austen affirms her hopeless love because she has worked so hard to love rightly, even if she fails sometimes. No one else in the novel has put in such a degree of self-examination and effort to ensure the beloved is done justice, is loved selflessly.

Austen draws the curtain on their story with an image of equality, hominess, and affection, yet it too includes an apophatic statement reminding the reader that earthly happiness is not the only kind of happiness that exists: "With so much true merit and true love, and no want of fortune and friends, the happiness of the married cousins must appear as secure as earthly happiness can be. Equally formed for domestic life, and attached to country pleasures, their home was the home of affection and comfort" (III.17.547). Although "the happiness of the married cousins must appear as secure as earthly happiness can be," and thus must have its limitations, only here at the close are we presented with a couple who share "true love." No one else in the novel has merited this description. Amid the wreckage of domestic lives we have seen in so many forms, Edmund and Fanny seem to live in a little utopia, but it is crafted by themselves and their own habitual virtues and way of life. Their home is made up of what they bring to it. And their fairy-tale ending continues as Dr. Grant, according to the accurate early prediction of Tom Bertram, soon "pops off," leaving the reader in no doubt that the author can indeed kill off inconvenient characters if she so chooses, to grant their homes to the more deserving, as Mary Crawford had also hoped when she came close to wishing Tom would die.[43] This is what Sheila Kindred calls *Mansfield Park*'s "second ending," the second of the final two paragraphs. She sums up why she believes Austen has "two endings" in *Mansfield Park*: "Austen's acknowledgement of Fanny's history of painful sensations is telling, for it reminds us that, as the novel progresses, Fanny did find the strength to be less timid and the courage to be more autonomous. Fanny was greatly discomforted but not cowed by her tormentors. In fact, Fanny displays courage, fortitude, and forbearance … Happiness in marriage is, in Austen's lexicon, only achieved with someone both truly loved and esteemed."[44] Kindred understands the confrontation with Mansfield parsonage as something more than the inheritance of property so often a part of the mechanics of a comic ending. For Fanny, this last step is one towards conquering the tyranny of painful memory, and an assertion of her right to create a happy future.

In *Mansfield Park,* Austen is more concerned with constancy, memory, and time than in any of her previous novels, themes she will return to in *Persuasion*. It is forward looking and projects a secure future for its heroine because of constancy, because of memory. These are the things over which time has no sovereignty, yet these are also the very things whose "sterling" worth is eventually proven by time. "I, that please some, try all, both joy and terror / Of good and bad, that makes and unfolds error," Shakespeare said in *A Winter's Tale* (IV.1.1–2). "Time will do almost every thing," says Jane Austen, including changing Sir Thomas's mind about the marriage of Edmund and Fanny:

> It was a match which Sir Thomas's wishes had even forestalled. Sick of ambitious and mercenary connexions, prizing more and more the sterling good of principle and temper, and chiefly anxious to bind by the strongest securities all that remained to him of domestic felicity, he had pondered with genuine satisfaction on the more than possibility of the two young friends finding their natural consolation in each other for all that had occurred of disappointment to either; and the joyful consent which met Edmund's application, the high sense of having realised a great acquisition in the promise of Fanny for a daughter, formed just such a contrast with his early opinion on the subject when the poor little girl's coming had been first agitated, as time is for ever producing between the plans and decisions of mortals, for their own instruction, and their neighbours' entertainment. (III.17.545–6)

The comic ending of *Mansfield Park* ratifies and re-echoes all that has gone before: Sir Thomas's value for money rings through this paragraph with its language of "prizing," "sterling good," "securities," and "acquisition," but his earlier values are upended, even as Austen assures the reader of the worldly comfort of her characters. All these things are found in "principle" and "temper" united; they are no accidents of fortune. Through apophasis, Austen makes the reader realize that "for ever" is the temporal framework to which all other times are compared. The "instruction" is anchored in "the poor little girl," for whom "as nearly for ever as possible" is not enough.

CHAPTER SEVEN

"The Perfect Happiness of the Union": Undeceiving Mr. Knightley and the Reader in *Emma*

Emma is not a character created to make the ordinary reader happy, or the ordinary man comfortable. She is a character Austen creates in order to make the character herself, and perhaps even the author, happy. The creation and reshaping of Mr. Knightley are her means to that end. However many readers have thought that he is a perfection to which Emma's waywardness must eventually submit, Emma's conversion, or *desengaño,* is not the only one required for the final happy union. As is generally the case for Austen, her hero too must change to deserve the heroine, must come to some realization that makes the scales fall from his eyes. The conversion necessary to an Austenian novel of education is not just a change in the woman who lives in an illusion, whether that be an illusion of superiority or of inferiority. To make Mr. Knightley's conversion necessary to the trajectory of the novel, Austen must make the errant Emma a good of which he is unworthy. The closure of the novel will reveal just how much the reader has overlooked her goodness, in the main because Mr. Knightley's dissatisfaction with her – and Emma's own reflections – has guided the reader to be blind to the virtues that offset her vices. Austen constructs the novel to invite the readers to their own *desengaño*, but she is both the creator of the illusion and the architect of its cure. She offers the reader Emma as a mixed character in a novel that proposes perfection as its telos. Austen proposes perfect happiness as the end towards which she aims her heroine; in so doing, she guides her reader to desire perfect happiness for her imperfect heroine and hero. If they do not achieve moral perfection, they aim at it, and their hearts are united in part because of their common valuing of what is good. As Hugh Blair maintained in his *Sermons*, "the issues of life are justly said to be out of the heart, because the state of the heart is what determines our moral character, and what forms our chief happiness or misery."[1] Thus, the final *desengaño* that the novel prepares for Emma is not her attainment of moral perfection, which Austen considers unattainable and unrealistic, but the discovery of the secret about herself that even her own heart has not revealed to her.

Hiding the Heroine's Virtues

One of Jane Austen's deep purposes in *Emma* seems to be not too distant from her purpose in *Mansfield Park*, which of course is the fruit of the same period of artistic endeavour. She is hiding the heroism of the heroine. Only the "small band of true friends" mentioned in the final sentence of *Emma* will see the merit and the justice of the reward. It is not for nothing that *Emma* is the novel in which Austen most insistently repeats the action of the heroine hiding her face from others to avoid discovery of the truth about her. In fact, Mr. Knightley takes refuge in exactly the same action. Austen is giving us a very broad hint that what is truest about Emma is secret. Why would Austen choose to narrate this action so often in *Emma*? Very simply, because Austen is revolutionizing the conception of the novelistic heroine. She has been working at this revolution since the juvenilia, finding her own way through experiment after experiment to create a protagonist who is at the same time not a "picture of perfection" and yet still a heroine. As Vera Tobin writes in the *Elements of Surprise*, "the most profound surprise in *Emma* is not that Emma loves Mr. Knightley, but that Emma deserves someone like that as her partner in life."[2] Austen does not frustrate poetic justice in her novel but requires the reader to re-evaluate the whole narrative to discover Emma, the Emma hidden even from herself, who is capable of perfect happiness, and whom Mr. Knightley will make happy.

Emma is about the true goal of the inner life of the human being, which is happiness. According to the Western philosophical tradition, happiness cannot be found outside a life of virtue. For Austen, in her novels at least, that happiness consists of a marriage of friendship between a woman and a man capable of friendship, friendship in its highest form. Although Mr. Knightley and Emma speculate throughout the novel about who might be the best friend for Emma,

Austen resolves on neither Jane Fairfax nor Harriet Smith. She resolves on Mr. Knightley.

Austen describes the happiness she foresees for the couple in two ways, preparing the careful reader for this union, which is the summit of the novel's marital matches every bit as much as Elizabeth Bennet and Mr. Darcy's is in *Pride and Prejudice*. Like Wayne Booth, I argue for its suitability according to both reason and feeling. Neither Emma nor Mr. Knightley is faultless, from the reader's perspective and from Austen's. However, the reader has been guided, or misguided, by the author to accept Mr. Knightley's overemphasis on Emma's flaws and to dismiss Mrs. Weston's excusal of them. Mr. Knightley's anxiety over Emma becomes the reader's anxiety; we learn from him to overlook her many virtues and to focus on her errors. The ending of the novel functions to force the reader to re-evaluate precisely how erroneous Emma has been throughout the novel and to imagine what kind of happiness could be available to so imperfect a heroine as to be called "perfect." Austen needs more than an unexpected marriage proposal to accomplish the goal of inducing reflection on this issue in the reader.

If one is just looking for poetic justice to be done, one might well ask, does Austen unjustly reward Emma with Mr. Knightley when she should have married her co-schemer, Frank Churchill? And then is Jane Fairfax's marriage to Frank Churchill an authorial punishment? As Lynda Hall observes, "Jane Fairfax is saved from 'mortification' through her marriage to Frank Churchill. By examining this relationship, however, we can see that this kind of marriage is not necessarily a reward."[3] Though Hall asserts that

Austen likes Jane even though Emma does not, this assertion is arguable. Indeed, the narrator never affirms Jane and Frank will be happy together, though clearly a burden has been lifted from Jane once the engagement is made public. It is hard to know how Frank will treat his wife. On the other hand, the last few chapters of *Emma* make it very clear how Mr. Knightley and Emma will get along. Those who believe Emma is Mr. Knightley's inferior perhaps expect the lively heroine to be subdued by her author, who should fashion the closure of the novel to subordinate her to her husband. But then is Emma really inferior to Jane, as Mr. Knightley has long argued, when Jane has laboured under a secrecy agreed upon with Frank in order to retain Mrs. Churchill's fortune? Does not Austen create this moral blemish in Jane to elevate Emma? Is Mr. Knightley, conversely, brought into line by his creator so that he too allows Emma primacy in a world he ought to govern with his benignity and good sense? Is she in the end the idol he worships rather than the subject he governs? Or is his love for her a positive good, which the reader may rejoice in?

To some commentators, it is as if Mr. Knightley has finally conceded to Emma's world of seeming rather than being, and as if the end of the novel depicts him as one who has lost his way because of the cloud of erotic attraction that baffles him. Such readers would see Austen offering us the possibility of considering Emma an idol, much as Joseph Poorgrass does Bathsheba Everdene when he contemplates her marriage to Gabriel Oak at the end of Thomas Hardy's *Far From the Madding Crowd*: "'Yes; I suppose that's the size o't,' said Joseph Poorgrass with a cheerful sigh ... 'and I wish him joy o' her; though I were once or twice upon saying today with holy Hosea, in my scripture manner, which is my second nature. "Ephraim is joined to idols: let him alone." But since 'tis as 'tis why, it might have been worse, and I feel my thanks accordingly.'"[4] However, even in Hardy's novel, the narrator compares the joy Bathsheba and Gabriel experience in their final commitment to each other to the love of the Song of Songs, "the only love which is strong as death – that love which many waters cannot quench, nor the floods drown, beside which the passion usually called by the name is evanescent as steam."[5] Joseph Poorgrass's final, damning comment is the last word of the novel but not the only – or the most important – word on the subject, since the narrator's authority outranks his.

To read *Emma* outside its genre and, more importantly, outside its author's narrative habits would be the same as concluding that *Tess of the D'Urbervilles* is a comedy because it ends with the implied marriage of Angel Clare to the executed Tess's sister. Austen is not writing tragedies or even tragi-comedies, and the endings of the novels, which are all complex narratively and tonally, must be read with that generic classification in mind. If *Emma*'s theme is simply the duping of the rational male hero, then Mr. Knightley occupies the same unenviable role as Demetrius in *A Midsummer Night's Dream* – the only one still under an illusion at the end. "The course of true love never did run smooth," is the only actual quotation of Shakespeare in the novels, and it occurs in *Emma* (I.9.80).[6] As Austen is metanarratively meditating on the influence Hartfield exercises over love relationships in this passage, it is possible that she might be planting parallels to Shakespeare's characters in the novel. But one can see Mr. Knightley as Demetrius only if one sees the Eltons as correct in their evaluation of his marriage to Emma. Austen is not writing a play, after all, but a novel, and one privilege of the novelist is to stand as an authority outside the chorus or cacophony of voices Bakhtin would call "polyphony."[7] A Bakhtinian would grant no one voice authority. Critic Marshall Brown does see the narrator as the ultimate authority, and considers the last words of a novel the most authoritative, but he reads the narrator's words though the lens of the embittered characters whose words precede the final statement.[8] This is to give the narrator's authority over to the final comments of the Eltons, who are surely bitter fools, and to ignore the fact that Austen never gives the last word to her heroine (or to her hero) and that she almost exclusively allows speech to dissident voices who, like Jaques in *As You Like It*, are not for comedy and marriage. For instance, we do not hear Henry or Catherine's voices at the end of *Northanger Abbey*, but the General growls his consent to Henry's marriage: "He might be a fool if he liked it" (II.16.260). To assume that Austen must give the last spoken word to the touchstones of the novel is naive and wilfully contrary; in no case does a protagonist speak the last line, not even in *Lady Susan*. It is to read anachronistically, to privilege characters over the narrator, who in the days before Bakhtin was the inheritor of many generations of narratorial authority and was untroubled by Henry James's pronouncements about objectivity and Bakhtin's dicta about the symphonic and heteroglossia.[9]

There are standards of worthiness at work at the end of *Emma*: much of the climax and dénouement of the novel is devoted to just this subject. Emma is very clear in her mind as we approach the last chapter that Frank Churchill, who *seemed* to be her perfect match when he was still a figment in the imagination of most of the inhabitants of Highbury, is not worth marrying. Frank's defects are obvious to most readers, and yet when we turn to Emma's rejoicing over her engagement to the superior man, we are distracted in a very different way than in the end of *Mansfield Park*: though Frank is not nearly so selfish and disloyal as Henry Crawford, there are few readers who would prefer him over Mr. Knightley as a match for Emma. Emma's defects are much more on readers' minds, though few feel compelled to ask why. Yet Austen gives more narrative space in the final chapters to the consideration of Frank's flaws than Emma's. It is likely that Emma's negative self-evaluation may simply be assisting the reader in following a misdirection planted in the text by Austen herself. The reader hears the warning in the coloured narrative at the end of the chapter featuring Emma's self-revelation, but little heeds it and rarely applies it to the act of reading a novel so deeply coloured by Emma's own vocabulary and moral perspective: "With unsufferable vanity had she believed herself to be in the secret of every body's feelings; with unpardonable arrogance proposed to arrange every body's destiny. She was proved to have been universally mistaken" (III.11.449). Austen's ability to reveal and to hide at the same time is nowhere more in evidence than in passages like these, where Emma herself leads the reader to think her incapable of reformation, doomed to backsliding. Austen includes the evidence that each examination of conscience Emma subjects herself to is a step forward on a faltering path, and at the same time obscures the progress in self-knowledge and love of the good by the force of the character's own focus on her failures.

Much has been said and written about *Emma*'s showcasing of free indirect discourse and of coloured narrative that mostly employs Emma's consciousness as focalizer. By this means, Austen makes it difficult to extricate Emma's judgments from the narrator's and perhaps makes the reader complicit in Emma's snobbery and her misguided treatment of Harriet. However, not enough has been said about Austen's use of these techniques and others to convey Emma's own tendency to think meanly of herself, in the line of Fanny Price and Anne Elliot.[10] Whose diction colours the above narrative? Emma's. Who thinks Emma "unpardonable," "universally mistaken," "unsufferable"? Emma. These hyperbolic words are all Emma's moral vocabulary, her own self-judgment. Austen makes it easier to critique Emma's egotism than to see her lancing examen of conscience, for Mr. Knightley and Emma herself assist the reader in discovering it. Austen invites us to compare and contrast Emma's estimate of herself with the facts of the matter right up to the penultimate chapter, when it is the theme about which she and Frank Churchill banter. In chapter 17 of volume 3, Mr. Knightley denies Emma's self-deprecating words about his brother John's opinion of the match. Emma responds to John's epistolary congratulations,

> "It is very plain that he considers the good fortune of the engagement as all on my side, but that he is not without hope of my growing, in time, as worthy of your affection, as you think me already. Had he said any thing to bear a different construction, I should not have believed him."
>
> "My Emma, he means no such thing. He only means –"
>
> "He and I should differ very little in our estimation of the two," interrupted she, with a sort of serious smile – "much less, perhaps, than he is aware of, if we could enter without ceremony or reserve on the subject."
>
> "Emma, my dear Emma –"
>
> "Oh!" she cried with more thorough gaiety, "if you fancy your brother does not do me justice, only wait till my dear father is in the secret, and hear his opinion. Depend upon it, he will be much farther from doing you justice. He will think all the happiness, all the advantage, on your side of the question; all the merit on mine. I wish I may not sink into 'poor Emma' with him at once. – His tender compassion towards oppressed worth can go no farther."
>
> "Ah!" he cried, "I wish your father might be half as easily convinced as John will be, of our having every right that equal worth can give, to be happy together." (III.17.506–7)

The reader may readily dismiss Mr. Woodhouse's prejudice in favour of Emma while approving John's more knowing preference for his brother. However, Mr. Knightley will have none of it.[11] He "cries" out against Emma's imbalanced view and announces that their future happiness will be rightly merited through "equal worth."

Does the reader abandon Mr. Knightley's judgment in favour of Emma's at this point? Austen brings other voices to weigh in on the issue. In the following chapter, Frank disallows Emma's claim to be his equal in enjoying the prospect of uniting themselves with partners who have characters superior to their own. In his mind, Emma can have no superior. Frank has never been jealous of Mr. Knightley, has never seen him, as Mrs. Weston has, as a potential suitor for Jane. Frank's opinion on Emma's equivalence to him may have less weight than Mr. Knightley's, since Frank is less upright and more inclined to flatter, but it is more disinterested. Emma once again herself diverts us from Frank's objection to her comparison by busily comparing Mr. Knightley with *him*, and rejoicing over her fortune as better than Jane's. The reader thinks in concert with her and does not seriously consider Frank's objection. But *is* Emma on the same moral level as Frank, who deceives everyone because he does not want to lose his aunt's fortune, and because he enjoys the intrigue and game playing? He inflicts emotional wounds on Jane for the fun of it, while Emma never intentionally inflicts pain, except when prompted by his malicious spirit at Box Hill to speak against Miss Bates. Emma does this once and repents, not having meant to hurt Miss Bates in the first place; in contrast, Frank's infractions are repeated, and he is never really sorry.

Just because Emma equates herself with Frank does not mean the reader should. Mr. Knightley does not, and neither does the narrator when she is not employing narrative coloured by Emma or free indirect discourse. Emma's negative self-assessment is overly harsh, but readers comply with it and class her with Frank. However, Mr. Knightley does not love the female version of Frank. Emma may be like Frank in marrying someone she does not deserve, but even here Austen makes fine discriminations, as in this exchange between Emma and Frank:

> "I think there is a little likeness between us."
>
> He bowed.
>
> "If not in our dispositions," she presently added, with a look of true sensibility, "there is a likeness in our destiny; the destiny which bids fair to connect us with two characters so much superior to our own." (III.18.522)

Frank puts the comparison differently in a letter to Mrs. Weston: "'If you think me in a way to be happier than I deserve, I am quite of your opinion. – Miss W. calls me the child of good fortune. I hope she is right'" (III.14.483). In both cases Austen drives the reader to compare Emma and Frank, but in both cases the comparison is mitigated in some way. In Emma's view, they are similar in finding they are to marry above their merit. Here she agrees with Frank's self-assessment, but his bow indicates he believes the comparison is a compliment. He then protests against any equivalency between them: "'No, not true on your side. You can have no superior, but most true on mine'" (III.18.483). In Frank's earlier view, however, Emma sees that he is always blessed with a happiness he does not deserve. He does not see Emma as sharing that kind of good fortune but as recognizing it in him. Frank invokes this judgment of Emma's as a hopeful one for him: it is not an insult or deprecatory in any way. Very like Captain Wentworth in *Persuasion*, Frank realizes the happiness he has been blessed with is unmerited.[12] He does not see Emma's union with Mr. Knightley in the same terms.

Mr. Knightley's assessment of Emma, his prizing of her, stands in for all the romantic conventions with which romance novels usually end. In the concluding chapters, Austen does not feature love scenes; instead, she invites the reader to compare levels of virtue and levels of happiness through the relationships of the main couples. More importantly, she invites the reader to compare Emma's self-evaluation with the new assessments of her offered by those who love and those who hate her. Mr. Knightley now ranks Emma as highest and admits he has long done so, and their marriage is clearly the one most to be envied.

As to ranking the other marriages, most would agree that the Westons rank second and Harriet and Robert Martin perhaps third – agreeable but not intellectually matched.[13] Isabella and John Knightley may also be said to be happy, though their marriage is disturbed by Isabella's fretfulness about health and John's testiness. Jane and Frank might come next, followed, on the bottom rung, by the Eltons. Yet they are happy. These are all happy marriages. Then how can we say that Emma's is best? Austen devotes these chapters, the longest dénouement in her oeuvre, to helping the reader understand that perfect happiness is not just a sentiment, but a moral quality. Emma and Mr. Knightley are both dutiful people with deep concern for others' comfort. They understand themselves as responsible for others, perhaps more so than even the Westons or the John Knightleys.

Some might claim that Austen gives them superior happiness because of their superior social status. Such a standard makes no sense, given her distaste for the aristocracy evinced in *Pride and Prejudice* and *Persuasion*. If anything, they are in positions of greater responsibility, and both discharge their duties well.[14] Both Emma and Mr. Knightley outrank the other couples in different, much more important ways: they are both excellent caregivers, and this is essential for the situation in which they will find themselves after their marriage.[15] As Emma thinks of her upcoming marriage, she contemplates above all the great comfort Mr. Knightley will be to her when her father's health worsens and he passes away: "Such a companion for herself in the periods of anxiety and cheerlessness before her! – Such a partner in all those duties and cares to which time must be giving increase of melancholy!" (III.15.490). For any man, marrying Emma means caring for Mr. Woodhouse, a task that even the Westons know Frank must be ill-suited to perform. Mr. Elton has probably never thought of it before his drunken proposal to her. No one else among the novel's characters rates as high in the ability to care for Mr. Woodhouse and, what might pass unnoticed, to care for Emma in her distress. This concern of Emma's is partly why friendship is an insufficient solution to her solitude. Austen is creating for her particular predicament a perfect companion, a friend who is also a comforter in affliction and safeguard from sorrow.

No other man in the novel's cast can be said to perform these duties for his wife or wife-to-be. The women also rate lower than Emma in the performance of their duties, although in Harriet's case, her situation does not permit any such work, except when she accompanies Emma on her rounds to the poor and sick. Although Jane's devotion to her aunt and grandmother raises her fairly high on the list, she has consented to a secret engagement to cooperate with Frank's plan to retain his fortune. That collusion is a source of unhappiness for her and makes her, to a certain degree, Emma's inferior, as Mr. Knightley's concern over the secrecy of "his favourite" makes clear.[16] Harriet needs guidance – Emma fears that her ability to be manipulated means that, in a different society, she would be prey to seducers, though Robert Martin's intelligence and steadiness promise a happy future for her.[17] Jane perhaps could be said to have fallen for such a one, though Frank honours his commitment to her in the end. However, Jane is not sure throughout the entire narrative if he will marry her. Does Emma ever need to worry about the lack of constancy of her intended? Does Mr. Knightley ever need to fear that Emma's heart is fickle and that she could love another once he knows she is his "own Emma"? No, for they, as a couple, outclass the other pairs. Frank may be a cad for assuming his flirtation with Emma is understood by her as a game, but he is not wrong. She is never susceptible to his charms in that way. Emma's preference for Mr. Knightley, as she realizes when she finally assesses her own heart, has been perfectly consistent.

Although the novel appears to lay the blame for everything that goes wrong in it on Emma's shoulders, it reveals the injustice of this scapegoating when Mr. Knightley chooses Emma for himself but does not exonerate Frank.

Where does the blame lie with respect to the issue of Jane's unhappiness and potential poverty? It does not lie with Emma's gossipy collusion with Frank about Mr. Dixon's potential interest in Jane. This insidious hint does not go further than the three of them, and while Frank knows it to be false as much as Jane does, he uses the misinterpretation to his own advantage to irritate and tease Jane. Not only that, but Mr. Knightley discovers in the course of volume 3 that Jane herself is not completely without blame. She is suffering, as she says, from her own infraction of the code against secret engagements and proving in her own person the value of the traditional rule. Secret engagements put the woman especially in a false position and even a precarious one. If Jane feels forced to take Mrs. Smallridge's offer to work as a governess, it is not because Emma has thought something slanderous about her but because Frank will not honour his promise to her and make her his lawful wife until his fortune is secured. Jane has broken with him for this reason. The two of them have been waiting for his aunt Churchill to die, or for some other providential resolution, but Jane is the one who has no control over the situation. This couple are not the moral equal of Emma and Mr. Knightley, though Frank's future wealth exceeds Mr. Knightley's and will place them both higher socially.

Although it is hardly worth arguing that the Martins and the Eltons will not share happiness equal to Emma and Mr. Knightley's either, it is worth pointing out that the Martins will be happier than the Eltons, even if Mr. and Mrs. Elton are perhaps more like-minded as a pair. The Westons too are happy, but Mr. Weston is too generally amiable, not particular enough in his friendships, and too willing to live without his own son, to rank with the greater domestic preoccupations of Mr. Knightley and Emma. He is like the amiable squire John Middleton in *Sense and Sensibility*, who is easily reconciled when he should continue being offended – on behalf of his wife, in Mr. Weston's case, and on behalf of the Dashwood girls, in Sir John's case. But Mr. Willoughby's dogs are so superior, and Mrs. Churchill is so unreasonable and manipulative – she is not even considered to be really sick until she actually dies. Frank's lack of real regret about his aunt is another strike against him, and yet Austen does not draw our attention to it, because we are in Emma's point of view for so much of the dénouement, and Emma is more concerned with her own failings than with his. It is Emma who would mourn sincerely at the death of her irritating parent, and Emma who regrets discomfiting her friends. She in fact has much more of the real tenderness of heart she allots to Harriet.

"There Is No Charm Equal to Tenderness of Heart"

Following Harriet's disappointment over Mr. Elton, Emma reflects on her friend's forbearance and sweetness in not blaming her for the misunderstanding, and rates Harriet's possession of these qualities as superior to her own: "'There is no charm equal to tenderness of heart,' said she afterwards to herself. 'There is nothing to be compared to it. Warmth and tenderness of heart, with an affectionate, open manner, will beat all the clearness of head in the world, for attraction: I am sure it will'" (II.13.289). Emma does not see that she herself is a forbearing and patient person. She is wrong about herself because she connects the tenderness of heart that is the usual characteristic of the heroines of sentimental novels with the ability to attract: charm. In *The Orphan of the Rhine*, a novel Isabella Thorpe recommends to Catherine Morland in *Northanger Abbey*, the author speaks of her heroine, Madame deRubine, as having a heart "'so finely tuned, so harmonized by nature,' that it vibrated at the slightest touch of human calamity."[18] This is a kind of sensitivity Austen casts doubt on even as Emma appears to admire it. Emma's sensitivity is of a different sort, and, unlike Mrs. Elton's misguided self-flattery, she can never congratulate herself on this quality because she is unaware of having it.[19]

Emma's dismissal of any attempt to be more like Harriet accords with her lack of desire to reform her heart to think on serious subjects.[20] One need only think of Emma's "sin of thought" – considering leaving her father behind to marry Mr. Knightley – to see that Austen is calling on registers of diction that have roots deep in the Christian moral tradition. Upon becoming engaged to Mr. Knightley, Emma thinks perhaps her most serious moral thoughts in the novel, about

> her father – and Harriet. She could not be alone without feeling the full weight of their separate claims; and how to guard the comfort of both to the utmost, was the question. With respect to her father, it was a question soon answered.

> She hardly knew yet what Mr. Knightley would ask; but a very short parley with her own heart produced the most solemn resolution of never quitting her father. – She even wept over the idea of it, as a sin of thought. While he lived, it must be only an engagement. (III.14.474)

Emma does indeed reject constancy in serious thoughts in volume 1 after visiting the sick, but she returns to serious thoughts at the most important junctures in her moral journey, as the end of volume 3 reveals. This is not "charm," because it is not on display to anyone. But the incident has its place in the novel to reveal to the reader alone Emma's "tenderness of heart." Emma's earlier rejection of the idea that she might have the same charm as Harriet, and perhaps in more abundant measure, is also Austen's signal to the reader that Emma is misinterpreting what makes a person attractive to someone else whose love is worth having. Mr. Knightley will not agree with Emma when she asserts Harriet's pliant disposition and prettiness are what every man desires: "'Her good nature too is not so very slight a claim, comprehending, as it does, real, thorough sweetness of temper and manner, a very humble opinion of herself, and a great readiness to be pleased with other people. I am very much mistaken if your sex in general would not think such beauty and such temper the highest claims a woman could possess.'" Instead, he responds, "'Upon my word, Emma, to hear you abusing the reason you have is almost enough to make me think so too. Better be without sense than misapply it as you do'" (I.8.67).

In this conversation, much of the rightness is on Mr. Knightley's side, but not all of it. He devalues and depersonalizes Harriet as he grows more and more angry, just as he grows more lenient with Frank Churchill at the end of the proposal scene in volume 3 in perfect correspondence to his estimation of the threat Frank poses to Emma.[21] Emma is unfair to Robert Martin, whom she does not know, but she is appreciative of Harriet's virtues in a way Mr. Knightley is not. However, later in the novel, he will come to appreciate those very things he derides here, and he attests to that change after Mr. Elton reveals his meanness of spirit. He is the angrier of the two in this earlier scene, and his anger, the narrator explicitly asserts, is in proportion to his judgment about his own compromised involvement in promoting the match between Harriet and Robert Martin. This scene is one of many the reader may recall in the proposal scene itself when Mr. Knightley says, "I have blamed you, and lectured you, and you have borne it as no other woman in England would have borne it" (III.13.469). The very fact that Emma emerges from her quarrels with Mr. Knightley with no ill will against him – an ill will he generally expects, and more especially risks, when he lectures her on her bad behaviour towards Miss Bates – is a sign of Emma's own very good nature. The woman who sustains with a complete lack of ill humour or envy the new bride Mrs. Elton's co-opting of her place as leader of her own ball is clearly possessed of great gifts of sympathy, understanding, and humility. And the narrator attributes a look of "true sensibility" to her near the end of the novel when she is conversing with Frank (III.18.522). Austen uses the term in this novel only one other time, in reference to Mr. Knightley's tone when he is trying to console Emma over Frank before his own proposal (III.13.464). Emma may not go into raptures upon hearing beautiful music, or imagine herself leading a donkey to a picnic to parade her simplicity and naturalness, but she forgives readily and holds no grudges. Emma tends to her father solicitously and never complains about him or feels put upon. In fact, Emma performs an act of service to him or some other character on nearly every second page of the novel.[22] Rather than resenting anything Mr. Knightley happens to correct her for – or indeed even treating his criticisms as a joke, as she tells her father she does in the first chapter of the book – Emma is discomfited, self-accusing, and in the end almost always in perfect agreement with him about what makes for right and what makes for wrong conduct. In her orientation towards a standard of right that she deplores her deviations from, in her concern for the good of others above her own, she is not like Frank Churchill. She is like George Knightley. The novel's narrative both deceives and undeceives the reader as to this similarity by making the comparison between Emma and Frank such an issue in the dénouement.

Emma has always taken great joy in teasing Mr. Knightley, and this often consists of taking an opposing side in an argument. Mr. Knightley himself ultimately realizes that what we would now call negative psychology has been at work in his berating of Emma. He claims at the end of the novel that his "interference was quite as likely to do harm as good" because "nature gave [her] understanding: – Miss Taylor gave [her] principles. [She] must have done well" (III.17.504). Emma protests, and the reader agrees with Emma perhaps, but it is an odd time to abandon

Mr. Knightley as the touchstone character whose guidance is always so valuable. Mr. Knightley indeed is the key Austen provides at the conclusion of *Emma* to the happiness Emma is able to earn. He is the key because he, like Emma, can change in an important way as regards tenderness of heart, while not changing in terms of his fundamental principles.

In *Deceit, Desire, and the Novel*, René Girard argues that novelistic endings feature conversion and redemption; these events occur through a renunciation of illusion, as Don Quixote finds salvation by renouncing the delusion that he is a knight errant.[23] Austen makes such moments of redemptive epiphany climactic, but usually not final, in all her novels, most famously in *Pride and Prejudice*: "Till this moment, I never knew myself" (II.13.230). In *Emma*, the corresponding moment of self-revelation is the famous sentence, "Her heart was before her in an instant … it darted through her with the speed of an arrow: Mr. Knightley must marry no one but herself" (*E*, III.11.444). Even Austen's more perfect heroines are generally acknowledged to have such encounters with truth, and to change.[24] Emma's moment is not her admission of her disgrace after her insult to Miss Bates but her realization that she is the one Mr. Knightley must choose. Austen is not simply repeating her themes and strategies from *Pride and Prejudice* but is focusing on a different kind of maturation in her later heroine.

The extraordinariness of Emma's epiphanic moment is often commented on, but what is less often conceded is that her heroes as well as her heroines demonstrate the ability to have moral epiphanies and to change. In this well-known passage, it is Mr. Knightley who must or must not act.

Emma can finally perceive her own heart, the shrouded centre of her own self that throughout the novel has lain hidden. Cupid's arrow is here, piercing her much as Frederick Wentworth's soul is pierced in *Persuasion*, and Emma's speedy powers of deduction assist its flight. Austen conveys so much in such short phrases, even falling into free indirect discourse to model Emma's thought process more closely. But Emma need do nothing. It is Mr. Knightley who must marry, and it is he who must choose her. But why should she be his choice if she is as defective and he as perfect as many readers and critics think?

Mr. Knightley's Change

Austen's men are less regularly subjected to critical scrutiny than her heroines, since they are secondary in importance to the women at the centre of each novel. Since Mr. Knightley is most often seen as the unchanging paragon in comparison to Emma's wilful self, his role in the conclusion of *Emma* is decisive when it comes to estimating the heroine herself and the "perfect happiness of the union" with which Austen closes the novel. No man in the novel is Emma's equal, and no man deserves her but he. This is so although Emma has erred – and although Mr. Knightley has made some serious mistakes as well. Mr. Knightley himself does not think he is entirely Emma's equal; he believes the good is all on his side in acquiring her as his wife.

Critics of *Emma* are in two minds about Mr. Knightley.[25] Those like Bernard Paris and Ward Hellstrom see him as the immutable standard of Englishness to which Emma must turn for redemption from her faults, while those like Mary Waldron, Margaret Kirkham, and John Hagan understand him as more or less flawed and chart a progress or decline for him, depending on their assessment of his love for Emma. John Hagan's negative assessment of Emma leads him to read Mr. Knightley's marriage to her as a fall and the conclusion of the novel as some kind of ironic pseudo-tragedy. Analysing Mr. Knightley's flaws leads him to argue that Mr. Knightley never changes, never really becomes aware, as Emma does, of his own defects and of emotion's rule over his own life, supposedly so dedicated to good sense and right judgment. This view can be disproved from Austen's own text, as we shall see. However, more recent contributions to the understanding of this character, such as Rosalind Meyer's "Mr. Knightley's Education," Mary Waldron's article on his "confusions," and Margaret Kirkham's more negative evaluation of his faults in her book on feminism and fiction seem, unfortunately, to have had little impact on the general apprehension of the dynamism of his role in *Emma*.[26] Yet, Rosalind Meyer and others demonstrate that he does change in some way that amounts to a renunciation of his didactic posture towards Emma. As Gillian Dooley notes, "Emma is certainly the queen of misconstrual, but Mr. Knightley is not immune to fallible assumptions."[27]

Mr. Knightley, however, settles one question himself when he says, "And I am changed also" (III.18.518). Here he and Emma are discussing Harriet, who moves in Mr. Knightley's estimation from being an abstract figure of "illegitimacy and ignorance" (I.8.65) to a real girl who is the

Eltons' superior in character and of whom Mr. Elton has shown himself unworthy. Desiring to do justice not so much to Harriet as to Emma, Mr. Knightley grows in his ability to value someone for her virtues and strengths as an individual, when previously he has considered her only in terms of class and education. This openness bodes well for his ability to learn to treat Emma herself as a wife, not a spoiled child.

But is this renunciation enough to turn Mr. Knightley the mentor into Mr. Knightley the lover: is "affection" merely overpowering "judgment"? That would be a fall rather than growth. To propose marriage acceptably to the heroine, he must knowingly extricate himself from his position as taskmaster and external conscience. Otherwise, he cannot occupy the role of lover in Emma's imagination or ours. He must become a suppliant. He must become, a term he decries early on, *aimable*, to both heroine and reader. Once he discovers his love for Emma through his jealousy of Frank, however, circumstances and the dynamic of his long relationship with her conspire to create an insuperable obstacle to his heart's desire. Having tried for years to correct Mr. Woodhouse's and Miss Taylor's indulgence of Emma by acting as guide and critic, he finds he has fatally miscast himself in a role unlikely to win a young girl's heart and hand.[28] He is paralyzed. This supposedly active and vigorous hero must wait passively for a *deus ex machina* to deliver his beloved to his arms. Austen constructs Mr. Knightley's story so that, on multiple encounters with the novel, the reader will see him as endangered by the same isolation that threatens Emma in the first chapter, and will feel the pathos of his situation in scenes that seem to demonstrate Emma's indifference to him. His ability to suffer for love and pay homage to his beloved in the end makes him the true romantic hero that he becomes and reshapes him from a critic into someone who can give credit for another's virtues.

Bernard Paris says of Emma's relationship with Knightley, "Emma's education is an example of moral growth through suffering. She is instructed not only by Knightley, but also by reality, which crushes her pride and forces her to abandon her delusional system."[29] This is a very typical reading of Emma's defeat and change and of Mr. Knightley's victory and immutability. It is a very traditional view of the role of *desengaño* or renunciation of illusions in the novel as a genre. While it is entirely true that suffering motivates Emma's self-knowledge and desire for improvement, Austen's narrative invites us to recognize a similar growth through suffering in Mr. Knightley. If Mr. Knightley did not demonstrate confusion, self-doubt, and humility, but were only Emma's moral superior, he would have little impact on the audience. As Elaine Bander has pointed out, "the problem with perfection is that it is static, impervious to growth or change."[30] We know that Austen's predilections make it nearly impossible for her to offer her reader a "perfect" and magisterial figure of this type.[31] When Mr. Knightley says, "I should like to see Emma in love, and in some doubt of a return; it would do her good" (I.1.41), he does not know that his author plans for him to be in love, and in grave doubt of a return, for many months, as opposed to Emma's single day of suffering for love of him. This longer period of suffering cannot be a mistake on Austen's part. Throughout the novel, Mr. Knightley's restraint and self-doubt reveal very gradually a man completely unsure of his position vis-à-vis the young woman at the centre of his and the novel's universe. He "blame[s her], and lecture[s her]" (III.13.430), presuming on one kind of intimacy and ceaselessly building higher and more impenetrable the wall between himself and love. At that point, he does not know how to be lovable to Emma. In the end, however, he will seize the opportunity to imagine himself in a different relationship to her and modify his behaviour accordingly.

The reader would certainly care about none of this if Austen did not succeed in making him lovable by creating scenes wherein the audience sympathizes with his vulnerability and powerlessness. Otherwise, one could well decry the union of the vigorous and powerful young woman with the man Sir Walter Scott called "the sturdy, advice-giving bachelor" – certainly a damning description.[32] But we sense all along he is more than that, for Austen gradually shapes our understanding of him just as she reshapes his understanding of Emma. She insists on *his* growth through suffering. Austen modulates the behaviour of Mr. Knightley in his interchange with Emma to build to the climactic moment of the proposal, in which he humbles himself before her.

There are multiple scenes throughout the novel in which Mr. Knightley suffers because of his love for Emma, though generally she is unconscious of inflicting pain, an important distinction Austen makes between her and Frank Churchill. The culmination of volume 1 – in which Emma plays devil's advocate, defending Frank Churchill to irritate Mr. Knightley – reveals to the careful first-time reader and the alert second-time reader Mr. Knightley's jealousy.

More important, this scene validates early on Mr. Knightley's recognition at the end of the novel of his own role in Emma's errors: it is not for nothing that he himself will declare to her, "'My interference was quite as likely to do harm as good. It was very natural for you to say, what right has he to lecture me? – and I am afraid very natural for you to feel that it was done in a disagreeable manner. I do not believe I did you any good. The good was all to myself ... My interference was giving you two bad feelings instead of one'" (III.17.462). Emma, of course, will deny the justice of his self-evaluation, as will the reader at first, swayed by Emma's self-mockery. But why should we brush aside his statement as exaggeration? Even here he is provoking an argument rather than correcting a real mistake in Emma's judgment. Emma is not poised to love Frank but is unwilling to let an aggressive Mr. Knightley see that she already agrees with him.

Emma notices a *moral* failing in Knightley, whose character she has always admired. She has "often laid to his charge" a "high opinion of himself," and here she sees him being unjust as a result (I.18.151). Emma's reaction to his tirade shows that he is also unjust to the merits of her forbearance. The irritation to his feelings makes him far from amiable in this scene. His defence of manly resolution sounds bluntly like a fondness for "bending little minds," as Emma puts it (I.18.147). He wants Emma to concede to his encomium of the dutiful man's will but offers her a display of the high-handed bossiness that would be repulsive in a love relationship. Obvious throughout the novel is his conceit about his good principles and others' lack of them.

While Mr. Knightley does not really act rudely to Emma, she must conciliate him and change subjects. He does not attempt to see the better points of her argument, as Mary Waldron has noted;[33] the ability to do so will be a step on the road to agreeableness he is not yet ready to take. The degree of pique (Elaine Bander's word) he displays shows he does not like to be contradicted, but a second reading of the novel reveals that he is wounded by Emma's words and her enthusiasm. We see anger and even hatred in his description of a young man who "'at three-and-twenty [is] to be king of his company – the great man – the practised politician, who is to read every body's character, and make every body's talents conduce to the display of his own superiority; to be dispensing his flatteries around, that he may make all appear like fools compared with himself!'" (I.18.150). As long as Emma perceives Frank as "king of his company," Mr. Knightley cannot bear him. It is not for nothing that Austen makes this argument the culmination of volume 1. It is not really about Frank, but about the way in which Emma and Mr. Knightley converse and argue. It showcases his irritation at the thought of another man's being "king."

Mr. Knightley blusters away at Emma, not even thinking of her reaction to his angry and alliterative, sputtering speech. If true amiability is closely linked to virtue in Austen's work, as Sarah Emsley has shown,[34] it will be a growth in virtue for Mr. Knightley to improve on this hot temper. The reader is easily blinded to Knightley's own failure at this moment to live up to the ideal he proposes (in regard to Emma) because he objects in such strong language to

Frank's deserving the term "amiable." Austen deliberately sidetracks the reader:

> "'Your amiable young man is a very weak young man, if this be the first occasion of his carrying through a resolution to do right against the will of others … No, Emma, your amiable young man can be amiable only in French, not in English. He may be very "aimable," have very good manners, and be very agreeable; but he can have no English delicacy towards the feelings of other people: nothing really amiable about him.'" (I.18.148–9)

To say that English amiability is constituted by genuine delicacy towards the feelings of other people, while in the midst of an unnecessarily heated argument with a dear friend, in which he advocates dogged pursuit of duty regardless of the feelings of easily-irritated adoptive parents, reveals Mr. Knightley's own less than sensitive approach to human relations.

Emma detects an important quality in his imagination of Frank's ideal response: a lack of the habit of "early obedience." Mr. Knightley does not know or remember what it is like to answer to another person, to yield rather than to oppose all that is "unworthy" in "authority" (I.18.147–8). That is certainly one reason why he strikes us as so mature and self-sufficient. But in his discussion of the "scale of vanity" in *Emma*, Mark Schorer does not see that Mr. Knightley's self-confidence comes in part from his position as elder son and his lack of living parents and of a wife. He is, Schorer says, "only a little pompous,"[35] but Schorer does not consider the question of why Austen made him so. The reader cannot overlook it, especially when the heroine does not: Mr. Knightley already suffers the symptoms of solipsism and rigidity that come from valuing his own opinion above those of all others.

Yet, Knightley's sense of self-importance and independence is being threatened, even as he argues with an already convinced Emma about Frank Churchill. It is for this reason that the reader forgives him and even favours him: the reader who sees the aching heart that the "unamiable" behaviour here reveals will pardon the weakness. This recognition is really only possible after the first reading of the novel, once we know his secret. Then one does not like Mr. Knightley simply because he is right; as Waldron reveals, he argues very inconsistently in this scene, a sure sign of prejudice. Rather, as Lionel Trilling said, we like Mr. Knightley "because we perceive that he cherishes Emma not merely in spite of her subversive self-assertion but because of it," just as we like Darcy because he rightly dislikes Caroline Bingley and falls in love with the critical Elizabeth Bennet.[36] In the "drama of the soul's choice," Austen's heroes pick the correct object of love. Mr. Knightley's heart has already accommodated Emma's bad qualities and has already been drawn to her good ones. If he is in danger of losing his place as first in Emma's life, he will react bitterly, and he continues to do so.

Another scene that displays once again Mr. Knightley's sensitivity to Emma's romantic detachment from him yields on a second reading proof that his displeasure and shyness are signs of a wounded heart. When a strangely anxious

Emma provokes him to speak about his potential attachment to Jane Fairfax, Mr. Knightley responds to her inquiries with little of the manly resolution he touts. He does not laugh off Emma's intrusion as absurd, nor does he tease her in response. Mr. Knightley is not averse to being teased elsewhere, an activity he participates in with greater ease and zest than the much younger Mr. Darcy (see, for instance, his remarks to Emma about his arriving at the party in a carriage "like a gentleman" [I.8.213], during which conversation, incidentally, Emma again observes character defects in the famously "perfect" hero). Faced with Emma and Mrs. Weston's curiosity, he eludes observation deliberately and will not look directly at Emma at crucial moments:

> Mr. Knightley was hard at work upon the lower buttons of his thick leather gaiters, and either the exertion of getting them together, or some other cause, brought the colour into his face, as he answered …
>
> He seemed hardly to hear her; he was thoughtful – and in a manner which shewed him not pleased, soon afterwards said,
>
> "So you have been settling that I should marry Jane Fairfax." (II.15.287)

Words usually come readily to Mr. Knightley. He and Emma enjoy vigorous repartee in their earlier conversations. He speaks in lists and syllogisms, favouring order, energy, and clarity. Yet, in this scene the pace slows, and he seems unwilling or extremely careful in his responses. The author conceals his thoughts from us, and though what he does say is rife with meaning, it does not reveal his love for Emma in a detectable fashion. The author coyly refuses to tell us the cause of his blush, but she does hint strongly that it has nothing to do with his gaiters. Why does he choose that particular moment to occupy himself in such a way as to avoid observation? More importantly, why does the narrator choose this particular moment to refuse to show her authorial face to the reader? "Either the exertion of getting them together, or some other cause, brought the colour into his face." Although Austen claims ignorance, she cannot be ignorant. When the narrator gives us two alternatives, and the first is clearly a sufficient explanation if true, the second cause is the true cause. We know this because she refuses to identify that alternative. He "seemed hardly to hear her": the verb "seemed" is the first verb in the entire novel, and seeming versus being is a theme that Austen maintains throughout the text. As Emma observes him for clues, Austen exposes to the reader – while telling us nothing definite – that Mr. Knightley is hiding something. On a second reading, we have no difficulty identifying the real source of his attempted concealment. He is wounded that Emma could imagine him as the husband of another, just as earlier he was nettled by Emma's assertion that Harriet would be the perfect wife for him, as Waldron observes.[37] He is embarrassed to be linked with Jane, to have his heart be the object of others' scrutiny in this more serious conversation.

Mr. Knightley and Emma, however, have now broached a topic that opens the way to the future; he tells her (in his usual aphoristic, generalizing way) what "a man would wish for in a wife," something very different from what

Emma had accused him and men in general of wanting earlier. He then continues, "And I love an open temper" (II.7.289). Mr. Knightley here begins to be willing to speak of himself personally rather than to submerge his desires in the vast ocean of universal statements about mankind. He does not want a cowed or subdued wife such as he has imagined Mrs. Weston becoming. The closure of the novel is in part designed to assure the reader that Emma will continue to be this way, and he will continue to enjoy her "open temper" after marriage.

In this scene, Mr. Knightley also provides one of his general rules of good behaviour, one that he does not apply in his conduct towards Emma. The contrast between his principle and his own behaviour towards her implies that open criticism, such as that to which he often subjects her, may have always been his way of being intimate: "'We all know the difference between the pronouns he or she and thou, the plainest-spoken amongst us … We cannot give any body the disagreeable hints that we may have been very full of the hour before. We feel things differently'" (II.15.286). We cannot, that is, except in the exceptional case of a person to whom plain-spokenness is welcome. Mr. Knightley does not generally favour Emma either with French "agreeableness" or even "English delicacy." As in *Pride and Prejudice*, open criticism of each other's faults manifests a growing or already established attachment, but it also entails some misconduct. The difference in *Emma* is that Mr. Knightley becomes aware of the connection between the two. The novel begins with a display of this kind of closeness as Emma soothes her father's dismay at Mr. Knightley's criticism with the assurance that it is all a joke and that "we always say what we like to one another" (I.1.10). But Austen does not end on a Shakespearean comic note of mutual criticism. If Mr. Knightley still finds it difficult to praise Emma, to bite his tongue when a "teaching moment" comes, Austen wants him to see his flaw before giving him her heroine.

She thus takes opportunities to show that his pride and complacency, unlike the Eltons', are far from unassailable. Even at this early stage, he demonstrates the potential for allowing the warmth of particular love for one person alone to humble him in his own eyes. Austen intensifies the reader's awareness of Mr. Knightley's emotional engagement when the narrative reveals the degree of disquiet Emma causes Mr. Knightley as she seems to assure him she and Frank are attached (III.5.351). The narrative highlights his emotional reaction to her confidence in Frank's indifference to Jane. The narrator, not given to hyperbole, says that Emma's confidence "staggered" him. It is a graphic verb, which Austen uses infrequently, meaning to sway or reel from a blow, drunkenness, or dizziness. Once again, we see a wounded Knightley, whose reaction to his beloved's supposed attachment can only be "silence" and immuring himself in isolation in "the coolness and solitude of Donwell Abbey" (III.5.351).

This silencing of the hero and his abrupt departure emphasize his paralysis in this situation, his utter helplessness in the face of what he sees as his replacement in Emma's affections by another man. Here his standards of duty and forthrightness cannot help him. He cannot "by vigour and resolution" (I.18.146) conquer his own real problem, which he has already identified in Frank Churchill's conduct: "Had he begun as he ought, there would have been no difficulty now" (I.18.148). Austen continually shows us the characters in Highbury in difficulty because they have not begun as they ought, and Mr. Knightley is no exception. It is not by being a very fine man alone that he can secure romantic love, and he cannot command it. At this point, how can anyone claim, as Hagan does, that Mr. Knightley is unaware of his subjection to emotion? He knows that he cannot even trust himself to talk rationally with Emma by chapter's end. He may attribute his fever to Mr. Woodhouse's fire, but only in part: "he found he could not be useful, and his feelings were too much irritated for talking" (III.5.351). From what he tells Emma a few chapters later, the reader can be certain that he knows why his feelings are irritated.

Once one sees that Mr. Knightley is not just criticizing and commanding, but suffering and despairing, one's sympathies are engaged, although Emma remains ignorant of the wounds she inflicts. Nonetheless, he must do more than suffer for love; he must learn to credit Emma's virtues and empathize with her pain. The first he does grudgingly early in the story in conversation with Mrs. Weston, but how different is his warm and open "fond praise of" Emma to her father at the end of the novel (III.17.467). At that point, he can speak openly and honestly words that he found difficult to articulate before. His empathy for her develops, too: Mr. Knightley can view with concern the Eltons' vicarious jab at Emma through Mr. Elton's refusal to dance with Harriet, and later, much more intensely, he can participate in her imagined anguish at the discovery of Frank's engagement to Jane. He has ridden through the rain from London on the latter occasion not to propose but to comfort an Emma he wrongly supposes to be heartbroken over Frank. This new and emotionally charged attitude of service bridges the distance between his actual self-offering and what comes so soon before, the uncompleted kissing of Emma's hand.

The sign of deference and service that Austen ascribes to Mr. Knightley as he flees to London indicates his advancement towards the kind of amiable behaviour he might earlier have scorned as French gallantry. To escape the distress he endures thinking of Emma in the toils of another man, he plans to avoid her. Before he leaves, however, he hears of her attempts to humble herself to Miss Bates. Austen chooses the act of kissing Emma's hand as his response. It is true that he does not complete the action, and it is also right: the act indicates "*hommage*," the offering of the self to one's lady as her man, her servant.[38] There are few novelistic choices so perfect as Austen's selection of this kind of romantic gesture for this couple in particular, few novelistic choices so perfect as her decision to delay the commitment. Even before Harriet's revelation, Emma finds herself wondering at the action and desiring its fulfilment, seeing in his eyes in this moment that he "at once caught and honoured" "all that had passed of good in her feelings" (III.9.385). Mr. Knightley has sufficient time to give full credit to Emma's humble choice to make amends without his prompting before he really does plead for her love. But the moment stands as a finely drawn compromise between French courtliness and English delicacy. Emma herself observes this move towards gallantry and is sure "the intention ... was indubitable" (III.9.386).

Mr. Knightley's progress in the novel is not towards blindness but towards the humility Austen thinks necessary in romantic love; he is humbled by his realization of his dependence on Emma for all his happiness and by his recognition of his earlier arrogance towards her (III.17.461–2). If readers and critics adopt his earlier attitude towards Emma, seeing him as the touchstone character he is in many but not in all ways, it is easy to miss or misinterpret the progress Austen charts for him. Even her touchstone character is a mixed character. However, the reader can recognize this sentiment of one's own unworthiness of the other from both Darcy and Elizabeth at the end of *Pride and Prejudice*. Emma's humiliation and self-condemnation have received much comment, but for Mr. Knightley to be a lover and not a master, Austen makes him judge his own conduct towards Emma in particular as wrong and undeserved. We rightly praise Mr. Knightley for being, as the narrator tells us, one of the few "who could see faults in" Emma (I.1.9), but he himself says later he has imagined many of those faults (III.17.504).

The reader might have missed that Emma also has a remarkable acuity when it comes to Mr. Knightley's faults, but her love for him in the end fills her with a humble appreciation of his worth. Austen brings them both to a point where they can speak of themselves in the same self-abasing terms. Emma unknowingly reveals to us that her love for Knightley is true, as Harriet's is not, because Austen characterizes her feeling as one of unworthiness of him:

> Harriet Smith might think herself not unworthy of being peculiarly, exclusively, passionately loved by Mr. Knightley.

> *She* could not. She could not flatter herself with any idea of blindness in his attachment to *her* ... How directly, how strongly, had he expressed himself to her on the subject! ... far, far too strongly to issue from any feeling softer than upright justice and clear-sighted good will. – She had no hope, nothing to deserve the name of hope, that he could have that sort of affection for herself which was now in question. (III.12.453)

Mr. Knightley's subsequent confession to her proves her right about the connection between "softness" and "that sort of affection." Charitably overlooking the foibles of Miss Bates because of her poverty and of Mr. Woodhouse because of his age, Knightley finally gives himself permission, seeing his own imperfection, to allow Emma's, or at least to allow her own conscience now to be her corrector and guide. The mentor has truly yielded to the lover.

Mr. Knightley runs the same risk Emma does of moulding his own character into that of an unapproachable monarch of all he surveys, free but unlovable. He recognizes in the end that he is indebted for all the domestic security he has enjoyed over the years to Emma's powers of forbearance. He can now see she has exercised them most perhaps in regard not to her father but to him; she has treated him with a deference and patience he has taken for granted. But he does not want to be tolerated. To be loved is his aim, and it is only his great good luck that Harriet Smith's infatuation with him has already startled Emma into knowledge of her own attachment. He approaches her now with "tenderness," a word Austen repeats several times in the proposal scene, and when the opportunity presents itself, he accepts her proposal of amity and begs permission for the last thing one might have expected: to become amiable. His request is not yet for her hand, but for her tolerance of him as a suitor. That means he now intends to approach her as one seeking favour, not conferring it. At this point, the reader is given the estimation of Mrs. Weston, whose earlier partiality now looks more like fairness, whereas Mr. Knightley's disagreeable hope that he should see Emma in love and in some doubt of a return appears in retrospect mean-spirited. Austen's irony makes him the one to endure that state for around two-thirds of the novel, while Emma endures only one day and one night. Mrs. Weston is delighted to hear of their engagement and observes that "he deserved even her dearest Emma" (III.17.510). Mrs. Weston's perspective is a corrective. We are unlearning our habit of blaming and lecturing Emma ourselves as readers.

For Emma's tastes, loathing excessive gallantry as she does, Mr. Knightley really has not needed to change much to gain her hand, though she certainly feels the change. From the author's perspective, however, something has been lacking. Emma herself need not ratify his evaluation of his behaviour towards her for us to recognize the author's point. Though Emma still cannot call him George, he knows enough now to want her to do so. His anxiety to attach Emma to him, to please Emma, has to become an element in his love for her so that he will not merely be a father or teacher. At the end of *Emma*, Mr. Knightley thinks his beloved "a woman worthy of being pleased" (*PP*, III.16.410) and can finally live up to his name through his truly chivalrous attitude towards the one woman he cannot live without.

The drama of the soul's choice is exactly what Austen sees marriage as revealing. In having both Emma and Harriet scorn the idea of being interested in Frank Churchill, Austen invites the reader to draw a conclusion about Jane Fairfax. Even Frank himself shows better judgment in choosing her than she does in choosing him. Mr. Knightley is always holding up Jane as a paragon to Emma (even in the proposal scene), but his heart chooses Emma. The Eltons are in some sense the most perfectly matched of all the couples in the novel, and yet their suitability for each other is just the characteristic that will ensure their continued and worsening shallowness and envy. Emma and Mr. Knightley truly do make each other better. The desire to be the other's object of affection, when there is so much true merit and true love on both sides, makes each character grow emotionally and morally. It is not enough that Emma be undeceived: Mr. Knightley must be undeceived as well, and readers must share in his *desengaño*.

CHAPTER EIGHT

The Oracles of Kellynch and Uppercross: Predicting the Future in *Persuasion*

Predicting What Lies Beyond the Novel's End

What is an end for Jane Austen? Aristotle, speaking of a tragedy, says an end is "an imitation of an action that is complete, and whole, and of a certain magnitude" and adds that "a whole has a beginning, a middle, and an end."[1] A beginning is something that is not caused by something else and from which something follows. A middle follows something and is followed by something. An end follows something and is not followed by anything. Investigations of novel endings over the past few decades have questioned Aristotle's concept of closure, which after all, does not account for the fact that even his premiere example of the best tragedy, Sophocles' *Oedipus*, has sequels. When is the end ever really the end? When Austen writes the end of a novel, does she think of it as an end? Has she provided us with an end at the conclusion of *Persuasion*? In that novel, we envision a happy future for the heroine, but the probability of real-life problems encroaching on even the most perfect happiness nevertheless lies in wait. Within the narrative, various characters actually predict different endings on our behalf.

Austen clearly thinks that a plot point she has begun must reach a culmination. The two problems we witness in the first chapters of the novel are worked out: the foiling of the petty Sir Walter's self-aggrandizement on the one hand and the elevation of the downtrodden daughter Anne on the other. Part of our satisfaction at the end of the novel comes from the "derangement" of Mr. Elliot's plans for domestic happiness and the humiliation of Elizabeth and Sir Walter in discovering the duplicity of Mrs. Clay. But Sir Walter, Mr. Elliot, and Mrs. Clay are decoy villains. The real thing that has kept Anne from happiness all these years is Frederick Wentworth's resentment. However, since he is the object of Anne's affections, as Edward Ferrars and Edmund Bertram (and even Reginald De Courcy) are the beloveds of their heroines, he must not come in for too much condemnation. We should probably be happy – and we are happy – that Anne and Frederick are looking forward to a lifetime together with no doubts about their own contentment. Like Austen's other novels, however, *Persuasion* also ends by giving the reader an impulse to prognosticate about the future of the cast of characters, and in this way it ventures outside the bounds of Aristotle's sense of wholeness and completion.

As D.A. Miller notes in *Narrative and Its Discontents*, Austen transformed the tenor of her conclusion when she added the word "perhaps" to the revised version of her closure:[2] "There they returned again into the past, more exquisitely happy, *perhaps*, in their reunion, than when it had been first projected; more tender, more tried, more fixed in a knowledge of each other's character, truth, and attachment; more equal to act, more justified in acting" (*P*, II.11.261; my emphasis). "Perhaps" puts the truth of the superior happiness into question but at the same time does not let us deny that it is true. The narrator slips from guessing, from conjecture, to what sounds like asserting. Austen likes this kind of equivocation, and she subjects Anne's happiness to the same doubts several times.

Persuasion presents two alternative futures through the anxiety of Anne and the premonitory musings of her sister Mary. We might not be aware that these two futures are in play until we examine the final chapter closely and attempt to define the tone Austen creates through the information she gives. The novel presents a challenge to the reader who is trying to visualize what exactly is going on in Austen's ending – or to the filmmaker who wants to display a satisfactory visual image. Austen's endings are never visual in this way. If Austen's lens has panned out from close-ups and dialogues, it is still fixed on the central characters and their stories, and even on the future of their hearts and their happiness. Perhaps there is no way to show that Anne Elliot could be both happy and sad in her future life, but Austen is not interested in giving us a tableau frozen in time in a passing moment of joy. Instead, she reminds the reader that the vicissitudes of human life make the future unpredictable. By comparing Anne's and Frederick's conflicting visions of the future happiness of Louisa Musgrove and Captain James Benwick with the narrator's own forecast of future happiness for the main couple, I hope to show that Austen leaves the reader to imagine what is most probable, but she does not close the question. Will Anne and Frederick eventually have a stable home? Will he survive the coming war, or will she be left a widow? The role of Providence in the novel, as Kathryn Davis has discussed, tips the balance perhaps in the direction of the positive.[3]

Several times in *Persuasion,* Austen's narrator or her characters make predictions about the future.[4] Of these the most important are those her heroine and hero make, and those made about them. One of the longest discussions Anne Elliot and Frederick Wentworth have in *Persuasion* actually concerns another couple, Louisa Musgrove and James Benwick. In this electrifying tête-à-tête at the concert in Bath, Captain Wentworth seems to offer a counter to Anne's earlier, more positive assessment of the pair's chance for happiness. Since Austen never shows us the future of the young Benwicks (who, like the other married couples in the novel, are foils for Anne and Wentworth), we as readers have only these predictions as guides. Here Austen is doing two things she very often does in regard to the futures of her married couples at the close of a novel: she has others within the narrative predict the characters' chances of prosperity and contentment, and she places the readers in the position of judge, to be guided by her instruction in producing a more refined or accurate prophecy by assessing the prophets themselves.

Aside from testing judgment, there can be no other motive for presenting the reader with the two differing opinions of her heroine and hero. The reader's judgment is engaged in regard to Louisa and Benwick, but also in regard to our protagonist and her future husband. Anne or Wentworth: who is right? Coming to a conclusion produces a mimesis of Austen's ideal of marriage, as readers balance both prophesies and see what is accurate and reliable in each. Anne is too sanguine, perhaps, but Frederick, only just learning that there may be reason to doubt the sincerity of Benwick's claim to lasting grief, may be too alarmist. As in the case of Mr. and Mrs. Bennet's predictions about Jane and Mr. Bingley, and the Westons' and Mr. Knightley's about Jane Fairfax and Frank Churchill, the truth lies in between. We must care what happens to Louisa and Benwick because Austen shows the main couple doing so. Their prophecies show what they value and their own attitudes about the marriage bond's resilience under the tension of the divisive power of individual differences.

Anne says very little in the conversation at the concert; she is mostly absorbed in interpreting how Frederick feels about her, the primary reason that what he says about Benwick and Louisa is important. These additions to the material of the story advance us towards the reunion of the heroine and hero. "With a little smile, a little glow," upset at the recollection of Louisa's fall and then, "half smiling again," Frederick brings up the topic of Louisa and Benwick: "'The day … has had some consequences which must be considered as the very reverse of frightful. – When you had the presence of mind to suggest that Benwick would be the properest person to fetch a surgeon, you could have little idea of his being eventually one of those most concerned in her recovery'" (II.8.198). Anne's reply is that of a well-wisher with nothing but good to say: "'I should hope it would be a very happy match. There are on both sides good principles and good temper'" (II.8.198). The reader is asked to assess Anne's statement because Frederick's agreement is only partial:

> "Yes," said he, looking not exactly forward – "but there I think ends the resemblance. With all my soul I wish them happy, and rejoice over every circumstance in favour of it. They have no difficulties to contend with at home, no opposition, no caprice, no delays. – The Musgroves are behaving like themselves, most honourably and kindly, only anxious with true parental hearts to promote their daughter's comfort. All this is much, very much in favour of their happiness; more than perhaps – ." (II.8.198)

The first count on which Frederick separates himself from Anne is in fact part of his agreement with her. He concurs that Louisa and Benwick do not have difficult personalities and are virtuous. Anne, however, has not brought up the family's reaction to Louisa's engagement. To him, thwarted in his early suit by Sir Walter's cold reception and Lady Russell's advice against him, this point is salient in advancing the young couple's chances. From his point of view, rapid and heartfelt consent from the parents is a considerable advantage.

But he struggles to show Anne his interest in her and has to stop himself from saying more because what he is about to add is no doubt a reflection on their own encounter with difficulty. He does not look exactly forward. Anne blushes, and Wentworth too has an emotional pause before he can continue with his view of the problems that might beset the Benwicks' relationship: "'I confess that I do think there is a disparity, too great a disparity, and in a point no less essential than mind. – I regard Louisa Musgrove as a very amiable, sweet-tempered girl, and not deficient in understanding, but Benwick is something more. He is a clever man, a reading man – and I confess that I do consider his attaching himself to her with some surprise'" (II.8.198–9). Even if his bafflement is tempered by relief, Wentworth is deeply troubled in a way Anne was not when she received the first news of the engagement in Mary's letter. The injection of this warning voice after Anne has painted a rosy picture of the Benwicks' future happiness is worth heeding.

Wentworth speaks so intimately in this conversation that the reader all of a sudden realizes just how close the two were eight-and-a-half years ago. The reader also realizes he is not ashamed at all to discuss Louisa in front of Anne, as he coolly assesses her character in a most un-lover-like way. His detachment from Louisa conveys a great deal. The speech must mean many things to Anne: she is in his confidence, and he clearly thinks they can discuss such things as what attracts a man to a woman; he does not love Louisa; he is disappointed in Benwick. The list goes on. Frederick is perplexed and troubled but not condemnatory. His speech, however, starts from a presumption that equality, or parity, should exist between spouses, an equality he estimates the pair cannot boast: "'I confess that I do think there is a disparity, too great a disparity, and in a point no less essential than mind'" (II.8.198). As others have observed, Austen often uses the word "mind" to mean the whole person, the heart and soul, not just the intellect:[5] this word operates as a red alert.

Perhaps more astonishingly, as Frederick continues confessing his doubts to Anne, he disparages a spontaneous love, where the man has no idea if the woman is attracted to him or not:

> "I confess that I do consider his attaching himself to her with some surprise. Had it been the effect of gratitude, had he learnt to love her, because he believed her to be preferring him, it would have been another thing. But I have no reason to suppose it so. It seems, on the contrary, to have been a perfectly spontaneous, untaught feeling on his side, and this surprises me. A man like him, in his situation! With a heart pierced, wounded, almost broken! Fanny Harville was a very superior creature, and his attachment to her was indeed attachment. A man does not recover from such a devotion of the heart to such a woman! – He ought not – he does not." (II.8.199)

There is only one conclusion to be reached by this reasoning: Benwick is not a man – not in Frederick Wentworth's eyes. He has recovered.

The speech begins with lengthy clauses, even with subordination. But it devolves into briefer, staccato exclamations, punctuated with dental consonants that ring out decision and scorn, perhaps shock: "hear*t*," "pierce*d*," "woun*ded*," "almos*t*," "*d*oes no*t*," "*d*evotion," "hear*t*," "*t*o," "ough*t* no*t*," "*does not*." Wentworth is the master of short, impassioned sentences ("You pierce my soul. I am half agony, half hope" [II.11.257–8]). 'He ought not – he does not" could not be shorter or more powerful, and yet it is richly polyvalent. At the beginning of the paragraph, "a man" was Benwick, or any man, but by the end of the speech, it is clear, to Anne as well as to us, that "a man" is Wentworth. Benwick's close friend gives the most decidedly negative account of his unfaithfulness, more influential than Mary Musgrove's, because he speaks from the point of view of a person who has remained constant, even in spite of himself. This is what a man is: constant even past the brink of death.

Jocelyn Harris has described Benwick as fickle.[6] Her view agrees with Wentworth's, who seems to find the spontaneity of Benwick's affection the biggest strike against it. Austen's most passionate lover is the one who sees "untaught feeling" as most troubling. He could accept the relationship with greater equanimity and confidence if Benwick were responding to Louisa's interest in him. The fact that Benwick himself seemed to initiate the romantic overtures so soon after Fanny's death makes him think for the first time that he does not know his friend as well as he thought. Harris's discussion of Benwick's dramatized emotion, comparing it to Mrs. Musgrove's over the loss of her worthless son, is apropos here, for Wentworth is perhaps coming to the realization that Benwick is not sincere and is not the feeling, heartbroken man he took him to be. And Wentworth is the man who curled his "handsome mouth" in scorn at Mrs. Musgrove's laments for the worthless Dick (I.8.73).

Wentworth, like Anne, is not dealing at all with disappointed expectations of the romantic kind. He is re-evaluating his friend in the light of his choice of a mate. Austen shows us Wentworth awaking to the possibility of weakness in what he thought was a firm and upright character. That awakening has some claim on our attention, since Anne's knowledge of Benwick is not shaken but confirmed: she thought him "not inconsolable" (II.6.181). But Wentworth thought him like himself. On the surface, that seems to be true – each values Anne; each flirts with Louisa. But below the surface, the two men could not be more unlike: Benwick wants consolation and an understanding ear. Any nice girl could provide that. Wentworth wants "only Anne."

Anne has provoked this confidence – their longest conversation to date – by the simple observation, "There are on both sides good principles and good temper." He agrees with this assertion, and thus whatever hope we have for them from Anne's earlier reverie remains. What has Anne thought up to this point, and has she taken into account the disparity in their minds and the problem of fickleness? Anne's power as charitable and candid judge is such that it is possible to read this passage as the author's confirmation of the couple's future, and not as Anne's rationalization, though Austen leaves both options open: "Captain Benwick and Louisa Musgrove! The high-spirited, joyous-talking Louisa Musgrove, and the dejected, thinking, feeling, reading Captain Benwick, seemed each of them every thing that would not suit the other. Their minds most dissimilar! Where could have been the attraction?" (II.6.181).

Looking back at Anne's earlier thoughts, the reader is struck by her first astonishment caused by the dissimilarity of Louisa and James Benwick's "minds." Talking and high spirits are too different from thinking, reading, and low spirits for Anne to accept that either could have been attracted to the other. Both Anne and Frederick seem to agree that the young pair could never echo what Elizabeth Bennet says to Mr. Darcy, "I have always seen a great *similarity in the turn* of *our minds*" (*PP*, I.18.103; my emphasis).

Austen's strategy in developing Anne's interior monologue, or the heavily coloured narrative, is interesting. Whereas Anne and Frederick agree on salient points, he thinks of his own disappointment and the influence of family; she thinks of the propitious situation of the two young people, constantly in proximity after Louisa's injury, which has made her, too, a guest at the Harvilles'. As Anne thinks about the reason for their attraction,

> The answer soon presented itself. It had been in situation ... Since Henrietta's coming away, they must have been depending almost entirely on each other, and Louisa, just recovering from illness, had been in an interesting state, and Captain Benwick was not inconsolable. That was a point which Anne had not been able to avoid suspecting before; and ... [it] served only to confirm the idea of his having felt some dawning of tenderness toward herself ... She was persuaded that any tolerably pleasing young woman who had listened and seemed to feel for him would have received the same compliment. He had an affectionate heart. He must love somebody. (II.6.181)

Anne begins with as much surprise and shock as anybody at the idea of Louisa and Benwick yoked for life. Her meditation centres on Benwick, not Louisa, and, unlike Captain Wentworth, she is unsurprised by his actions. Natasha Duquette has written of Anne's sympathetic understanding of Benwick's "compassionate sensibility."[7] Anne has also noted, however, that Benwick is "not inconsolable." His seeking consolation has opened him up to finding it. An affectionate heart in this case seems a good thing: "He must love somebody." Anne's final two sentences in this paragraph are worth noting. They are declarative, and their substance is affection and love. Benwick strikes her as being loving, not selfish. She believes his love only requires an object.

And thus she convinces herself that the two will certainly be happy together. Looking upon Benwick very much as Reginald De Courcy's mother and sister looked upon him, Anne sees no cloud from the first hovering over the second attachment:

> She saw no reason against their being happy. Louisa had fine naval fervour to begin with, and they *would* soon grow more alike. He *would* gain cheerfulness, and she *would* learn to be an enthusiast for Scott and Lord Byron; nay, that was *probably learnt* already; of course they had fallen in love over poetry. The idea of Louisa Musgrove turned into a person of literary taste, and sentimental reflection was amusing, but *she had no doubt* of its being so. The day at Lyme, the fall from the Cobb, *might* influence her health, her nerves, her courage, her character to the end of her life, as thoroughly as it *appeared* to have influenced her fate. (II.6.181–2; my emphasis)

Anne makes excuses for Benwick and invents a new Louisa, different from the one we know from the previous chapters. However, Benwick might have fallen in love with a very different Louisa from the one both Anne and Wentworth describe; the narrator does not confirm Anne's fanciful imagination of how the decision to marry was arrived at. Anne forcefully guesses and then muses in the conditional: "*she* had no doubt"; "The day at Lyme … *might* influence her [Louisa's] … character to the end of her life" (my emphasis). But such a guess at what might have happened and such a prophecy of what their future would be is all the reader gets, aside from Mary's ominous observations.

Why would Austen couch the fate of Benwick and Louisa in such dubious grammatical terms? Anne is not represented as an unrealistic dreamer in the novel, and here she is just a candid and generous woman who doesn't envy Benwick's choice of Louisa over herself. Anne seems to imagine a companionate marriage but one perhaps more along the lines of the ideal of the time, where the woman is helpmate and support. Although she does not imagine herself being guided and educated by Wentworth in this way, she is willing to see a weaker woman improved by a more intelligent mate. Frederick does not think of the disparities between Louisa and Benwick in this way, but Anne's words retain a good deal of their power over the reader's imagination. I believe we remember them as confident predictions rather than as conditional musings.

Anne finishes her assessment with the following free indirect discourse: "The conclusion of the whole was, that if the woman who had been sensible of Captain Wentworth's merits could be allowed to prefer another man, there was nothing in the engagement to excite lasting wonder" (II.6.182). Anne's problem is with the first premise, but that of course is the ironic or comedic point Austen inserts here. A woman who appreciated Wentworth prefers Benwick. Louisa is perfectly at liberty to choose; she did not know when she made her choice that Wentworth did not want her. Anne is so incomprehending of such a wonder, nothing else surprises her. Frederick does not approach the problem from this perspective: he does not care at all that Louisa has switched allegiances from him to his friend.

Louisa's general admiration of the navy might have led her to be drawn to someone else in the same profession as Captain Wentworth, but, to Anne, the two men are not comparable. Captain Benwick is an object of Anne's compassion and kindness but is not capable of capturing her heart. Moreover, Austen never invites us to imagine Louisa's youthful fishing for an admirer as an undying love for Wentworth in the first place. The relationship between the two seems to consist of Louisa's showing off as flirting and Frederick's use of Louisa as a sort of medieval troubadour's screen lady to obscure from himself as well as onlookers his continued devotion to Anne. His private conversation with Louisa on the long walk before the trip to Lyme, which Louisa probably interprets as growing intimacy between them, concerns Anne almost exclusively. Louisa, we feel, would show off to any eligible bachelor in her quest for a husband, but she has the potential, with her parents' good example and the sobering effects of her accident, as Anne imagines, to be satisfied with one man.

Change and Constancy: "She Would Not Have Forgotten Him So Soon"

Austen features another couple who prophesy concerning the Benwicks' future, both in their conversation and in their embodiment of a type of marriage: Charles and Mary Musgrove. Charles, who is Louisa's older brother, after all, and has known her all her life, says she is changed by the accident, telling Anne that she is "very much recovered; but she is altered: there is no running or jumping about, no laughing or dancing; it is quite different. If one happens only to shut the door a little hard, she starts and wriggles like a young dab-chick in the water; and Benwick sits at her elbow, reading verses, or whispering to her, all day long" (II.10.237). Anne laughs at Charles's description, but that does not mean he is wrong. He has some authority as an observer in this novel, though he loses a portion of it – and we are thankful that he does – when he is blinded by the allure of a gun and hands Anne off to Wentworth in the climactic chapter. Nonetheless, he is the observant young man who wanted Anne, not Mary, when he first went wooing and who detected Captain Benwick's penchant for Anne when the jealous Wentworth did not, an observation that Mary mocks in the letter that reveals his proposal to Louisa.

Mary, for her part, says, "Miss Harville only died last June. Such a heart is very little worth having" (II.2.142). We might be tempted to dismiss Mary's opinion because of her often annoying and invariably selfish behaviour, but her view resonates later with Frederick's doubts. Since her own husband married her within a year of having asked *Anne* to marry him, we can perhaps guess what standard Mary has in mind. Mr. Elliot has also not been a widower for even a year upon his courtship of Anne and his affair with Mrs. Clay. As for Benwick, Fanny Harville died in June 1813, but he does not know of it till August 1814. Three months later, Benwick meets Anne and the Musgroves on their visit to Lyme; by the end of January, he has proposed to Louisa. By February 21st, Frederick and Anne are discussing the engagement at Lady Dalrymple's sponsored concert.[8] So, about five months after he learns of his beloved's death, Benwick has been attracted to two vastly different young ladies and promised to marry the second, younger one, the one who by all accounts cannot compete with his dead fiancée's excellence or come up to his own intellectual level. We do not have to be like the early Christian author Tertullian and condemn all second marriages (or in this case, engagements) to be troubled by what those in *Persuasion* imply.

A suspicion that inconstant affections, affections not anchored by a steadfast heart, have led to such a rapid set of changes of course leads the reader to suspect as well that marriage itself might not be enough to keep the spouse from wandering. Only one man in the novel appears to be preparing to be guilty of something so bad as adultery, however, and that is William Elliot. If he intends to marry Anne and keep Mrs. Clay away from Sir Walter by installing her as his mistress in London, he obviously expects to be untrue to his marriage vows. Austen does not imply even in Captain Wentworth's darker view of him that Captain Benwick is going to be untrue in this way; we can imagine him to be much higher on the scale of marriageable men from the narrator's perspective. Though marrying William Elliot would make Anne mistress of Kellynch, marriage to the poetry-quoting Benwick seems in Austen's eyes to be a much preferable fate. If Wentworth had not come back to Anne, if Louisa had not fallen, and if he had had to marry her out of duty, might Anne and Benwick not have been thrown together a good deal? Benwick would by then certainly be in love with her; he is already well on his way. But the reader is certain Anne would never care for him. Her heart belongs to Wentworth exclusively.

For Austen, part of the end is setting the jewel – seeing what the pair looks like in comparison and contrast to the surrounding cast of characters. As discussed in the preceding chapter, Austen often seems to encourage us to rank her couples at the end of the novel, with those where at least one spouse can barely tolerate the other, like Mr. and Mrs. Bennet, Charlotte Lucas, and Mr. Palmer, near the bottom (the absolute nadir, an infernal circle occupied by the divorced Rushworths and the adulterous Admiral Crawford), and those who have companionate marriages, such as the Crofts and the Gardiners, at or near the top. The heroines' marriages always fall in that upper realm, with their blending of romance, esteem, and common love of what is right. Anne's guess about Louisa and Benwick sails us near to this territory of good-hearted and intelligent people, for we know their story is romantic and their personalities set on pleasing. We hear from Charles how eagerly Benwick reads poetry to the prostrate Louisa,[9] and we know from Anne how cheerful Louisa's disposition is. Louisa's little imperfections and Captain Benwick's perhaps partly dramatized suffering strike Frederick as not what he would want for himself – or what he would want to be himself – as he speaks with Anne in the Octagon room. But he agrees that the two young people have good principles.

Anne and Frederick do not argue about their views of this secondary couple whose coming together is the *deus ex machina* that permits their own final reunion. After Frederick speaks, Anne has no more time to think about the two who have provided the literal level of their conversation, for she is swept away by the moral and anagogical meanings she, like Frederick, is immediately reading into their own words. Responding even before he does to the clear *applicatio* to their own situation, Anne's cheeks are red, and her confusion turns into delight. They forget Louisa and Benwick, and so do the readers. Something more important is afoot.

If we evaluate the predictions of all the speakers on the subject in the novel, we cannot lodge Louisa and her sailor-rhapsode in the pantheon of Austen marriages we all envy, no matter how sunny Anne's outlook, for there stands Captain Wentworth's growing realization that Benwick, for all his gloominess and protestations, does not have the constant heart his friends assumed he did. Right before Frederick's proposal, Austen allows the generally admired Captain Harville to say of his sister, "She would not have forgotten him so soon" (II.11.252). The departed Fanny would have been more like Anne or Wentworth and would have found it hard if not impossible to dislodge the image of her beloved from her heart. As marriages in Austen novels go, Louisa Musgrove and James Benwick are probably going to be happier than the Collinses and Charles and Mary Musgrove, and far happier than the Bennets and Anne Elliot's poor mother. The reader, who has no other means of knowing, relies on Anne's optimism and acknowledges Captain Wentworth's concerned good wishes in coming to this conclusion. But the Benwicks will never be as happy as Anne Elliot and Frederick Wentworth, whose future happiness, the narrator tells us, is assured. Whereas Louisa and Benwick are all but forgotten in the concluding chapters of the novel, we follow Anne and Frederick to a quiet walk "where the power of conversation would make the present hour a blessing indeed; and prepare for it all the immortality which the happiest recollections of their own future lives could bestow" (II.11.261). Such delight and such assurance are the reward Austen gives only to the couple who cannot be consoled when "hope is gone" (II.11.256).

"She Had a Future to Look Forward to, of Powerful Consolation": Oracles of Envy or of Trepidation

However blissful this episode is, it is not the very end, and Austen follows it with more references to the couple's future. In fact, in her novels she always records the reactions of other characters to the main match, just as she recorded her readers' reactions to *Mansfield Park*, as Susan Allen Ford has recently discussed in her *What Jane Austen's Characters Read (and Why)*.[10] The judgments of others, however, generally reveal more about the judges than about the central couple. Often these assessments see the two in a way that highlights the outsiders' lack of understanding. This restricted view arises from material and societal concerns that have prevented and will continue to prevent the commenters' attainment of the kind of happiness and goodness the heroine and the hero have achieved. In *Persuasion,* the last word on Anne and Frederick is divided among several oracles. A strategy Austen repeats fairly consistently is elevating her main couple even when they do not speak in the final chapter by asking the reader to compare them with characters we do not regard so highly. She also assures us of the future material security of the main pair.

Anne is advancing to the glory of being a "sailor's wife," but it is also significant that Frederick is upwardly mobile. Anne's sense that her social or ethical position is elevated because her husband is a sailor is enough for her, but the narrator intimates that Frederick himself is going to achieve a higher status still. The novel that ends with the much-observed "tax of quick alarm" that comes from loving someone in a dangerous profession also ends with the fear, on the part of some characters, that Anne's husband will rise above them someday. In her conclusion, Austen not only implies that the coming war with Napoleon may endanger Frederick, she also suggests he may survive and continue his upward progress, eventually outranking at least his sister-in-law and her husband.

The two predictions about Anne Elliot's future at the end of *Persuasion* distance Austen's novel from the pat epilogues some readers see as her usual closure of the predictable marriage plot. D.A. Miller says the sentence "All suspense and indecision were over" after the proposal marks the closure of the novel, but, on closer examination, it does not.[11] He is concerned that what is narratable, tellable, should be laid to rest in the end of the novel. As long as there is suspense over the resolution of the romance, there are things to be told. But Austen clearly tells us there is a narratable future that we ourselves must prognosticate from the words of the character she also allows to predict the future for Louisa and Captain Benwick: Anne's sister Mary.

The comic element of envy in her sister's vision of *what might be* could and perhaps does blind the reader to the fact that we tend to favour Mary's version of the future – a future she fears – rather than the future Anne's trepidation might seem to predict. On the one hand lies the steady ascent of the confident, prize-winning Wentworth, until he perhaps will outrank the Musgroves and the Elliots themselves. On the other is the "dread of a future war," which could be a hint that the years to come hold wounds or even death for the adventurous captain. What reader does not prefer Mary's scenario? Which version of the future are we consciously adopting? Austen leaves a great deal only hinted at, a great deal unsaid.

One of the most unusual elements in *Persuasion*'s conclusion is a noteworthy ellipsis: Austen takes pains to avoid telling us where Anne is living after her marriage. She does not allow us to imagine Anne as housed or as endowed with the security and authority of home and property. Although Anne's house is situated in a true ellipsis at the end of *Persuasion*, Mary Musgrove is probably wrong that her sister will not eventually live in very nice home, given

Wentworth's £25,000 and the likelihood of his increasing his fortune in the war. Austen probably also meant her readers to understand that his money was secure against the looming bank collapses (collapses that profoundly affected Austen's family: when her brother Henry's bank failed, many members of the family lost a great deal of money). As Sheryl Craig has pointed out, all readers of *Persuasion* would have been aware that in the upcoming economic crash, naval men and farmers like the Musgroves would have been among the few whose money was not at risk.[12] Wentworth seems poised to live comfortably on his current thousand pounds a year, and, if his career continues as before, to increase his fortune by capturing more ships in upcoming battles and rising in the ranks as his brother-in-law, Admiral Croft, did. However, Austen does not assure us of any of this.

It is, moreover, unlikely Anne will spend all her future life onboard ship, particularly if her husband will soon be in combat. She will live in a house, but, in this novel, the size and location of that house are unimportant. Unlike most other characters in the novel, Anne is never imagined as residing in a place that characterizes her or bears her stamp, though she changes the atmosphere almost everywhere she goes. In the final chapter, Mary's consolation for Anne's reascending to her rank of elder sister through her marriage is Anne's lack of an estate. The narrator's portrayal of her satisfaction reveals that Austen is thinking very much about this theme: "Of all the family, Mary was probably the one most immediately gratified by the circumstance [of Anne's marriage]. It was creditable to have a sister married, and she might flatter herself with having been greatly instrumental to the connexion, by keeping Anne with her in the autumn; and as her own sister must be better than her husband's sisters, it was very agreeable that Captain Wentworth should be a richer man than either Captain Benwick or Charles Hayter" (II.12.272).

So far, so good. Mary's position as superior to Henrietta and Louisa can never be lost: they are married to men of inferior fortune. But her view is also retrospective thus far, not predictive: she congratulates herself on having helped make the match by asking for Anne to come to Uppercross. But then the narrator shows Mary in the toils of envy, practically sinister in her plotting to keep Wentworth away from any title:

> She had something to suffer, perhaps, when they came into contact again, in seeing Anne restored to the rights of seniority, and the mistress of a very pretty landaulette; but she had a future to look forward to, of powerful consolation.
>
> Anne had no Uppercross Hall before her, no landed estate, no headship of a family; and if they could but keep Captain Wentworth from being made a baronet, she would not change situations with Anne. (II.12.272)[13]

This deeply ironic section of the conclusion tells us all Austen wants us to know. It is enough for Mary at this early stage in Anne's marriage that she maintains prestige over her Musgrove in-laws through her brother-in-law Wentworth's wealth, but her self-importance suffers the blow of being forced by convention to "go lower" (as Lydia says to Jane in *Pride and Prejudice*), because Anne is no longer single.[14] It is not until now that we are abruptly made aware of the injustice that had prevailed for all the years since Mary wed Charles Musgrove: all this time, Anne's rank had been clearly signalled to family members, but not to the reader, as beneath her married younger sister's. Although she is older, that status had been superseded by Mary's elevation as a married woman. This means Mary walked into rooms ahead of her, sat higher at table, and took precedence over Anne in all things. Mary now loses that prestige. It is a blow to her. And, now that the order of age is restored, Mary fears an increase of that precedence through Frederick's gaining of a title. Charles will never have one, but he is the heir of a landed estate, Uppercross Hall. Mary feels this superiority will satisfy her enough so she will never envy Anne, but of course all her present satisfaction arises from envy.

It is possible Austen included Mary's vision of the future in the chapter just to tip the reader off to the possibility of Wentworth's still greater rise in eminence. Perhaps her prophecy is itself an instance of narrative apophasis, where the reader imagines the future precisely because Mary is wishing for it not to happen. Nonetheless, Mary's predictions of Anne's future may be about as accurate as the comments of Lydia Wickham at the close of *Pride and Prejudice* or of the Eltons at the end of *Emma*. Austen leaves the reader unsure. Will Frederick ever be able to buy a home rather than rent one? Does it compromise his status in the reader's eyes, as it does in Mary's, that he lacks a house?

Instead of hinting at future family get-togethers in some more modest version of Pemberley, Austen astonishingly gives us a description not of the place where her heroine will dwell securely, but of her new carriage, of which Mary is of course envious. Anne now owns a landaulette, which is the equivalent of a modern sports convertible, a vehicle that enables her to drive around the countryside by herself accompanied by one or two male servants.[15] This fact is the only evidence Austen gives that Anne is living anywhere. We don't even know where Mary visits her or if she is visiting Mary. But a landaulette requires a horse, and a horse requires a stable and thus a fixed abode. According to Mary, Anne has no landed estate – yet – so she and Frederick are tenants somewhere. Austen deliberately leaves out information about Anne's new home, yet she clearly focused on giving us this information in every preceding novel. This, then, must be a deliberate omission on her part. For Anne, the perpetual guest, the woman with no estate or parsonage to return to, having a vehicle but not a house reminds the reader that "We none of us expect to be in smooth water all our days," as Sophia Croft says (I.8.75).[16] One of the first things that we hear about sailors' wives in the novel is that they need to be conveyed from port to port and that their mobility is a primary concern to the husbands who miss them. Perhaps Anne's mobility is more important than the place where she stays.

Austen sometimes makes houses manifest the characters of their inmates, the most famous example of this being the uncompromised natural beauty of Pemberley, but they tend to exhibit taste rather than flaunting wealth, unless the inmate be Lady Catherine de Bourgh or General Tilney. Even the Harvilles' little home in Lyme Regis is a place of neatness and comfort, whereas the dirtiness and unhealthiness of the cramped and slovenly quarters of Fanny's family at Portsmouth reflect the unkempt habits and unpleasant personalities of Mr. and Mrs. Price. In Austen's novels, houses are not primarily for showing off. Unlike some filmmakers, she is not overly impressed by magnitude. The narrator even adds concerning Captain Harville's small home, "his taste, and his health, and his fortune all direct[ed] him to a residence unexpensive." The term that strikes the reader here is "taste," since we already imagine his lack of wealth and health to have dictated his choice in real estate. But he is unpretentious and does not yearn for extensive grounds, unlike Augusta Elton.[17]

As Nicolson points out, Jane Austen did not allow herself to be carried away by the grandeur of mansions. "She was in no sense a snob. She never boasted to her family of the distinction of her new acquaintance, never stood in awe of their rich porticos and furnishing, nor of the family portraits which hung like a second set of occupants on the walls."[18]

Austen is moving away from a focus on the heroine's search for a home in the last two completed novels. Fanny Price is the last Austen heroine to move to a new home, Mansfield parsonage. At her novel's close, Emma is located at least for the time being at Hartfield: in her case the hero uproots himself for her sake. We have no idea what Austen planned for Charlotte Heywood of *Sanditon,* though the Parkers' old house, which she spies from their carriage, appears comfortable and attractive: "in a sheltered dip within two miles of the sea, they passed by a moderate-sized house, well fenced and planted, and rich in the garden, orchard and meadows which are the best embellishments of such a dwelling."[19] Will she eventually live there with Sidney Parker? We are not even sure he is the hero.

The restrained but comfortable estate featured as an ideal in eighteenth-century novels, as the Christian-Stoic ideal celebrated in the Renaissance English country-house poem was incorporated into the prose narrative. In Ann Radcliffe's *The Italian*, for instance, we are introduced to the heroine Ellena's house almost at the very moment we first see her face:

> From the style of their residence, he imagined that they were persons of honourable, but moderate independence. The house was small, but exhibited an air of comfort, and even of taste. It stood on an eminence, surrounded by a garden and vineyards, which commanded the city and bay of Naples, an ever-moving picture, and was canopied by a thick grove of pines and majestic date-trees; and, though the little portico and collonade [*sic*] in front were of common marble, the style of architecture was elegant. While they afforded a shelter from the sun, they admitted the cooling breezes that rose from the bay below, and a prospect of the whole scope of its enchanting shores.[20]

The picture is an attractively elegant type of "moderateness." It might still rate as a cottage in Robert Ferrars's eyes, because of its size, but the beauty and orderliness of the image bespeaks a beautiful and orderly family within the walls.

Austen was clearly drawn to these kinds of general images of order and respectability, but she has left us few very particular descriptions of any of the dwellings in her novels. This was a deliberate aesthetic choice. She said in a letter to her niece Anna, "You describe a sweet place, but your descriptions are often more minute than will be liked. You give too many particulars of right hand and left."[21] Anna's overly detailed descriptions were something Austen herself deliberately avoided, and in *Persuasion* she seems to end by eradicating place entirely.

Jane Austen is so revolutionary that she dares to propose a conclusion that goes against the reader's instincts: she dares to create a heroine who neither desires nor receives an estate like Pemberley. If Anne Elliot's financial security is never put in doubt, her stability in a home and with land is. She has undergone a kind of mendicant reform, throwing off father and ancestral holdings to run loose in the world. One reason *Pride and Prejudice* and *Emma* maintain their ascendancy over Austen's other novels is almost assuredly the location of the heroines in impressive estates in the end. Whether the husband-to-be is an elegant, partly reformed snob or a generous but "sturdy and advice-giving" neighbour, the promise of "extensive grounds" appeals equally. Anne, Fanny, Elinor, and Catherine must make do with less. The author who invented Pemberley must surely have, in the end, preferred to challenge her reader with more modest gains. *Persuasion* as a novel is most open to the perils of the future, and the lack of the house indicates this openness.

Anne has been disgusted by the family's need to pay court to Lady Dalrymple; however, she has never envied her elder relative's position. Although Anne has felt envious of others in the course of the novel – above all, the Musgrove girls for their affectionate familial ease – she has not expressed any desire to rise socially in spite of her possessing all the delicacy and refinement that would be appropriate for such a position. Austen has discovered the paradox that bedevils Disney to this day: how does one reward merit and constancy in a narrative without the social structures of monarchy and aristocracy? The mythic, Cinderella underpinning that Austen so successfully makes use of in *Pride and Prejudice* is almost necessary to provide satisfaction to one's audience. Austen has played with it throughout her career. The three less-loved novels of the six not coincidentally find the heroine becoming a pastor's wife, not lady of the manor. It is one argument recently made for Marianne's being the true heroine of *Sense and Sensibility* and Colonel Brandon's being the hero; how happy can we be with Elinor's movement into a rectory with the prevaricating Edward Ferrars, who has lost his place as eldest son through defying his mother? If we suspect that Susan Price might be the next Lady Bertram, as Joan Aiken's continuation of *Mansfield Park* claims,[22] how dull and unsatisfactory must be the heroine's placement in Mansfield parsonage? She could have been mistress of Everingham. Her younger sister – someone else, at any event – will outrank her in the neighbourhood. And who will Frederick Tilney eventually bring home to reign at Northanger Abbey while Catherine Morland sits in her parlour at Woodston looking at a cottage out the window?

A turn Austen takes in half of her novels is probably not a mistake, however. She challenges us to rejoice in her heroines' choices. And along comes the sixth completed novel, and once again the heroine rejects the role of mistress of an estate. In removing the certain satisfaction of that kind of Cinderella ending, Austen tips the scales against the reception of an estate as necessary for happiness: only a third of her finished novels favour a closure that raises the heroine to the highest available social status.

Anne's choice breaks upon her other suitor with the suddenness of a thunderbolt: "The news of his cousin Anne's engagement burst on Mr. Elliot most unexpectedly. It deranged his best plan of domestic happiness, his best hope of keeping Sir Walter single by the watchfulness which a son-in-law's rights would have given. But, though discomfited and disappointed, he could still do something for his own interest and his own enjoyment" (II.12.272–3). William Elliot's calculations to ensure his own future ascendancy reveal the same kind of cold-blooded desire for money and prestige Mary Crawford had revealed in *Mansfield Park* and thus instruct the reader at the end of *Persuasion* what *not* to value. Guiding our wishes to what she considers truly valuable, truly worth pursuing, Austen exposes but does not deny Mr. Elliot's prime desire. Because he desires it so fixedly, so heartlessly, the reader begins to devalue what William Elliot wants, just as we learned early on to devalue what Sir Walter prizes.

So *Persuasion* gives the reader an Aristotelian end: we are satisfied that our divided couple so unable to communicate, so unwilling to proclaim Anne's excellence confidently at the outset, has reunited permanently; they will be happy together, though we do not know for how long. A combination of circumstances has conspired to allow Anne to rise above her position as disregarded and disprized faded blossom. She herself has contributed to that ascent. It is not an ascent to a throne or even an estate, but to having her merit recognized by the offering and commitment of love. The love comes from a flawed but worthy man who sees her excellence.

Some have seen parallels between *Persuasion* and *The Odyssey*, with Anne as a faithful Penelope and Wentworth the returning Odysseus who has dallied with Circe and Calypso.[23] If Austen is harking back to that work, Penelope Clay's name and Louisa Musgrove's role are fantastic jokes. More importantly, the reader remembers that *The Odyssey* ends not just with the reunion of the king and queen of Ithaca but also with Odysseus's prediction to Penelope (ratified by the prophet Teiresias in the underworld) that he will die in an unwarlike way, in a sleek old age. He also tells her that, for now, he has to go raiding to provide for their diminished household. Wentworth, like Odysseus, is a seafarer who has to go back to work and whose voyages entail risk. The tax of quick alarm Anne has to pay is a warning that the risk is real. But is it an omen?[24] Or is the vision of prosperity and happiness that is the fruit of the envious fear of the Sibyl of Uppercross, Mary Musgrove, a more probable vision of the future?

Aristotle does not advise projection into the future or forecasting events as an element in the conclusion of a tale. In his *Poetics*, he advises the creation of a beginning, middle, and end of an action. Insofar as that action is the reunion of Anne Elliot and Frederick Wentworth, Austen provides an Aristotelian sense of completeness in *Persuasion*. On the other hand, Jane Austen always includes the kind of projections and predictions the ancient idea of unity precluded; in *Persuasion*, she imagines Louisa and Benwick's future through Anne and Wentworth, and then Anne and Wentworth's through Mary and the narrator. Because the future is less assured than in the case of *Pride and Prejudice* or *Emma*, the closure has its own, distinct tone. Austen, as an author who is dedicated to what is natural and probable, invites us to pass a judgment on what will happen within the perimeters she has set up within the narrative. Thus, we too become oracular readers, weighing the evidence, judging the likelihood of things unknown, unspoken of, and yet to come.

Conclusion

Austen herself says that conclusions should "speed truth to the world." Her view may seem naive to us, but it was not so to her. She had a consistent view of what truth is, but it was nonetheless not simplistic, even if it did not accord with the modern world's post-Nietzschean evacuation of all stability from the term. Not synonymous with historical fact, "truth" for Austen has something to do with her interest in verisimilitude and probability. Those two desirable elements in artistic representation meant for her that "pictures of perfection" or unmitigated representations of virtue – or vice – were untruthful. Even her most admirable heroines, those who do not need to change their moral compass much as their novels progress – Elinor, Fanny, and Anne – are not flawless. She spends time in each novel humorously divulging their foibles even while displaying her affection for her creations.[1] At the close, they have all matured, even if they have not substantially changed. And one could argue that, even with their epiphanies about their own behaviour, Catherine, Marianne, Elizabeth, and Emma do not transform much, either, and it is in her conclusions that Austen demonstrates this truth about all her heroines. They are still comical in some way to their creator, even if she fondly crafts a happiness appropriate to each woman, appropriate to the tone and trajectory of each one's story. Nor does she think her cads are all thoroughgoing villains, or her heroes paragons of sanctity. The reader can imagine that happy as he is, Mr. Darcy will still find laughing at himself a difficult thing, and Captain Wentworth may still indulge the occasional sneer at the ironies of parents rewriting the histories of their wayward children. Willoughby feels content more often than not in his unromantic marriage, and Henry Crawford probably feels regret, even wretchedness, when he thinks in the future about having lost Fanny. Frank Churchill heads off into a future of happiness with Jane Fairfax, though Austen family lore predicted an early death for that lady, who, as Mr. Knightley knows, has acted against her conscience, though he still thinks her a paragon – a paragon he has never had any desire to marry.[2]

Conclusions ratify the changes to the protagonists, but also end them. Austen is sure that even a chastened Emma, an Emma who dines regularly with the Martins and the Coles, will look out upon her world with many of her "musts" and "oughts" intact.[3] She is also sure that not even

Mr. Knightley is unchanged. Austen is sure that Marianne Dashwood can change, but, like Emma, she retains characteristics that make her identifiably herself. She cannot love by halves; we are sure Willoughby can.

Conclusions place the protagonists in their final locations. Austen is sure Catherine Morland, Elinor Dashwood, and Fanny Price will be happy in parsonages, even if Elizabeth Bennet and Emma Woodhouse are far more suited to life in a stately home. Anne Elliott may be the only heroine ready to bear the trepidation that her future of being married to a navy man entails, but it is still a better future than that which marrying Sir Walter's heir would secure for her. And she, unlike any other heroine, has her own landaulette, a sign of mobility and a degree of independence.

Austen's endings confirm or reject the basis of the protagonist's values, giving the audience the narrator's final view of the shape of the universe in which the characters reside. Austen does not reject Christian belief or ethics, but she wonders about the scope of the Christian rules that are the bedrock of her view of the world. Since her heroines are all on the brink of marriage, she is particularly concerned with what the commandment that seems to require a parent's blessing on marriage means for the morality of their decisions and desires. Marriage is the telos of the novels but, to an even greater degree, so is happiness – and a particular kind of happiness at that. It is a happiness that is distinct from the satisfaction of appetites I discussed in chapter 1; for Austen, it cannot be a happiness attained through vice.

Famous Last Words: Tone and Unity in the Conclusion

Because Austen relies so heavily on narrative coloration and irony, tone is especially important in her work. This is an element of prose the reader always responds to, generally unconsciously, but it accounts for many of the varying responses to the novels' different closures. As Willa Cather said in her 1922 essay "The Novel Démeublé," "Whatever is felt upon the page without being specifically named there – that, it seems to me, is created. It is the inexplicable presence of the thing not named, of the over-tone divined by the ear but not heard by it, the verbal mood, the emotional aura of the fact or the thing or the deed, that gives high quality to the novel or the drama, as well as to poetry itself."[4] Sensitivity to verbal mood or tone is essential to reading Austen's conclusions. She generally ends with a combination of playful irony and seriousness. She is never melancholy or wistful. Her notes never turn to tragic (however many critics would like to see *Mansfield Park* as tragic, it utterly lacks tragic tone). These exclusions alone tell us a great deal about what Austen wants in an ending. As she announces famously in the final chapter of *Mansfield Park*, "Let other pens dwell on guilt and misery. I quit such odious subjects as soon as I can, impatient to restore everybody, not greatly in fault themselves, to tolerable comfort, and to have done with all the rest" (III.17.533). One can concede that this is a deliberate drawing of a boundary around her subject matter, but it is also an announcement of her commitment to a certain tonal range. That does not mean her tone is uniform;

it is always mixed, but the final sentence provides the reader with the final notes, and it is to those that I now turn.

Not consistently advancing or undermining traditional forms of closure, Austen allows for the ambivalences and vicissitudes of a future wherein even the good characters are mixed characters, not simply good or evil, and earthly fortune, especially in *Persuasion*, may not always be secure. Austen makes no heroine faultless, even Anne Elliot, whose tendency to think too little of herself and too much of what others around her think of her colours her story from beginning almost to the end. She is no Esther Summerson, but she does not see herself accurately, and Austen understands accurate sight as a good to be attained, if only partially, by her best characters, Anne included.

Persuasion was, of course, not meant to be a last novel. How she intended to end *Sanditon* must always remain a mystery, but it should be clear that she meant it to be different from the preceding novel, because all of Austen's novelistic conclusions, as similar as they may be in uniting the heroine and hero in a happy marriage, as similar as they are in providing *desengaño* to heroine or hero, differ from each other. While it is tempting to imagine Austen launching into more modern ambiguity as she matures as an artist, in fact that element is present from the outset, and her readers cannot chart a smooth progress from hermetically sealed, naively optimistic closure to daring openness and doubt. The last piece to come from her pen is the comic "Venta," a poem on the St. Swithun's Day races she composed just three days before her death.[5] That does not mean she had in mind a similarly funny ending to *Sanditon*, but it does mean that critics like Virginia Woolf who saw the autumnal qualities of *Persuasion* as charting Austen's path forward into greater romanticism were almost assuredly wrong.[6] Woolf predicts that, if Austen had lived, she would have been in London more, known more, would have been less funny, less sure of herself – in short, she would have been more like Virginia Woolf. That is a supremely arrogant, one might almost say misogynistic, assessment of Austen's confidence and élan. Moreover, it is all suppositious. The endings we have are what we can analyse and judge, and what manifests itself in them is a desire for difference and range within her own boundaries. What Austen seems to care about in her novelistic endings is Cather's "whatever is felt upon the page without being specifically named there." She cares about tone and even admixtures of tone that bid us attend to the storyteller's voice as it moves out to a wider temporal scope. The storyteller is both ironic and serious, playful and moral. However, she herself is never confused about what she is doing and how she is leaving her characters or her readers.

Austen takes as much care over her conclusions as she does over her first chapters, but her strategies perhaps take a different form. Whereas the first sentences of several of her novels have been extensively examined, especially that of *Pride and Prejudice*, the final sentences have not been subjected to as much scrutiny. However, comparing the final sentences of both her juvenilia and novels to each other demonstrates Austen's concern for thematic and tonal unity in each work. What will immediately leap out at the reader is the shift after the juvenilia (not all of which are quoted here) and *Northanger Abbey* to *Sense and Sensibility*. There is a clear break. These last sentences are as follows:

"Love and Freindship": "Philippa has long paid the Debt of Nature; Her Husband, however, still continues to drive the Stage-Coach from Edinburgh to Sterling: –"

"The Three Sisters": "Watts is going to Town to hasten the preparations for the Wedding. I am your affectionate Freind, G.S."

"Frederic and Elfrida": "Tho' in any threatening Danger to his Life or Liberty, Frederic was as bold as brass, yet in other respects his heart was as soft as cotton & immediately on hearing of the dangerous way Elfrida was in, he flew to her & finding her better than he had been taught to expect, was united to her Forever. – "

"Jack and Alice": "In the mean time, the inhabitants of Pammydiddle were in a state of the greatest astonishment & Wonder, a report being circulated of the intended marriage of Charles Adams. The Lady's name was still a secret. Mr. & Mrs. Jones imagined it to be Miss Johnson; but *she* knew better; all *her* fears were centered in his Cook, when to the astonishment of every one, he was publicly united to Lady Williams – "

"Henry and Eliza": "No sooner was she reinstated in her accustomed power at Harcourt Hall, than she raised an Army, with which she entirely demolished the Dutchess's Newgate, snug as it was, and by that act, gained the Blessings of thousands, & the Applause of her own Heart."

Lady Susan: "For myself, I confess that *I* can pity only Miss Manwaring, who, coming to Town & putting herself to an expense in Cloathes which impoverished her for two years, on purpose to secure him, was defrauded of her due by a Woman ten years older than herself."

Northanger Abbey: "I leave it to be settled, by whomever it may concern, whether the tendency of this work be altogether to recommend parental tyranny, or reward filial disobedience."

Sense and Sensibility: "Between Barton and Delaford, there was that constant communication which strong family affection would naturally dictate; – and among the merits and happiness of Elinor and Marianne, let it not be ranked as the least considerable, that although sisters, and living almost within sight of one another, they could live without disagreement among themselves, or producing coolness between their husbands."

Pride and Prejudice: "Darcy, as well as Elizabeth, really loved them [the Gardiners]; and they were both ever sensible of the warmest gratitude toward the persons who, by bringing her into Derbyshire, had been the means of uniting them."

Mansfield Park: "On that event they removed to Mansfield; and the Parsonage there, which, under each of its two former owners, Fanny had never been able to approach but with some painful sensation of restraint or alarm, soon grew as dear to her heart, and as thoroughly perfect in her eyes, as everything else within the view and patronage of Mansfield Park had long been."

Emma: "But, in spite of these deficiencies, the wishes, the hopes, the confidence, the predictions of the small band of true friends who witnessed the ceremony, were fully answered in the perfect happiness of the union."

Persuasion: "She gloried in being a sailor's wife, but she must pay the tax of quick alarm for belonging to that profession which is, if possible, more distinguished in its domestic virtues than in its national importance."

The tonal differences among these various endings are immediately noticeable. Like the juvenilia, the first two novels end with a jaunty tone; however, there is a shift even before the Chawton novels: even *Northanger Abbey*'s final sentence does not sound like the end of "Henry and Eliza." The startlingly funny amorality is gone, even if the narrator is still joking. Now the reader is dared to find the narrator unreliable in the moral sense, but for that very reason the reader must consider morality and amorality, a question Austen poses to the audience via apophasis. The juvenilia generally do not leave room for such judgment. The end of *Northanger Abbey* interacts the most openly with its reader and invites an assessment of the work, which none of the others do, with its references to the style and moral concerns of conduct books and sermons. The endings of *Northanger Abbey*, *Emma*, and *Persuasion* are the most concise and quotable, but none of them has the aphoristic quality of the famous opening line of *Pride and Prejudice* that all readers recall. Austen seems to want to avoid the aphoristic in her final words.

There are other kinds of interesting similarities among the endings. *Pride and Prejudice* and *Emma* end with warm confirmations of marital and familial union, and *Mansfield Park* and *Persuasion* with more recollection of the heroine's worries than the other four. *Sense and Sensibility* and *Persuasion* both end with reflections about the heroines' husbands, highlighting the role of the men. *Pride and Prejudice, Mansfield Park,* and *Persuasion* locate us in the point of view of the heroine one last time: we are looking through Fanny's eyes when we bid farewell to Mansfield Park. Although all the novel endings except that of *Northanger Abbey* refer to the marriage of the heroine more or less explicitly, only *Emma* ends with the wedding. The closing sentences of *Sense and Sensibility* and *Mansfield Park* – and *Pride and Prejudice* to a lesser degree – reorient us geographically and refer to the heroines' homes. *Persuasion* pans out to the nation in its final words, something none of the other novels is concerned with at the close, and points out the one ominous feature of marriage to a naval captain.

These final sentences all suit their particular novels. *Northanger Abbey*'s flippant refusal to draw its own moral and to offer two equally unacceptable options as to its main purpose continues the satire of "virtue" education in chapter 1 and seems to take Catherine's side in the education as torment debate with Henry Tilney. At the same time, it challenges the reader to discern what the book is really about, asking the reader to complete an exercise in interpretation.

Sense and Sensibility affirms the strong sisterly bond of the dual heroines and satirizes the qualities that cause families to fragment. It reminds us that strong affection naturally compels people to stay close to each other, the geographical closeness demonstrating the closeness of hearts. Elinor and Marianne conquer the vicious tendency of society families to fracture through the fierce rivalries over money and property that have been on display in their own family as well as those of Edward Ferrars, Mr. Willoughby, and Colonel Brandon.

The concluding sentence of *Pride and Prejudice* boasts the strongest vocabulary relating to love: "Loved," "warmest gratitude," "uniting" – we leave Elizabeth and Darcy in a glow of feeling, although it is for the Gardiners and not specifically for each other. Yet it is their own marriage that compels this feeling of gratitude towards their elders. The elevation of the Gardiners at the close completes a political or moral message of the novel as well by giving them, rather than the higher-ranked de Bourghs or the wealthier Bingleys, this privileged position.

Mansfield Park's closure, in keeping with its difficulty as a novel, presents Fanny as both beloved heroine and formerly downtrodden poor relation. The last sentence is what Sheila Kindred has called *Mansfield Park*'s "second ending," since the novel is difficult enough to need more than one: The shadow of Mrs. Norris and the Crawfords persists for just a moment in this last statement.[7] As Richard Jenkyns claims, "lovelessness … is … a condition recurrent in *Mansfield Park* and it is perhaps this more than anything that gives the book its cold, clear, desolate character."[8] Jenkyns attends more to tone in the book than many other critics tend to, observing about the unresolved outcomes of the Crawfords that "it is part of the serious, rather somber air of *Mansfield Park* that so many of the characters are engaged in the moral wrestle. The book's spirit is summed up in Jane Austen's concluding words about 'the advantages of early hardship and discipline and the consciousness of being born to struggle and endure.'"[9] That, even with the security of the married cousins' happiness and the hint of Fanny's pregnancy, we should look back to the unhappy days the novel has mostly chronicled seems true to Austen's depiction of this mistreated heroine. An ending for a heroine less concerned with memory – and less worried that she merits her low position – would not convey such a feeling.

Emma laughs at the trivial comments of the jealous Mrs. Elton the author has just recorded, and speaks of the friends of Emma and Mr. Knightley as perfect prognosticators of a perfect union – they "wish," "hope," and have "confidence." These are all things Emma has done with bad results throughout the novel, but they are now powers the narrator endorses in the friends who attend the ceremony. What was dangerous is now freely indulged in; readers may feel as if they have passed into Dante's Earthly Paradise, where, as Virgil tells Dante the pilgrim, not to follow your will would be wrong. Perfection in imperfection is a theme Austen underscores. Emma's improvement has always been rather like Petrarch's up Mount Ventoux: she knows she has to move forward and upward, but somehow ends up taking the easier path; then, all of a sudden, unlike Petrarch, she has landed at the summit, in spite of that. Austen's tone in recounting the surprise of such a conclusion is cheerful and confident.

Persuasion, on the other hand, ends with the oft-noted "tax of quick alarm" Anne Elliot has to pay for being a sailor's wife. She "glories" in her married state as no Austen heroine has done before her but, also unlike any other Austen heroine, she is promised a more perilous future. Joan Klingel Ray has said, "Anne is taxed with worry about the re-continued war with France, unlike her other heroines, because Anne has the greatest soul and maturity."[10]

Austen has in the past connected maturity with suffering – famously, in *Mansfield Park*'s elevation of those who have had to suffer and endure – but we have the least assurance of Anne's future happiness in the final lines. That assurance has come before, in the assertion that Anne and Frederick's happiness is greater at this second engagement than it was at the first. Austen always moves past the first éclaircissement in her final chapters, but it is only in *Persuasion* that she hints that Anne's fear for her husband's future might be an alloy in her happiness.

Looking at these different endings leads us to the deduction that Austen is interested in the artistic unity of each work, and that she has this unity in mind when she writes each conclusion. She is not tossing her stories aside, fatigued with the effort of invention. She is concerned with how her readers receive her moral and also with her realistic representation of human nature, of life. Her characters are not the unmixed heroines and villains of the eighteenth-century novel, and yet she has presented the protagonists to her readers as young women worthy of love and respect in spite of any human flaws they might have. What will happen to these beloved characters after we turn the last page? Austen's endings allow us to consider that future outside the book.

Thus, there is always a tentativeness as well as a firmness in Austen's closures. Her participation in the levity occasioned by the constant destruction of the "plans and decisions of mortals" in the end of *Mansfield Park* should alert the reader to her understanding of her power over her characters, whose ability to foresee the future is always inferior to her own. Yet Austen is indulgent about the minor infractions of most of those characters. One thinks of Reinhold Schneider's observation about even some of the most tragic writers: "So few tragedians have ended as tragedians after suffering death again and again with their hero; their heart softened and a presentiment came over them of the peace that spreads out on the far side of guilt."[11] Jane Austen has not ventured so close to death or tragedy, except perhaps in the near-death experience of Marianne Dashwood. She nonetheless is now bringing her characters to the conclusion of their novels, which could be thought of as a kind of death. They exist no more once she lifts her pen from the page for the last time, and everything to be said of their foibles and virtues, their worries, anger, exultations, and sufferings has been said.

John Wiltshire has argued that "the world assumes that Jane Austen is a romantic novelist and that all 'Jane Austen novels' are alike. But they are all distinct, and equally serious, and, as her re-readers know, there certainly is a hidden Jane Austen."[12] The purpose of the present study has been to show, building on Wiltshire's point, that Austen's consistent tendencies in her conclusions are generally hidden from the public and, likewise, those consistent tendencies exist in conclusions that are nonetheless distinct from one another. Her endings are by no means mechanical or programmed; the agility, lucidity, and profundity, with her admixture of humour and irony, is always there, but in different proportions, with different emphases. That Austen insistently retained the ending to *Mansfield Park* that she had written, even against her sister Cassandra Austen's arguments, and that she rewrote the ending of *Persuasion* to suit her own vision – just these two late pieces of evidence show us a conscious artist at work, not a fatigued ironist anxious to dismiss her characters offstage. Even Wiltshire argues that Austen takes refuge in clichés at the end of *Mansfield Park* (120–1), but Austen never takes refuge. To introduce complex characters is not to approve of vice, nor is a complex ending a veil over the unsophisticated and unsubtle desire for happiness for the protagonist. That assumption prevents us from engaging authentically with Austen's endings. If our last impression of her is that she will allow us happiness in spite of the imperfections of her characters and the imperfection of the world in which they dwell, has she not achieved her telos? Is it not proof that critics have often swept away consideration of her artistic ends by saying we need not consider them? D.A Miller, comparing her to de Sade, states, "Jane Austen lets all the evidence of the incompatibility stand, knowing that her text will eventually pass over to the side of the law, where the rest doesn't count ... The limiting prestige of Jane Austen as a miniaturist does not encourage comparisons with Scott or Sade."[13]

Even John Wiltshire says of the romance between Fanny and Edmund, "the defensive, uneasy irony misfires: could anyone believe that Edmund and Mary's romantic relationship conforms to the romantic clichés that are mocked with such glibness here? ... With its vagueness about time, so sharply contrasted with the day-to-day accuracy of the preceding chapters, *Mansfield Park* propels its characters into a future for which the author now takes no responsibility."[14] When the reader knows that Austen plays with clichés, becomes vague about time, and makes the reader imagine and predict the futures of her characters consistently in all her novelistic conclusions, these assertions seem naive. They are not attentive to her habits of composition; they are resentful of her artistic choices; they will her to be someone she is not, very much like a Sir Thomas with Fanny Price. But as Elizabeth Bennet's argument with Lady Catherine de Bourgh demonstrates, Austen's heroines will not be defined by others' insults and putdowns.[15]

Austen uses apophasis, metalepsis, analepsis, forced retrospection, and more, to engage the reader's imagination and direct us rhetorically. She gives the reader so much information, such an array of rhetorical strategies, that her conclusions are dizzying, drawing the reader to go ever deeper into the story, to go ever more insistently back to the story, to see the unity, to see in what way Austen's providential hand has prepared every final step. We look back because she has surprised us; she has done just the right thing, even if at first we think it is wrong. She was glad to earn her pounds and pence from her professional excellence, but she also was seeking, like her character Eliza in "Henry and Eliza," the applause of her own heart.

Artists can execute their compositions defectively. They can be sloppy, or tired – "even Homer nods." But Austen is consistent, persistent, and, above all, joyous about what she is doing in her conclusions. The moment the reader says, "This is unexpected and unpleasant" is the moment she is most intent on saying what she is saying, and she will not change it for anyone. A reader can dislike an ending, but if that dislike is based on misunderstanding some quality essential to Austen's world view or her rhetoric, then it is best to correct the misunderstanding before advancing those judgments as certainties. The assessments I have just quoted from critics I admire are not based in the novels. They bypass the actual endings in search of something Jane Austen never wrote and probably would not write. No one has ever seen a Jane Austen conclusion on film or in a television series – they are truly invisible to the non-reading public. But they ought not be invisible to her readers. Austen hides information to surprise her readers with the enjoyment of discovery. Up to the very last word, she is trying both to delight and to instruct, as Horace advised. However apophatic Austen is, her last impressions on the reader should be, not dull reflections in a mirror, but speedy arrows from her bow striking the mark of truth.

Notes

1. Austen's Telos: Speeding Truth into the World

1 Newton, *"Pride and Prejudice,"* 84.
2 Mudrick, "Irony as Discrimination: *Pride and Prejudice,"* in *Jane Austen,* 120.
3 Poovey, "Ideological Contradictions and the Consolations of Form: The Case of Jane Austen," in *The Proper Lady,* 205.
4 C.L. Johnson, *"Pride and Prejudice* and the Pursuit of Happiness," in *Jane Austen,* 74–5.
5 Potkay, "Narrative Possibilities," 523.
6 Kaufmann, "Closure as Covenant," 92. Kaufmann cites Kermode, *The Sense of an Ending.*
7 Emsley, *Jane Austen's Philosophy*; Ruderman, *The Pleasures of Virtue.*
8 Valihora, *Austen's Oughts,* 14.
9 Potkay, "Narrative Possibilities," 523, 533.
10 Pope, "An Essay on Man: Epistle IV," 395–8, 545; Kenney, "'Abjuring All Future Attachments.'"
11 See Dadlez, *Mirrors to One Another*; Valihora, *Austen's Oughts.*
12 Valihora, *Austen's Oughts,* 27.
13 Torgovnick, *Closure in the Novel.*
14 Toner, *Jane Austen's Style,* 3.
15 Clark, "Shaftesbury's Art of 'Soliloquy,'" 59.
16 Though one should always note that the famous phrase appears in a self-deprecating apology for not producing "strong, manly, vigorous sketches, full of variety and glow," sent to a nephew she must have known did not exceed her talent. Jane Austen, letter to James Edward Austen, 16 December 1816, in Austen-Leigh and Austen-Leigh, eds., *Jane Austen,* 331.

17 Jane Austen to Cassandra Austen, Castle Square, 9 December 1808, Southampton, in Le Faye, ed., *Jane Austen's Letters*, 155–6.
18 *Spectator*, in Knox, *Elegant Extracts*, 23.
19 Jefferson, *Two Sermons*, 17. Austen not only purchased this book, as did several other of her family members, but she also sought others to subscribe to aid the poor clergyman with his numerous family (her name is on the list of subscribers on p. viii). In other words, this is the book Austen helped "crowdfund" for. Its importance as a representation of attitudes that were significant for her should not be underestimated.
20 Shaftesbury, *Letters of the Earl of Shaftesbury*, s. 1; Valihora, *Austen's Oughts*.
21 Bacon, "Of Truth," 341.
22 Knox, *The Spirit of Despotism*.
23 Nietzsche, "On Truth and Lies," 45.
24 Watt, *The Rise of the Novel*, 296–8. See also Sayre-McCord, "Moral Realism."
25 See Kubic, "Aristotelian Ethical Ideas" for a concise overview of the arguments of Ryle, Ruderman, Emsley, and Mooneyham White for Austen's reception of (and departure from) Aristotelian ideas as well as a classification of the different virtues, including moderation, Austen consistently depicts. David Gallop gives what Dadlez calls "one of the most philosophically convincing" "Aristotelian" analyses of Austen: Gallop, "Jane Austen and the Aristotelian Ethic"; Dadlez, *Mirrors to One Another*, 51.
26 C.L. Johnson, *Jane Austen*, 350.
27 Haybron, "Happiness."
28 Austen, *Juvenilia*, 56.
29 Austen, *Juvenilia*, 45.
30 René Girard, *Deceit, Desire, and the Novel*, 290–314.
31 See MacIntyre, *After Virtue*, 239.
32 Nietzsche, *The Will to Power*, 267; Nietzsche, "On Truth and Lies," 45.
33 Nietzsche, "Twilight of the Idols," 24, 44.
34 Rieff, *My Life among the Deathworks*; MacIntyre, *After Virtue*, 239 and passim.
35 Vachris and Bohanon, "Human Nature and Civil Society," 364.
36 Smith, *The Theory of Moral Sentiments*, 171, 181–2, 187, 249, 251, 254, 261, 423–4, and passim.
37 Fergus, *Jane Austen and the Didactic Novel*.
38 I've italicized "human nature" in quotations throughout this section.
39 The fifth commandment, or the fourth in Roman Catholic and Lutheran tradition. St. Paul also recalls this commandment in the Epistle to the Ephesians 6:2.
40 Stovel, "'A Nation Improving in Religion.'" "Another intermediate model for Jane Austen's prayers is one of the twenty surviving books that she owned, *A companion to the altar: Shewing the nature & necessity of a sacramental preparation in order to our worthy receiving the Holy Communion, to which are added Prayers and meditations*. Apparently written by William Vickers and published in 1793 'this book of devotions always used by Jane Austen,' to quote her great-niece Florence Austen, is inscribed with her

signature and the date 1794 … It is a guide for those about to be confirmed in the Church of England; Jane Austen's copy was probably presented to her at the time of her own confirmation – she was 18 in 1794."

41 "I am very fond of Sherlock's sermons and prefer them to almost any." Jane Austen to Anna Austen, Letter 88, Chawton, 28 September 1814, in Le Faye, ed., *Jane Austen's Letters*, letter 108, p. 278. See my "Benevolence and Sympathy in *Emma.*"

42 Sherlock, "Commentary on the Epistle to the Hebrews," in *The Works of Bishop Sherlock*, 252–3.

43 Jefferson, *Two Sermons*, 23–4.

44 Girard, *Deceit, Desire, and the Novel*.

45 Herodotus, *Histories*, Book I, cited by Euripides, *The Trojan Women*, ll. 505–10 (Hecuba), and by Ovid, *Metamorphoses*, III. 131–252, Fable III.

46 Kermode, *The Sense of an Ending*, 7.

47 Toner, *Jane Austen's Style*.

48 Elaine Bander says that portions of "Blair's *Rhetoric* also formed the greatest part of Vicesimus Knox's *Elegant Extracts in Prose*, a one-volume anthology published in 1794 … [and] at least one of these versions of Blair's Rhetoric must have found its way into the Rectory at Steventon." See Bander, "Blair's *Rhetoric*." 124. Miriam Wolff asserts that Austen "in fact, … did own a copy": Wolff, "Jane Austen and Belles Lettres."

49 Genette, *Narrative Discourse*, 234–6.

50 Blair, *Lectures on Rhetoric*, S95, 21; Wolff, "Jane Austen and Belles Lettres," 21.

51 Brown, "The Comic Conclusion in Austen's Novels." 1583.

52 Norris, *Truth and the Ethics of Criticism*, 36. Norris clearly is writing in the tradition of Nietzsche mentioned above.

53 *PP*, II.8.195.

54 Jane Austen, to Cassandra Austen, on 29 January 1813: "There are a few typical errors; and a 'said he,' or a 'said she,' would sometimes make the dialogue more immediately clear; but 'I do not write for such dull elves' as have not a great deal of ingenuity themselves." In Le Faye, *Jane Austen's Letters*, 210. The quotation clearly concerns a reader's ability to interpret correctly in spite of omissions, as did Sir Walter Scott's original lines: "I do not write to that dull elf / Who cannot image to himself," *Marmion* (vi.38).

2. "Abjuring All Future Attachments": Teaching the Reader to Desire the Right Object in *Lady Susan*

1 This chapter is a slightly reduced and edited version of my "'Abjuring All Future Attachments': Concluding *Lady Susan*," *Persuasions On-Line* 41, no. 1 (2020), https://jasna.org/publications-2/persuasions-online/vol-41-no-1/kenney/.

2 Jane Austen, "Lady Susan," in *Later Manuscripts*, 75–8. Subsequent references to the text of *Lady Susan* will refer to page numbers from this edition.

3 Austen, *Later Manuscripts*, 77.

4 Tarpley, *Constancy and the Ethics of Mansfield Park*.

5 Brooks, "In Search of Austen's Missing Songs."
6 Austen, "Fredric and Elfrida," in *Juvenilia*, 3–12.
7 Blamires, "Women and Creative Intelligence."
8 Raia, "Women's Roles in Plautine Comedy."
9 As Northrop Frye has named the type in *Anatomy of Criticism*, 172. See Levine, "Lady Susan."
10 Raia, "Women's Roles in Plautine Comedy."
11 Wood, "The Birth of Inwardness."
12 See Kaplan, "Female Friendship and Epistolary Form."
13 The seemingly surprising exception was, in fact, conventional and can be dated back to rabbinical commentaries on the Hebrew Scriptures. These commentaries on the commandments had long made at least two exceptions to the rule of obedience: one, that the law of God always takes precedence, and so no child could be compelled to obey a parental order to disobey God's laws; and two, that a child could not be compelled to marry against his or her wishes. Fordyce also makes these two exceptions in his sermon on good works. James Fordyce, "On Good Works," 189.
14 Forster, *Aspects of the Novel*, 69–78.
15 Jane Austen to her niece Fanny Knight, 23 March 1817, Chawton, in Le Faye, ed., *Jane Austen's Letters*, 350.
16 It is impossible to resist the temptation of comparing Lady De Courcy's joy at her son's wretchedness with Fanny Price's at Edmund's misery in *Mansfield Park*. Already, Austen is interested in the fact that an event might affect two persons who love each other in a very different way, and that something that brings sorrow to one might bring joy to the other. Shakespeare has Rosalind comment on this problem in marital relationships in *As You Like It* IV.i, but Austen might already have been fascinated by the fact of discordant emotions in her own life.
17 Although De Courcy is originally derived from a place name, Austen could have had many reasons to associate it with heroism. She might be thinking of the legendary descent of the De Courcy family from Charlemagne; the presence of Richard De Courcy at the Battle of Hastings, which resulted in the settlement of that family member in her neighboring Somerset; the upper-class associations of Anglo-Norman descent or even of the impressively heroic defiance of Richard I by Sir John De Courcy as an earl in Ireland.

3. Parental Tyranny and Filial Disobedience: Socratic Irony and Metalepsis in *Northanger Abbey*

1 Cohn and Gleich, "Metalepsis and Mise en Abyme," 105. They cite Genette, *Narrative Discourse*, 234–5.
2 Cohn and Gleich, "Metalepsis and Mise en Abyme," 105.
3 Modern readers might be more familiar with a figure more recent than Socrates: Lieutenant Columbo. His famous "Just one more thing" always leads to "adroit questions" meant to expose the responder.
4 Jane Austen to Cassandra Austen, 9 December 1808, in Le Faye, ed., *Jane Austen's Letters*, 155–6.

5 S. Johnson, "*Rambler* 148," 5.25. See Gloria Gross, "Mentoring Jane Austen.'"

6 However, one of the few contemporary comments on *Northanger Abbey* criticizes precisely the improbability of General Tilney as a character. See Le Faye, *Jane Austen: The World of Her Novels*, 221.

7 In the last chapter of *Mansfield Park*, Sir Thomas even holds himself responsible for his daughter's adultery because he did not intervene to prevent Maria's marriage to Mr. Rushworth decisively enough.

8 See Probert, "Control over Marriage in England and Wales." See also O'Connell, *The Origins of the English Marriage Plot*.

9 See O'Connell, *The Origins of the English Marriage Plot*: "As clandestine weddings and the unruly culture that surrounded them began to threaten power and property, questions about where and how to marry became urgent matters of public debate. In 1753, in an unprecedented and controversial use of state power, Lord Chancellor Hardwicke mandated Anglican church weddings as marriage's only legal form. Resistance to his Marriage Act would fuel a new kind of realist marriage plot in England and help to produce political radicalism as we know it" (quote from back cover).

10 O'Connell, *The Origins of the English Marriage Plot*.

11 See Adkins and Adkins, *Jane Austen's England*, 7.

12 See Stillman, *Love and Friendship*.

13 Southam, *Northanger Abbey and Persuasion*, 32.

14 Fordyce, "On Good Works," 184–6.

15 Hull, *A Sermon on the Duty of Obedience*, 1–13.

16 Blackall, *The Lord Bishop of Exeter's Answer*, 54 (emphasis in original).

17 Boswell, *Boswell's Life of Johnson*, 373.

18 See Ellen Moody, "A Calendar for Northanger Abbey," http://www.jimandellen.org/austen/na.calendar.html.

19 Fordyce, "On Good Works," 189. These exceptions might have come down to Anglican theological scholars through study of rabbinical commentaries. Fathers and husbands were warned against giving their anger free rein in a household and acting as tyrants. This was the case not only in Christian traditions. "Rabbinic literature is fully aware of the potential for abuse of parental power, and there are many passages in which parents are warned of the ill effects of physical and emotional abuse. We read in the Gittin 6b: 'Rabbi Hisda said: A man should never impose excessive fear upon his household, or else he may be the cause of great tragedy.'" Rabbi Peretz Rodman, "Must One Honor an Abusive Parent?" n.d., https://www.myjewishlearning.com/article/must-one-honor-an-abusive-parent/. Jesus had criticized the Pharisees for allowing self-serving exceptions to this particular commandment:

> And he said unto them, "Full well ye reject the commandment of God, that ye may keep your own tradition. For Moses said, Honour thy father and thy mother; and, Whoso curseth father or mother, let him die the death: But ye say, If a man shall say to his father or mother, It is Corban, that is to say, a gift, by whatsoever thou mightest be profited by me; he shall be

> free. And ye suffer him no more to do ought for his father or his mother; Making the word of God of none effect through your tradition, which ye have delivered: and many such like things do ye." (Mark 7:9–13)

However, John Calvin's commentary on the fifth commandment was informed by this tradition and could equally have inspired Fordyce and other Anglican writers of the eighteenth century in providing the exception of necessarily disobeying commands to do wrong:

> It ought to be observed by the way, that we are ordered to obey parents only in the Lord. This is clear from the principle already laid down: for the place which they occupy is one to which the Lord has exalted them, by communicating to them a portion of his own honour. Therefore the submission yielded to them should be a step in our ascent to the Supreme Parent, and hence, if they instigate us to transgress the law, they deserve not to be regarded as parents, but as strangers attempting to seduce us from obedience to our true Father. The same holds in the case of rulers, masters, and superiors of every description. For it were unbecoming and absurd that the honour of God should be impaired by their exaltation – an exaltation which, being derived from him, ought to lead us up to him.

Calvin, *Institutes of Christian Religion*, 260, 2.8.8. Calvin adds "that we are forbidden to detract from their dignity either by contempt, by stubbornness, or by ungratefulness" (2.8.35).

20 Interestingly, another exception to the law of filial obedience in rabbinical tradition is adopted children. This, too, seems to have come down to the reformed interpretation of the commandment. Whereas in Elizabeth Bennet's case, her defiance of her mother is mitigated by her father's approval of her choice, in Fanny Price's much more difficult situation, Sir Thomas says explicitly, "*You* are not to be judged by the same rule. You do not owe me the duty of a child" (III.14.368). Austen makes this comment doubly vicious by having Sir Thomas explicitly point out that Fanny has not even been adopted. However, even if she were, adoption had such an ambiguous status in Austen's day it is likely he could have said the same thing in that case. Like his predecessor General Tilney, Sir Thomas for all intents and purposes evicts the unworthy parasite from his home.

21 Nabokov, "Jane Austen," 57. Austen is repeating some elements of her conclusion to *Lady Susan* here with the swipe at a person sacrificing her conscience as a mere inconvenience.

22 Wolfson, *Northanger Abbey*, 40.

23 Spurr, "La frivolité chez Jane Austen," 393, 398.

24 Spurr, "La frivolité chez Jane Austen," 395: "Ce discours est fermement ancré dans la critique anglaise du XVIIIe siècle, avec son double impératif de plaire et d'instruire. L'accent est mis non pas sur la forme de l'œuvre, mais sur les qualités d'esprit et de jugement qui y sont mises en valeur. Austen ne réclame donc pas une nouvelle esthétique, même si son œuvre en prépare le terrain" (This discourse is firmly anchored in English criticism of the eighteenth century, with its double imperative of pleasing and

instructing. The accent is not placed on the form of the work, but on the qualities of wit and judgment that are valued therein. Austen does not lay claim to a new aesthetic, even if her work prepares the terrain for one) (my translation).

25 Spurr, "La frivolité chez Jane Austen," 397–8: "Il y a quelque chose de subversif dans cette absurde caricature de la pruderie, surtout au moment où les événements catastrophiques du récit semblent vouloir nous persuader de la fatale vérité des dangers posés à la vertu féminine. La brillance du style d'Austen réside dans le maintien de cette fine tension où la raison tient la dérive, voire le délire, en bride" (my translation).

26 Burns, "Comic Resolutions," 243.

27 Wallace, "*Northanger Abbey* and the Limits of Parody," 262.

28 Wallace, "*Northanger Abbey* and the Limits of Parody," 265.

29 See Litvak, "The Most Charming Young Man in the World," 54.

30 Litz, *Jane Austen*, 139.

4. Forced Retrospection in *Sense and Sensibility*: Willoughby's Desire for "Something Like Forgiveness" on "More Reasonable Grounds"

1 Twain, "Letter to Joseph Twitchell," 220 (my emphasis). One wonders why he subjected himself to the torture of rereading. Likewise, in his unpublished essay, "Jane Austen," Twain begins by saying, "Whenever I take up *Pride and Prejudice* ..." See E. Auerbach, "'A Barkeeper Entering the Kingdom of Heaven.'" I agree with Auerbach that Twain clearly reads Austen repeatedly and though he claims never to have made it past the first third of any of her novels, he cites events in the second and third volumes of *Sense and Sensibility* and *Pride and Prejudice*, so this claim is clearly untrue.

2 See Alter, *The Art of Biblical Poetry* 37–8, 46, 75, 115, and passim, and *The Art of Biblical Narrative*, 19, 22, 55, 63, 76, 89, 11, 177, and passim; Bloomfield, "Interlace as a Medieval Narrative Technique," 54; Vinaver, *The Rise of Romance*, 68–9, 85. See also Kukkonen and Klimek, eds., *Metalepsis in Popular Culture*. On repetition and its effect on closure and rereading, Genette says, with reference to Proust's *À la recherche du temps perdu*, "not only is the *Recherche*, as Blanchot says, a 'completed-incompleted' work, but its very reading is completed in completion, forever in suspense, forever 'to be taken up again,' since the object of that reading is constantly thrown into a dizzy rotation." Genette, "Proust Palimpsest," in *Figures of Literary Discourse*, 222.

3 See also Snow, "The Judgment of Evidence in *Tom Jones*."

4 See Genette, *Narrative Discourse*, 114–15.

5 de Behar, *Rhetoric of Silence*, 59–80.

6 Kaufmann says this is the ending *Mansfield Park* calls for: "Closure as Covenant," 91.

7 Brunton, *Self-Control*. The two novels came out in the same year, 1811 (Brunton's in February, Austen's in late October. Austen's first mention of it is the information that she could not get ahold of it) and have very similar

concerns. If Austen did not read Brunton's book before working out the story of Willoughby's relationship with Marianne, she certainly was thinking of precisely the same problems with the reformed lecherous heroes of many eighteenth-century novels. Above all, both women are concerned with the improbability, not the impossibility, of such a person reforming, and the projection of a less than rosy future for the heroine if married off to such a man in real life. In conversation with Laura and Julia, Laura's father, Montreville, adds that Fielding artificially elevates Tom by comparing him with Blifil, an easy target, and that he makes religion contemptible by putting religious prattle in the mouths of inferior persons, Thwackum and Blifil. However, Montreville is taken in entirely by Hargrave, and though he never learns that Hargrave originally propositioned Laura instead of proposing to her, he does tell her that young men of his station should be expected to commit such peccadilloes before they marry, whereas the strictures against female straying are, as he sees it, rightly more rigid. Laura is shocked and upset but does not change her resolution. Austen admired this book a little, but famously found it hysterically improbable; however, its thematic influences can be clearly seen in *Mansfield Park* in particular.

8 As Brenda Cox says, "the weakest part of his confession … is in his treatment of Eliza … Thus, his most serious sin is treated most lightly": "Marianne Dashwood's Repentance." Also see Dooley and Dufour, "'A More Gentle, Less Dignified, Forgiveness.'"

9 Colonel Brandon's very long "confession" to Elinor is *about* Willoughby.

10 Morris, *Jane Austen.*

11 Forster, *Aspects of the Novel*, 73–6.

12 Carroll, "Willoughby's Apology"; Poovey, *The Proper Lady*, 187.

13 Poovey, *The Proper Lady*, 186–8.

14 Carroll, "Willoughby's Apology."

15 Tomashevski, *Theory of Literature*, 268.

16 See Cox, "Marianne Dashwood's Repentance."

17 To some outcry, in his plenary talk at the 2022 Jane Austen Society of North America's meeting, Robert Morrison speculated that Marianne is pregnant: "Deeper in a Life of Sin." Arnie Perlman said the same in a question-and-answer session at the Jane Austen Society of North America meeting in 2009. Marianne is clearly not victimized in this way: otherwise her comments about what could have happened and what she was spared would not make any sense. For instance, she says, "I have nothing to regret – nothing but my own folly" (III.11.398). Austen would not use such language if Marianne had succumbed to Willoughby's sexual advances, what Elinor will call a few lines later, describing his seduction of Eliza Williams, his "first offense against virtue" and his "crime." In her penitent state, it is utterly impossible that Marianne would describe fornication as "nothing."

18 St. Jerome's interest in conscience and synderesis had been revived by Jeremy Taylor, among others, in England in the seventeenth century: Taylor, *Ductor Dubitantium.* St. Augustine said, "There is no soul, however perverted in whose conscience God does not speak." Augustine, "On the

Sermon on the Mount," quoted in Mahoney, *The Making of Moral Theology*, 187. Austen demonstrates this underlying conviction in her portrayal of ambiguous or mixed characters, among whom Willoughby stands out as the most charming and attractive to many of her readers.

19 William Lyons, "Conscience," 478.

20 Emsley, *Jane Austen's Philosophy of the Virtues*, 59.

21 Carroll, "Willoughby's Apology."

22 Jane Austen to Cassandra Austen, 15–16 October 1808, in Le Faye, *Jane Austen's Letters*, 147.

23 Wiltshire, *Jane Austen and the Body*, 48–50.

24 See Kenney, "*Mansfield Park*."

25 Carroll, "Willoughby's Apology." Wiltshire even more forcefully attributes sincerity to Willoughby's confession and is more positive than I am about Willoughby's discovery that he has a conscience. See *The Hidden Jane Austen*, 46–7. For his troubled pausing over Willoughby's exultation over his ability to imagine what Marianne might look like dead, he credits Claudia Johnson's essay "A 'Sweet Face White as Death,'" 168.

26 Tomashevski, *Theory of Literature*, 268.

27 See Todorov, "Les catégories du récit littéraire," 128.

5. "The Happiest, Wisest, Most Reasonable End": Silence, Spatial Dislocation, Secrets, and the Sublime in *Pride and Prejudice*

1 Portions of this chapter have appeared as articles or parts thereof. See "'The Happiest, Wisest, Most Reasonable End': Silence and the Sublime in *Pride and Prejudice*," *Persuasions* 45 (2024): 127–37; "Anne De Bourgh Smiles," *Persuasions On-Line* (2013); and "'Slyness Seems the Fashion': Dexterous Revelations in *Pride and Prejudice*," *Persuasions* 27 (2005): 263–69.

2 Ellen Moody says in her timeline for *Pride and Prejudice*, "A Calendar for Pride and Prejudice," that the novel "closes in indeterminate time, projecting into the future." She also notes that the letters that appear in the closing are undated: "Three letters inserted, described, quoted from: Elizabeth to her aunt, a letter from Darcy to his, a letter from Mr Bennet to Mr Collins given whole. Four more mentioned, all unmoored, briefly described: Miss Bingley to her brother, Miss Bingley to Jane and Jane back to Miss Bingley; Georgiana sends 'four sides of a paper' Look[ing] forward to [the] 'time' they retreat into Pemberley (III:18, 324–5, Ch 60)."

3 Their second walk, to Oakham Mount, during which they decide how to go about asking for her parents' blessing, is entirely narrated. Its importance lies in the fact that Mr. Bingley, already in on the secret, slyly arranges for the two to be alone, dissuading Kitty from accompanying them, and also that Mr. Darcy, taking up Mrs. Bennet's suggestion obediently, professes "a great curiosity to see the view from the Mount" (*PP*, III.17.416).

4 Lascelles, *Jane Austen and Her Art*, 126.

5 Wiltshire, *The Hidden Jane Austen*, 70.

6 McMaster, "*Emma*," 34.
7 C.R. Miller, "Jane Austen's Aesthetics," 244.
8 C.R. Miller, "Jane Austen's Aesthetics," 257.
9 However, the word "wonder" very often occurs when the novel's theme of gossip and curiosity about one's family and neighbours is in the foreground; it does not always connotate amazement or admiration.
10 Brann, "Opening Lecture."
11 See Burke, *A Philosophical Enquiry*, 53–9, 65, 67, 70.
12 Natasha Duquette and Elizabeth Lenckos claim in reference to Fanny's meditation on the night sky in *Mansfield Park* that Austen may have followed the lead of women writers who "moved beyond Burke's emphasis on fear to include social affection and community within their definitions of the sublime": *Jane Austen and the Arts*, xxvi.
13 Austen's timelessness thus has some of the features of the art on Keats's Grecian urn, without the futile yearning, sterility, and nostalgia.
14 Although I will focus on this topic later in the chapter, it is worth noting that Jane accuses Lizzy of being sly: "But Lizzy, you have been very sly, very reserved with me" (III.17. 415). The paragraph in which this remonstrance occurs contains Jane's very last words in the novel.
15 Toner, "Apophatic Austen."
16 Ray, *Simply Austen*, n.p. Ray speaks of the use Austen makes of Colonel Brandon's gravity in *Sense and Sensibility*; it has an explanation, but we (and the Dashwoods) must wait a long time to discover it.
17 Patricia Meyer Spacks points out that here the narrator pretends not to know for sure what Mr. Darcy is thinking, a playful way of telling us exactly what he is thinking. She notes that Austen uses this technique infrequently. Readers of Thomas Hardy will recall that he makes use of this pretense quite often. Whether he learned it from Austen or not, he is almost always telling us what a character is thinking but preventing us from being sure because of his metaphysical premises. It goes without saying that Austen is far more interested than Hardy in being coy to be amusing. Spacks, *Pride and Prejudice* 407n2.
18 Spacks has also noted the similarity between these two excerpts, but not the fact that all the novels include qualms over the potentially subversive moral tenor of the work. Spacks, *Pride and Prejudice*, 423n4.
19 Another example of this kind of verbal circularity is Lady Catherine's "And this is your real opinion!" (III.14.397). We cannot fail to hear the echo of Mr. Darcy's "And this is your opinion of me!" from volume 2 (II.11.214). Thus Lady Catherine's visit is an anti-proposal as well as an ante-proposal, devolving into a revelation to Elizabeth's interlocutor of her real opinion rather than the securing of a promise from her.
20 Wiltshire, *The Hidden Jane Austen*, 70.
21 As usual, however, he corrects Elizabeth's impression of his behaviour, which he probably will have to do his whole life because she has now begun criticizing him for imaginary deficiencies just to get a response from him.

22 In writing the first letter to Elizabeth at Rosings, Darcy exceeded what was allowable in epistolary communications between unmarried young men and young women. Letters were permitted only between the engaged, as we have seen in *Northanger Abbey*, although a man could propose by letter, as John Mullan points out (*What Matters in Jane Austen*, 274–5). In writing the letter, Mr. Darcy is acting as if they are engaged, although he promises Elizabeth in his missive that he is not repeating his proposal: "Be not alarmed, Madam, on receiving this letter, by the apprehension of its containing any repetition of those sentiments, or renewal of those offers, which were last night so disgusting to you. I write without any intention of paining you, or humbling myself, by dwelling on wishes, which, for the happiness of both, cannot be too soon forgotten" (218). Having once outraged etiquette in this way, perhaps he would have ventured to do so again, especially if the happiness of both were at stake.

23 Kenney, "Anne De Bourgh Smiles."

24 Spacks observes that it is difficult to tell whether this is Elizabeth thinking or the narrator speaking, but it is irony aimed at her: *Pride and Prejudice*, 283.

25 Fraiman, "The Humiliation of Elizabeth Bennet." See also Hirsch, "Shame, Pride and Prejudice." Mary Crawford thinks of marriage in these terms and imagines marriage to Edmund as her potential conquest over his persistence in his course to the priesthood. She is sure if he does not obey her, he does not love her.

26 Ray, "Do Elizabeth and Darcy Really Improve?"

27 Ray, "Do Elizabeth and Darcy Really Improve?"

28 *The Female Instructor*, 266.

29 Although there is no space here for a separate essay on this subject, Darcy begins the novel with a conviction that he cannot change and in fact that everyone has a dominant vice that never can be overcome. He insists in his later conversations with Elizabeth that her rejection made him change, made him want to change. In a sense, he is an anti–Henry Crawford, who has confidence in his own ability to adopt a new role but whose habits dominate him more than he suspects. At Netherfield, Darcy says, "There is, I believe, in every disposition a tendency to some particular evil – a natural defect, which not even the best education can overcome" (I.11.63). But he himself, although unwillingly, recognizes his habits of selfishness when Elizabeth accuses him. And unlike Henry, he exerts himself to overcome those habits.

30 Vickery, "A Man's Place."

31 Jane also uses the adjectival form in her last conversation with Lizzy: "But Lizzy, you have been very sly, very reserved with me" (III.17.415).

32 Lascelles, *Jane Austen and Her Art*, 105.

33 Page, *The Language of Jane Austen*, 185.

34 Sherry, "*Pride and Prejudice*," 616–17.

35 Gillie, *A Preface to Jane Austen*, 93.

36 Sherry, "*Pride and Prejudice*," 616.

37 Van Ghent, *The English Novel*, 129.
38 Ray, "Do Elizabeth and Darcy Really Improve?"
39 Page, *The Language of Jane Austen*, 29.
40 Sherry, "*Pride and Prejudice*," 612.
41 Fergus, "The Power of Women's Language," 104–5. See also Casal, "Laughing at Mr. Darcy": she observes that Caroline Bingley uses laughter as a weapon.

6. "As Nearly for Ever as Possible": Apophasis in *Mansfield Park*

1 Glover, "The Erotics of Restraint." Glover adds later: "The basis of self is apophatic: the ability to say, I am not that, and I am not that either. What the world offers is contingent, mired in circumstance, calculation, and history, rated by pre-existing discourses (habits, traditions, forms). The soul proceeds by denial." Glover nonetheless accuses Austen of creating a weak finale: "Even the narrator is only dimly celebratory about the upshot."
2 Toner, "Free Speech." See also Toner, "Apophatic Austen," 73.
3 Fanny's resistance to the trajectory plotted out for her by all the characters surrounding her may be one source of readers' dislike of her, as the audience participates in the unity against which she stands. However, it is clearly Austen's purpose to create this tension and to distinguish Fanny by that resistance from every other heroine she had created thus far.
4 Jocelyn Harris has discussed Austen's probable references to yet another Hargrave: Sir Hargrave Pollexfen, Harriet Byron's unwanted suitor in Richardson's *Sir Charles Grandison*, a novel we know ranked very high in Austen's opinion. Since the hero was designed as a "good man" to provide an example of one after the very bad Lovelace of *Clarissa*, Sir Hargrave is of course designed to be the novel's "bad man." Harris, "*Mansfield Park*," in *Jane Austen's Art of Memory*. She sees compelling parallels between Harriet's reasons for rejecting Hargrave and Fanny's reasons for rejecting Henry.
5 Le Faye, *Jane Austen's Letters*, 234.
6 Letter, November 1813, in Le Faye, *Jane Austen's Letters*, 283.
7 Austen, "Plan of a Novel."
8 Gibbons, *Rhetoric*, 157–8.
9 Oddly, she gives pride of place to *Villette* in really pioneering the technique, even after pointing out Austen's use of it in this passage: Dannenberg, *Coincidence and Counterfactuality*, 192–3.
10 Booth, *The Company We Keep*, 279.
11 Austen knew of Rev. Thomas Jefferson's opinion that the world does not reward the good or punish the wicked. According to Jefferson, "from the very Nature of general Laws, Good and Evil must frequently happen indiscriminately to the Righteous, and to the Wicked. Calamity and Success ought not, therefor, to be confounded with Punishments and Rewards. They are equally the Portion of the Good, and of the Bad; for

they are not the inseparable Attendants of Merit and Demerit. The time of strict and impartial Retribution is not yet come." Thomas Jefferson, *Two Sermons*, 32.

12 Brunton, *Self-Control*, 143–4.

13 Brunton, *Self-Control*, 144.

14 Brunton predicts a future damnation for her villain, Hargrave, as he fixes on his final plan to kidnap and then marry the heroine: "On that [the path] in which he trode the night was stealing, slow but sure, which closes at last in outer darkness" (*Self-Control*, 288).

15 Henry will have £4,000 per annum, which is about £308,600 or US$395,000 in modern currency, and Edmund only £700, about £53,900 or US$69,000, according to Katherine Toran's calculations: see "The Economics of Jane Austen's World." Toran cites Charlotte Runcie and Scott Campbell's table for her estimate of Edmund's income: "Could Mr. Darcy Afford a Stately Home Today?" To update these numbers, given the fluctuation of the pound, the numbers would be £439,205 for Henry and £76,861 for Edmund.

16 Pope, "Essay on Man, Epistle II," 281. Austen in an 1813 letter misquotes this poem, which she had earlier parodied: see "A Collection of Letters," in *Juvenilia*, 190–214.

17 Watt, "On Sense and Sensibility," 43. One could turn to the *Stanford Encyclopedia of Philosophy* for a thorough definition of it as a concept, but not as a literary one.

18 *Oxford English Dictionary*, s.v. "hereafter."

19 Jane Austen's sister Cassandra Austen "tried to persuade [Jane] to alter the end of *Mansfield Park* and let Mr. Crawford marry Fanny Price." Austen, *Later Manuscripts*, 231. Louisa Knight, daughter of Austen's brother Edward Austen Knight, later remembered "their arguing the matter but Miss Austen stood firmly and would not allow the change": quoted in Le Faye, *Jane Austen: A Family Record*, 275. Although Jan Fergus has suggested that this was "almost certainly … a mock argument," she offers no evidence for the claim (*Jane Austen: A Literary Life*.

20 Sheehan, "To Govern the Winds."

21 Tarpley, *Constancy and the Ethics of Mansfield Park*, 20.

22 Tarpley, *Constancy and the Ethics of Mansfield Park*, 241. Tarpley refers to Emerson and Holquist, "Introduction to M.M. Bakhtin," xviii.

23 Austen, *Juvenilia*, 194. In the introduction to that volume, Sabor dates "A Collection of Letters" to 1792; Austen was seventeen that December (xxviii).

24 As an aside, we could note that Austen's memory, like her heroine's, is long – she did not forget her favourite set of names when writing her later novels, but christened a Willoughby, a Crawford, an Edward, and a Fitzwilliam rather than a Fitzowen.

25 See the timeline in Ellen Moody, "A Calendar for *Mansfield Park*," http://www.jimandellen.org/austen/mp.calendar.html. The author guesses that Henry and Maria live together until around September, so about four months.

26 See Moody, "A Calendar for *Mansfield Park*," http://www.jimandellen.org/austen/mp.calendar.html.

27 As in *Northanger Abbey*, Austen is responding to Samuel Richardson's essay "Coquetry," in which he says the following: "That a young lady should be in love, and the love of the young gentleman undeclared, is an heterodoxy which prudence, and even policy, must not allow" (280).

28 D.A. Miller, "Good Riddance," 45. Miller asks if Mary "is removed from the foreground of the novel so that this [knowledge of her real character] may be more easily secured – behind her back, as it were?" He asserts that the closure removes her "linguistic polyvalency." Austen has done the same with Willoughby in *Sense and Sensibility*. What Miller sees as a betrayal of a complex character, I would argue, could well be a reinforcement of Austen's Shakespearean sense that such linguistic dexterity can be a smokescreen. As Catherine Morland says, "I cannot speak well enough to be unintelligible." The dexterous speech of Elizabeth and Aunt Gardiner, as I have remarked elsewhere, can be used to advance affection – but it can also be a weapon. It is not a virtue in and of itself. Kenney, "'Slyness Seems the Fashion.'" See also chapter 5 above.

29 Duffy, "Moral Integrity and Moral Anarchy," 71.

30 Mudrick, *Jane Austen*, 155. A. Walton Litz adds that the "form of *Mansfield Park* expresses all too clearly its author's conviction that the values of art are not the ultimate ones": Litz, *Jane Austen*, 130.

31 Trilling, "*Mansfield Park*"; Byrne, "*Mansfield Park*"; Edwards, "The Difficult Beauty of *Mansfield Park*."

32 Not according to the *Book of Common Prayer*'s table of forbidden affinities, however, which accounts for "cousins marrying" being a theme after the Reformation in England.

33 David Kaufmann, for instance, argues that

> even good stories may appear specious … when at the end they seem to violate their own ethics. For example, while the conclusion of Austen's *Mansfield Park* is complete in the sense that the marriage of Fanny and Edward [*sic*] finishes the story, it remains closurally disjunctive because it violates the meaning that emerges from the validating process. Fanny *ought* to marry Crawford. In stories of this type we may be seeing the hand of the author too clearly. Of course we must ask ourselves if our own ethic is at fault. Is the meaning wrong or can we not translate the handwriting on the wall? Or is it both? These kinds of questions depend upon our understanding of closure for both their enunciation and exploration. (Kaufmann, "Closure as Covenant," 91.)

34 Some of these continuations are respectable forays into reproducing Austen's style, and the last mentioned, by the well-known Joan Aiken, delightful in its own right.

35 McMaster, "Surface and Subsurface," 142.

36 See Toran, "The Economics of Jane Austen's World." See also Copeland, "Money." It is worth noting that though both gifts are given

"clandestinely," Edmund wishes to avoid Fanny's gratitude and Henry wishes to capitalize on it. As Thomas Stanford argues about *Pride and Prejudice*, Mr. Darcy so little wants Elizabeth to feel obligated to him for his generosity to Lydia that, when she expresses her gratitude to him at the beginning of the second proposal scene, "Darcy … responds 'in a tone of surprise and emotion,' making clear that he did not intend that she know of his actions: 'I am sorry, exceedingly sorry … that you have ever been informed of what may, in a mistaken light, have given you uneasiness'" (III.16.406). Stanford, "'What Do I Not Owe You?'" I am grateful to my former doctoral student Augusta Hardy, who brought this article to my attention.

37 Moody, "A Calendar for Mansfield Park," last updated 3 July 2012, http://www.jimandellen.org/austen/mp.calendar.html.

38 He does say Mary is one of his two dearest, when urging Fanny to wear Henry's chain: "'I would not have the shadow of a coolness arise,' he repeated, his voice sinking a little, 'between the two dearest objects I have on earth'" (II.9.209). This passage supports McMaster's observation about the strange way Austen has Edmund pair the two of them up in his thoughts. McMaster, *Jane Austen on Love*, 35–6.

39 Sheila Kindred believes Fanny and Edmund have become parents, though she overlooks the potential inconsistency of keeping two livings at the same time: "It is evident that they will be more financially secure (it has been estimated that the two livings of Thornton Lacey and Mansfield could be worth as much as £1500 annually). This fact, together with their wish to be closer to the 'paternal abode,' prompts speculation about why these changes in circumstances are so welcome. It seems as if Fanny may be pregnant, if not already the mother of young children, a state of affairs which would surely add to their married happiness." See Kindred, "The Happy Endings." Richard Jenkyns also speaks of the ending of *Mansfield Park* as indicating Fanny's pregnancy: "A Park with a View," in *A Fine Brush on Ivory*. Ruth Bernard Yeazell, conversely, had argued that "Austen's novels keep out children, especially from a heroine's future, and this exclusion is particularly apparent in *Mansfield Park*": "The Boundaries of Mansfield Park," 151–2.

40 There may be one other explanation. Austen is not averse to showing little hypocrisies in her heroines and heroes – the ending of *Sense and Sensibility*, with its reference to Edward's experience in proposing and Elinor's willingness to excuse any misbehaviour of his because she was flattered at his valuing her above Lucy, is a perfect example. Emma placidly recalls her earlier fear that Jane Fairfax's children with Mr. Knightley, should they marry, will displace Isabella and John's oldest son as heirs of Donwell and does not abandon her determination to marry Mr. Knightley. But that Edmund is impecunious or greedy is never hinted in the novel's text – rather the opposite. In an essay on the death of Dr. Grant, Cheryl Kinney argues that "in the ending paragraphs of the novel, Jane Austen uses Dr. Grant's death to expose Sir Thomas' and Edmund's hypocritical defense of the clergy with their stance on multiple

incumbencies. The death also reveals that both Fanny and Edmund could fall prey to the very mercenary motives that they found so reprehensible in Mary Crawford: a larger income and a bigger house" (Kinney, "Why Tom Bertram Is Right"). However, as Edmund has said earlier, "Sir Thomas ... undoubtedly understands the duties of a parish priest. We must hope his son may prove that *he* knows it too" (II.vii.288; emphasis in original). Edmund would indeed be a hypocrite if he were not to surrender the living at Thornton Lacey back to his father, who could then further make up for the financial losses Tom has imposed on the family by his early extravagance. The narrator does not suggest any resolution to this potential problem at the close of the novel, but Thornton Lacey is in Sir Thomas's gift, and he is not only opposed to multiple incumbencies, but also recently has become far more interested than in the past in living up to his principles. Nabokov discusses this situation in his "Jane Austen: *Mansfield Park*," 17.

41 As Nora Bartlett argues, "The two sisters [Fanny and Susan] have made their way into Mansfield as two earlier sisters did, and one, Fanny, has brought moral depth and moral meaning to the emptiness and silence she found there, but at such a cost. One remembers, almost too late, that these two sisters are called 'Price.' I draw from these disquieting events one consolation: Fanny and Edmund's children will love their parents and know themselves loved by them. Theirs will be a more blessed generation." Bartlett, "What's Wrong with Mansfield Park," 174.

42 de Rougemont, *Love in the Western World*, 7. See especially the chapter, "Beyond Tragedy."

43 See my "Why Tom Bertram Cannot Die."

44 Kindred, "The Happy Endings of *Mansfield Park*."

7. "The Perfect Happiness of the Union": Undeceiving Mr. Knightley and the Reader in *Emma*

1 Hugh Blair," Sermon 17," *Sermons*, 2:17.

2 Tobin, *The Elements of Surprise*, 170.

3 Hall, "Jane Fairfax's Choice."

4 Hardy, *Far from the Madding Crowd*, 308.

5 Hardy, *Far from the Madding Crowd*, 303–4.

6 Shakespeare, *A Midsummer Night's Dream*, I.i.134. See also Harris, *Jane Austen's Art of Memory*, 169–87. Harris oddly compares Mr. Knightley to "Lysander, Who Loves Hermia/Jane," 177. More helpfully, she draws our attention to Mr. Knightley's own statement, "'But I ... who have had *no such charm* thrown over my senses, must still see, hear, and remember. Emma is spoiled" (I.5.37) (my emphasis).

7 Bakhtin, *Problems of Dostoevsky's Poetics*, 6–7.

8 Brown, "Emma's Depression."

9 Collins Hemingway misunderstands Austen's use of metalepsis as authorial intrusion in exactly the way James mandates. See his *Jane Austen*, 44–5.

10 Although Austen probably never read Chrétien de Troyes, his Enide in *Erec and Enide* similarly berates herself for lamenting over her husband's lack of interest in chivalry, never attributing his decision to stay in bed with her till noon every day to his own desire or choice. The critical debate over whether Enide is at fault or not is proof that even moderns cannot discern when a storyteller is having a character say something she believes to be true but that is not. If a twelfth-century narrative artist can imagine a good character being mistaken and accepting blame for something that is not her fault, so can Austen.

11 Michele Larrow refers the reader to Adam Smith's definitions of the sympathetic imagination to showcase Austen's tracing of Mr. Knightley's growth in sympathy towards Emma: "'Could He Even Have Seen into Her Heart.'"

12 Astonished at the weight his own free will had in creating his eight years of unhappy separation from Anne Elliot, Wentworth exclaims, "'I have valued myself on honourable toils and just rewards. Like other great men under reverses,' he added with a smile, 'I must endeavor to subdue my mind to my fortune. I must learn to brook being happier than I deserve'" (II.11.268–9).

13 See Tarpley, "Manhood and Happiness in *Emma*." Tarpley's discussion of the men in the novel centres on their education and the language they speak. While she sees Mr. Knightley as exemplifying a "key qualification for the teachable man: the proper understanding of and use of leisure" (25), she maintains that "Mr. Weston knows only how to speak one language: the utilitarian language of success. Their brief, unhappy union ends in his indebtedness and his wife's death" (27). On the other hand, Tarpley sees Robert Martin as best enacting what she defines as a "cornerstone marriage," because he "chooses Harriet for the good (rather than the gain) he sees in her" (36).

14 See Kenney, "Benevolence and Sympathy in *Emma*."

15 Austen emphasizes this aspect of the heroines and heroes in most of the novels. Elinor cares for Marianne when she is ill at Cleveland. Darcy objects to Elizabeth's claim that he "knows no actual good" of her by bringing up her devoted care of Jane when she was sick at Netherfield. Fanny spends most of *Mansfield Park* catering to her Aunt Bertram, and Edmund ends the novel nursing his brother Tom back to health. In *Persuasion*, Anne is caregiver to her sister Mary, little Charles, and Louisa Musgrove, and Captain Wentworth assists her when she is being harassed by her nephew and when she is tired after a long walk. Catherine Morland is the only exception, as at the close of *Northanger Abbey* the narrator presents her to the reader as an object of solicitude, not as a caregiver herself.

16 In coloured narrative, Austen relates Mr. Knightley's disappointment in Jane when he observes her and what he surmises is her silent communication with Frank: "How the delicacy, the discretion of his favourite could have been so lain asleep! He feared there must be some decided involvement. Disingenuousness and double dealing seemed to meet him at every turn" (III.5.377).

17 "No objection was raised on the father's side; the young man was treated liberally; it was all as it should be: and as Emma became acquainted with Robert Martin, who was now introduced at Hartfield, she fully acknowledged in him all the appearance of sense and worth which could bid fairest for her little friend. She had no doubt of Harriet's happiness with any good-tempered man; but with him, and in the home he offered, there would be the hope of more, of security, stability, and improvement. *She would be placed in the midst of those who loved her, and who had better sense than herself; retired enough for safety, and occupied enough for cheerfulness. She would be never led into temptation, nor left for it to find her out.* She would be respectable and happy; and Emma admitted her to be the luckiest creature in the world, to have created so steady and persevering an affection in such a man; – or, if not quite the luckiest, to yield only to herself" (III.19.526) (my emphasis).
18 Sleath, *The Orphan of the Rhine*, chap. 2.
19 Lindstrom, "*Sense and Sensibility* and Suffering," 1076–7. "As readers trying not to pass over the scene having only noticed its most brutal ironies and obvious pieties of judgment against Marianne's narcissism, we need to interpret nimbly after the sharp turn taken by her pattern of seeking knowledge, her pointed and false conclusion regarding Elinor that *she doesn't really feel*, or *couldn't*, based on her sister's way of talking" (emphasis in original). What Lindstrom notes is that Marianne cannot see the concealed sensibility of her sister. I would argue that Austen puts Mr. Knightley and the reader in the same position vis-à-vis Emma.
20 See my "Benevolence and Sympathy in *Emma*." Aside from the medieval resonances of the names Donwell Abbey and George Knightley – and Emma, for that matter – references to Christianity and sin are subtly woven into the story.
21 For a complete study of the ways in which Austen strategically uses description as a mode of argumentation that necessarily involves ethics, see Bourbon, *Jane Austen and the Ethics of Description*.
22 Thanks to Dr. Cheryl Kinney for this observation.
23 René Girard, *Deceit, Desire, and the Novel*, 97, 144.
24 See Astell, "Anne Elliot's Education" and Pawell, "Fanny Price and the Sentimental Genealogy."
25 What follows is a slightly edited version of the previously published "'And I Am Changed Also': Mr. Knightley's Conversion to Amiability," *Persuasions* 29 (2007): 110–20.
26 Hagan, "The Closure of *Emma*"; Meyer, "Mr. Knightley's Education"; Kirkham, *Jane Austen, Feminism and Fiction*.
27 Dooley, "'My Fanny.'"
28 Sir Thomas Bertram finds he has similarly failed as a father at the end of *Mansfield Park*, when he realizes he has set himself up as the grave and unbending voice of principle, unwittingly sending his daughters to their Aunt Norris for indulgent treatment – and submitting Fanny to her bullying. Austen is clearly thinking about the problems attending upon moral correction.

29 Paris, *Character and Conflict*, 70.
30 Bander, "*Emma*," 158.
31 Waldron, "Men of Sense and Silly Wives," 141–6.
32 Scott, "Rev. of *Emma*," 42.
33 Waldron, "Men of Sense and Silly Wives," 147.
34 Emsley, "Learning the Art of Charity in *Emma*," in *Jane Austen's Philosophy of the Virtues*, 61–70.
35 Schorer, "The Humiliation of Emma Woodhouse," 177, 185.
36 Trilling, *Sincerity and Authenticity*, 77.
37 Waldron, "Men of Sense and Silly Wives," 150.
38 Austen rarely features kisses in her novels, and only once between the heroine and her husband to be, when Edmund kisses Fanny's hand out of gratitude after he confesses to her his despair over Mary and she seems to reassure him (*MP*, III.313). Only Edmund hugs his wife to be (*MP*, II.915.514–15). Mr. Wickham kisses Elizabeth Bennet's hand after his marriage to Lydia and their final contretemps (*PP*, III.10.364). Mrs. Weston kisses Emma with tears of relief and joy on finding out Emma is not in love with Frank Churchill. Harriet kisses Emma's hand "in silent and submissive gratitude" (*E*, III.4.371). That the act of kissing the hand signifies submission rather than just affection is clear from these examples, even if some might argue Emma is not sure just who took whose hand. See Harvey, *The Kiss in History*, 192. The use of the kiss for feudal contract was ceasing to be widespread in England long before Austen's day, but the survival of the salute on the hand in France, Germany, and Poland is well documented. Austen almost certainly associated the act with French gallantry.

8. The Oracles of Kellynch and Uppercross: Predicting the Future in *Persuasion*

1 Aristotle, *Poetics*, 52.
2 D.A. Miller, *Narrative and Its Discontents*.
3 Davis, "Austen's Providence in *Persuasion*."
4 What follows is an edited and much expanded version of my article "A Tale of Two Captains: Whose Heart Is Worth Having?" *Persuasions On-Line* 39 no. 1 (2018).
5 Ryle, "Jane Austen and the Moralists," 17–18.
6 Harris, *Jane Austen's Art of Memory*, 183.
7 Duquette, "The Sensibility of Captain Benwick," 105, 108.
8 I have reproduced Ellen Moody's dating of events in the novel, which she attributes in the main to Chapman and Jo Modert. See Moody, "A Calendar for Persuasion."
9 I wonder if, in joining the two while Louisa is bedridden after her coma, Austen has not created a "deathbed" scene for Benwick's benefit, as he was not able to see Fanny before her death. In such a reading, Louisa would be a kind of substitute for Fanny in a way Anne Elliot could not be. It is interesting that she is referred to (along with the fainting Henrietta) as

a "dead young lady" after the fall at the Cobb (*P*, II.12.120). If Austen were thinking in this way, Louisa became the perfect match for Benwick *because* of her injury. The situation is also reminiscent of Willoughby's pleasure in thinking he knows what Marianne would look like in death.

10 Ford, *What Jane Austen's Characters Read*, 6–8.

11 D.A. Miller, *Narrative and Its Discontents*.

12 Craig, "The Persuasion of Pounds." With £25,000 invested in naval bonds, Wentworth would be living on around £1,000 a year. Mr. Darcy has £10,000 a year, so we can see that an estate like Pemberley will not be within Wentworth's grasp, or even the Netherfield of Mr. Bingley, who has £5,000 a year.

13 It is unclear here whether Austen means Mary assumes Anne is too old to have children or if she considers headship of a family something entirely attached to the estate and not the people. This would be typical of Mary, the negligent mother and socially conscious snob, and Austen could of course mean to convey both senses.

14 "Elizabeth could bear it no longer. She got up and ran out of the room, and returned no more till she heard them passing through the hall to the dining-parlour. She then joined them soon enough to see Lydia, with anxious parade, walk up to her mother's right hand, and hear her say to her eldest sister, 'Ah, Jane, I take your place now, and you must go lower, because I am a married woman!'" (*PP*, III.9.350).

15 See Eastaugh and Sternal-Johnson, "Persuasion Season." Anne's landaulette would have cost in today's money about £10,800 pounds or US$14,000. Nye, "Pounds Sterling to Dollars."

16 Lewis, "When a House Is Not a Home." Lewis argues that upper-class women often seem to have inhabited spaces controlled and designed by the men who owned the homes and did not always feel the emotional sense of "home" we ascribe to the term now.

17 *E* II.14.295: Mrs. Elton: "'People who have extensive grounds themselves are always pleased with any thing in the same style.' Emma doubted the truth of this sentiment. She had a great idea that people who had extensive grounds themselves cared very little for the extensive grounds of any body else; but it was not worth while to attack an error so double-dyed."

18 Nicolson, "Jane Austen's Houses," 91.

19 Austen, *Lady Susan, The Watsons, Sanditon*, 169.

20 Radcliffe, *The Italian*, 10.

21 Cited in Le Faye, *Jane Austen: An Austen Family Record*, 214.

22 Aiken, *Mansfield Revisited*.

23 See De Forest, "*Persuasion* as a *Penelopeia*."

24 Some might argue that Austen does not leave the reader in much doubt about Wentworth's safety, since Napoleon was defeated at Waterloo in 1815. This is to ignore the fact that in 1816, perils remained for all active naval men. After all, Napoleon was not England's only enemy: the navy was involved in the bombardment of Algiers in 1816. Austen's brother Charles's ship *The Phoenix* sank in 1816 on a mission against pirates. Even though the war is over in *Persuasion*, the hazards of naval life remain, as Austen well knew.

Conclusion

1 See Gillooly, *Smile of Discontent*, 79–80.
2 Wilt, "The Powers of the Instrument."
3 See Justice, "Must and Ought"; Morton, "Emma's 'Serious Spirit'"; and Valihora, *Austen's Oughts*.
4 Cather, "The Novel Démeublé," 5–6.
5 Austen, "Venta."
6 Woolf, "Virginia Woolf Wonders," 261.
7 Kindred, "The Happy Endings of *Mansfield Park*."
8 Jenkyns, *A Fine Brush on Ivory*, 98.
9 Jenkyns, *A Fine Brush on Ivory*, 137.
10 Ray, "The Professor Is In."
11 See von Balthasar, *Tragedy under Grace*.
12 Wiltshire, *The Hidden Jane Austen*, 167.
13 Miller, *Narrative and Its Discontents*, 272–3.
14 Wiltshire, *The Hidden Jane Austen*, 120–1.
15 See Bourbon, "Elizabeth Bennet."

Bibliography

Adkins, Roy, and Lesley Adkins. *Jane Austen's England: Daily Life in the Georgian and Regency Periods*. London: Penguin, 2013.

Aiken, Joan. *Mansfield Revisited*. New York: Doubleday, 1985.

Alter, Robert. *The Art of Biblical Narrative*. New York: Basic Books, 2011.

– *The Art of Biblical Poetry*. New York: Basic Books, 2011.

Aristotle. *Poetics*. Translated by Malcolm Heath. London: Penguin, 1997.

Astell, Ann. "Anne Elliot's Education: The Learning of Romance in *Persuasion*." *Renascence* 40, no. 1 (Fall 1987): 2–14. https://doi.org/10.5840/renascence19874011.

Auerbach, Emily. "'A Barkeeper Entering the Kingdom of Heaven': Did Mark Twain Really Hate Jane Austen?" *Virginia Quarterly Review* 75, no. 1 (Winter 1999): 109–20.

Auerbach, Nina. "Jane Austen's Dangerous Charm: Feeling as One Ought to About Fanny Price." *Women & Literature* 3 (1983): 208–21.

Austen, Jane. *Emma*. Edited by Richard Cronin and Dorothy McMillan. Cambridge: Cambridge University Press, 2005. Originally published 1815.

– *Emma*. Edited by R.W. Chapman. 3rd ed. Oxford: Clarendon Press, 1933. Originally published 1815.

– *Juvenilia*. Edited by Peter Sabor. Cambridge: Cambridge University Press, 2006.

– *Lady Susan, The Watsons, Sanditon*. Introduction by Margaret Drabble. Harmondsworth: Penguin Books, 2003.
– *Later Manuscripts*. Edited by Janet Todd and Linda Bree. Cambridge: Cambridge University Press, 2008.
– *Mansfield Park*. Edited by R.W. Chapman. Oxford: Clarendon Press, 1923. Originally published 1814.
– *Mansfield Park*. Edited by John Wiltshire. Cambridge: Cambridge University Press, 2013. Originally published 1814.
– *Northanger Abbey*. Edited by Barbara M. Benedict. Cambridge: Cambridge University Press, 2006. Originally published 1817.
– *Northanger Abbey*. Edited by R.W. Chapman. Oxford: Clarendon Press, 1923. Originally published 1817.
– *Persuasion*. Edited by Janet Todd. Cambridge: Cambridge University Press, 2006. Originally published 1817.
– "Plan of a Novel." In *Catharine and Other Writings*, edited by Margaret Anne Doody and Douglas Murray, 230–2. Oxford: Oxford University Press, 1993.
– *Pride and Prejudice*. Edited by Pat Rogers. Cambridge: Cambridge University Press, 2013. Originally published 1813.
– *Pride and Prejudice*. Edited by R.W. Chapman. Cambridge: Cambridge University Press, 1923. Originally published 1813.
– *Sense and Sensibility*. Edited by Edward Copeland. Cambridge: Cambridge University Press, 2006. Originally published 1811.
– "Venta." In *Minor Works*, edited by R.W. Chapman. Oxford: Clarendon Press, 1988.
Austen-Leigh, James. "A Memoir of Jane Austen." In *Persuasion*, edited by Jane Austen, 267–391. Harmondsworth: Penguin, 1965.
Austen-Leigh, William, and Richard A. Austen-Leigh, eds. *Jane Austen: Her Life and Letters – A Family Record*. London: Smith, Elder, 1913.
Bacon, Francis. "Of Truth." In *Francis Bacon: The Major Works*, edited by Brian Vickers, 341–2. Oxford: Oxford University Press, 1996. First published 1625.
Bakhtin, Mikhail. *Problems of Dostoevsky's Poetics*. Minneapolis: University of Minnesota Press, 1984.
Bander, Elaine. "Blair's *Rhetoric* and the Art of *Persuasion*." *Persuasions* 15 (1993): 124–30.
– "*Emma*: The Pique of Perfection." *Persuasions* 21 (1999): 155–62.
Bartlett, Nora. "What's Wrong with Mansfield Park." In *Jane Austen: Reflections of a Reader*, edited by Jane Stabler, 155–74. Cambridge:

Open Book Publishers, 2021. https://books.openedition.org/obp/18773.

Benson, Robert. "Elizabeth as Beatrice: A Reading of Spenser's Amoretti." *South Central Bulletin* 32, no. 4 (Winter 1972): 184–8. https://doi.org/10.2307/3186966.

Black, Jeremy. "Conclusions." In *England in the Age of Austen*, 299–314. Bloomington: Indiana University Press, 2021. https://doi.org/10.2307/j.ctv1c3pdt5.16.

Blackall, Offspring. *The Lord Bishop of Exeter's Answer to Mr. Hoadly's Letter*. London: W. Rogers, 1709.

Blair, Hugh. *Lectures on Rhetoric and Belles Lettres*. Edited by Harold F. Harding. 2 vols. Carbondale: Southern Illinois University Press, 1965.

– "Sermon 17: On the Government of the Heart." *Sermons*, vol. 2. Dublin: William Colles, 1784.

Blamires, Alcuin. "Women and Creative Intelligence in Medieval Thought." In *Voices in Dialogue: Reading Women in the Middle Ages*, edited by Linda Olson and Kathryn Kerby-Fulton, 213–30. South Bend, IN: Notre Dame University Press, 2005.

Bloom, Paul. *Against Empathy: The Case for Rational Compassion*. New York: HarperCollins, 2018. https://doi.org/10.1525/9780520351981.

Bloomfield, Morton W. "Episodic Narrative and Marvels in Epic and Romance." In *Essays and Explorations*. Cambridge, MA: Harvard University Press, 1970.

Booth, Wayne C. *The Company We Keep: An Ethics of Fiction*. Berkeley: University of California Press, 1988. https://doi.org/10.1525/9780520351981.

– "Point of View and Control of Distance in *Emma*." *Nineteenth-Century Fiction* 16, no. 2 (September 1961–2): 95–116. https://doi.org/10.2307/2932473.

Boswell, James.*Boswell's Life of Johnson*. Edited by George Birkbeck and L.F. Powell. Oxford: Oxford University Press, 1934.

Bourbon, Brett. "Elizabeth Bennet, the Socrates of Descriptive Reason." *Persuasions On-Line* 34, no. 1 (Winter 2013). https://jasna.org/persuasions/on-line/vol34no1/bourbon.html.

– *Jane Austen and the Ethics of Description*. New York: Routledge, 2022. https://doi.org/10.4324/9781003331445.

Brann, Eva. "Do You Know What an Odyssey Is?" (Opening Lecture for the Honors Program at Whitman College in Walla Walla, Washington in September, 1993.) *Imaginative Conservative*, May 2013. http://www.theimaginativeconservative.org/2018/10/odyssey-eva-brann-90.html.

Brooks, Jeanice. "In Search of Austen's Missing Songs." *Review of English Studies* 67, no. 202 (November 2016): 929–35. https://doi.org/10.1093/res/hgw035.

Brown, Lloyd. "The Comic Conclusion in Austen's Novels." *PMLA* 84, no. 6 (October 1969): 1582–7. https://doi.org/10.2307/1261504.

Brown, Marshall. "Emma's Depression." *Studies in Romanticism* 53, no. 1 (Spring 2014): 3–29. https://doi.org/10.1353/srm.2014.0036.

Brunton, Mary. *Discipline*. London: Unwin Hyman, 1987. First published 1814.

–. *Self-Control*. Edited by Anthony Mandal. Abingdon, UK: Routledge, 2016. First published 1811. https://doi.org/10.4324/9781315649405.

Burke, Edmund. *A Philosophical Enquiry into the Origin of Our Ideas of the Sublime and the Beautiful*. Edited by Adam Philips. Oxford: Oxford University Press, 1990.

Burns, Margie. "Comic Resolutions, Humorous Loose Ends in Austen's Novels." *Persuasions* 33 (2011): 238–43.

Byrne, Paula. "Mansfield Park Shows the Dark Side of Jane Austen." *Telegraph* (London), 26 July 2014. https://www.telegraph.co.uk/culture/books/10987048/Mansfield-Park-shows-the-dark-side-of-Jane-Austen.html.

Calvin, John. *Institutes of Christian Religion*. Translated by Henry Beveridge. Grand Rapids, MI: Eerdmans, 1957.

Carroll, Charles Durning. "Willoughby's Apology." *Persuasions On-Line* 30, no. 1 (Winter 2009). https://jasna.org/persuasions/on-line/vol30no1/carroll.html.

Casal, Elvira. "Laughing at Mr. Darcy: Wit and Sexuality in *Pride and Prejudice*." *Persuasions On-Line* 22, no. 1 (Winter 2001). https://jasna.org/persuasions/on-line/vol22no1/casal.html.

Cather, Willa. "The Novel Démeublé." *New Republic*, 12 April 1922, 5–6.

Clark, Lorrie. "Shaftesbury's Art of 'Soliloquy' in *Mansfield Park*." *Persuasions* 24 (2002): 59–70.

Cohn, Dorrit, and Lewis S. Gleich. "Metalepsis and Mise en Abyme." *Narrative* 20, no. 1 (January 2012): 105–14. https://doi.org/10.1353/nar.2012.0003.

Copeland, Edward. "Money." In *The Cambridge Companion to Jane Austen*, edited by Edward Copeland and Juliet McMaster, 131–48.

Cambridge: Cambridge University Press, 1997. https://doi.org/10.1017/CCOL0521495172.008.

Corfield, Penelope J. "Aristocrats, Plutocrats and Cross-Class Gentlemen." In *The Georgians: The Deeds and Misdeeds of 18th-Century Britain*, 245–65. New Haven, CT: Yale University Press, 2022. https://doi.org/10.12987/yale/9780300253573.003.0013.

Cox, Brenda S. "Marianne Dashwood's *Repentance*, Willoughby's 'Repentance,' and *The Book of Common Prayer*." *Persuasions On-Line* 39, no. 1 (Winter 2018). https://jasna.org/publications-2/persuasions-online/volume-39-no-1/marianne-dashwoods-repentance-willoughbys-repentance-and-the-book-of-common-prayer/.

Craig, Sheryl. "The Persuasion of Pounds." Jane Austen Society Annual General Meeting Plenary Lecture, Kansas City, MO, 29 September 2018.

Dadlez, E.M. *Mirrors to One Another: Emotion and Value in Jane Austen and David Hume*. London: Wiley-Blackwell, 2009. https://doi.org/10.1002/9781444310412.

Dannenberg, Hilary P. *Coincidence and Counterfactuality: Plotting Time and Space in Narrative Fiction*. Lincoln: University of Nebraska Press, 2008. https://doi.org/10.2307/j.ctt1dgn486.

Davis, Kathryn. "Austen's Providence in *Persuasion*." *Persuasions* 25 (2013): 212–24.

de Behar, Lisa Block. "Rhetoric: State of the Art." In *A Rhetoric of Silence and Other Selected Writings*, 14–18. Berlin: Mouton De Gruyter, 1995. https://doi.org/10.1515/9783110813555.14.

De Forest, Mary Margolies. "*Persuasion* as a *Penelopeia*." In *Jane Austen, Closet Classicist*, 109–26. Seattle: Amazon Press, 2017.

de Rougemont, Denis. *Love in the Western World*. Translated by Montgomery Belgion. Princeton, NJ: Princeton University Press, 1940.

Doody, Margaret. "Jane Austen, That Disconcerting Child." In *The Child Writer from Austen to Woolf*, edited by Christine Alexander and Juliet McMaster, 101–21. Cambridge: Cambridge University Press, 2010.

Dooley, Gillian. "'My Fanny,' and 'A Heroine Whom No One but Myself Will Much Like': Jane Austen and Her Heroines in the Chawton Novels." *Persuasions On-Line* 38, no. 1 (Winter 2017). https://jasna.org/publications-2/persuasions-online/vol38no1/dooley/.

Dooley, Gillian, and Charles Dufour. "'A More Gentle, Less Dignified Forgiveness': Willoughby's Apology in the Context of

Austen's Religious Beliefs." *Persuasions On-Line* 38, no. 3 (Summer 2018). https://jasna.org/publications-2/persuasions-online/volume-38-no-3/dooley-dufour/.

Duffy, Joseph M., Jr. "Moral Integrity and Moral Anarchy in *Mansfield Park*." *ELH* 23, no. 1 (1956): 71–91. https://doi.org/10.2307/2871784.

Duquette, Natasha. "'Motionless Wonder': Contemplating Gothic Sublimity in *Northanger Abbey*." *Persuasions On-Line* 30, no. 2 (Spring 2010). https://jasna.org/persuasions/on-line/vol30no2/duquette.html.

– "The Sensibility of Captain Benwick in Literary and Historical Context." In *Jane Austen and Masculinity*, edited by Michael Kramp, 97–112. Lewisburg, PA: Bucknell University Press, 2018.

Duquette, Natasha, and Elisabeth Lenckos, eds. *Jane Austen and the Arts*. Bethlehem, PA: Lehigh University Press, 2014.

Eastaugh, Ben, and Chris Sternal-Johnson. "Persuasion Season, Coaches and Conveniences Part II: Green-Eyed and Extravagant Monsters." *AustenOnly*, 18 February 2010. Archived 5 August 2017 at the Wayback Machine Archive. https://web.archive.org/web/20170805025446/https://austenonly.com/2010/02/18/austenonly-persuasion-seasoncoaches-and-conveniences-part-ii-green-eyed-and-extravagant-monsters/.

Edwards Thomas R., Jr. "The Difficult Beauty of *Mansfield Park*." *Nineteenth-Century Fiction* 20, no. 1 (June 1965): 51–67. https://doi.org/10.2307/2932492.

Emsley, Sarah. *Jane Austen's Philosophy of the Virtues*. New York: Palgrave, 2005. https://doi.org/10.1057/9781403978288.

Euripides. *The Trojan Women*. Oxford: Oxford University Press, 2009.

The Female Instructor; or, Young Woman's Companion; Being a Guide to All the Accomplishments Which Adorn the Female Character, etc. Liverpool, 1811. British Library; Shelfmark 8415.dd.17.

Fergus, Jan. *Jane Austen and the Didactic Novel: Northanger Abbey, Sense and Sensibility, and Pride and Prejudice*. New York: Barnes & Noble, 1983.

– *Jane Austen: A Literary Life*. New York: Macmillan, 1991. https://doi.org/10.1007/978-1-349-21665-9.

– "The Power of Women's Language and Laughter." In *The Talk in Jane Austen*, edited by Bruce Stovel and Lynn Weinlos Gregg, 103–22. Edmonton: University of Alberta Press, 2002.

Ford, Susan Allen. *What Jane Austen's Characters Read (and Why)*. London: Bloomsbury Academic, 2024.

Fordyce, James. "On Good Works." In *Sermons to Young Women, Corrected and Greatly Enlarged*. Southampton: Chawton House Press, 2012. Reprint of the text of the 10th edition of volume 2, 1796.

Forster, E.M. *Aspects of the Novel*. New York: Harcourt, 1927.

Fraiman, Susan. "The Humiliation of Elizabeth Bennet." In *Unbecoming Women: British Women Writers and the Novel of Development*, 59–87. New York: Columbia University Press, 1991.

Frye, Northrop. *Anatomy of Criticism: Four Essays*. Princeton, NJ: Princeton University Press, 1957. https://doi.org/10.1515/9781400866908.

Gallop, David. "Jane Austen and the Aristotelian Ethic." *Philosophy and Literature* 23, no. 1 (April 1999): 96–109. https://doi.org/10.1353/phl.1999.0016.

Genette, Gérard. *Figures of Literary Discourse*. Translated by Alan Sheridan. New York: Columbia University Press, 1982.

– *Narrative Discourse: An Essay in Method*. Translated by Jane E. Lewin. Ithaca, NY: Cornell University Press, 1980.

Gibbons, Thomas. *Rhetoric, or, a View of Its Principal Tropes and Figures, in Their Origin and Powers, with a Variety of Rules to Escape Errors and Blemishes and Attain Propriety and Elegance in Composition*. London: J. and W. Oliver, 1767. Reprint Scolar Press, 1969.

Gilbert, Sandra, and Susan Gubar. *The Madwoman in the Attic: The Woman Writer and the Nineteenth-Century Literary Imagination*. New Haven, CT: Yale University Press, 1979.

Gillie, Christopher. *A Preface to Jane Austen*. London: Longman, 1985.

Gillooly, Eileen. *Smile of Discontent: Humor, Gender, and Nineteenth-Century British Fiction*. Chicago: University of Chicago Press, 1999.

Girard, René. *Deceit, Desire, and the Novel: Self and Other in Literary Structure*. Baltimore: Johns Hopkins University Press, 1976. https://doi.org/10.56021/9780801802201.

Glover, Douglas. "The Erotics of Restraint, or the Angel in the Novel: A Note on Jane Austen's *Mansfield Park*." *Brooklyn Rail*, 1 March 2017. https://brooklynrail.org/2017/03/fiction/Erotics-of-Restraint.

Goodheart, Eugene. "Emma: Jane Austen's Errant Heroine." *Sewanee Review* 116, no. 4 (Fall 2008): 589–604. https://doi.org/10.1353/sew.0.0087.

Gross, Gloria. "Mentoring Jane Austen: Reflections on 'My Dear Dr. Johnson'." *Persuasions* 11 (1989): 53–54.

Hagan, John. "The Closure of *Emma*." *Studies in English Literature, 1500–1900* 15, no. 4 (Autumn 1975): 545–61. https://doi.org/10.2307/450010.

Hall, Lynda A. "Jane Fairfax's Choice: The Sale of Human Flesh or Human Intellect." *Persuasions On-Line* 28, no. 1 (Winter 2007). https://jasna.org/persuasions/on-line/vol28no1/hall.htm.

Hardy, Thomas. *Far From the Madding Crowd*. New York: Norton, 1986. First published 1874.

Harris, Jocelyn. *Jane Austen's Art of Memory*. Cambridge: Cambridge University Press, 1989.

Harvey, Karen. *The Kiss in History*. Manchester: Manchester University Press, 2005.

Haybron, Dan. "Happiness." In *The Stanford Encyclopedia of Philosophy*, edited by Edward N. Zalta. Summer 2020. https://plato.stanford.edu/archives/sum2020/entries/happiness/.

Hellstrom, Ward. "Francophobia in *Emma*." *Studies in English Literature* 5, no. 4 (August 1965): 607–17. https://doi.org/10.2307/449430.

Hemingway, Collins. *Jane Austen and the Creation of Modern Fiction*. Jefferson, NC: McFarland, 2024.

Herodotus. *Histories*. London: Penguin, 2003.

Hirsch, Gordon. "Shame, Pride and Prejudice: Jane Austen's Psychological Sophistication." *Mosaic: An Interdisciplinary Critical Journal* 25, no. 1 (Winter 1992): 63–78.

Holquist, Michael. "Introduction to M.M. Bakhtin." In *Speech Genres and Other Late Essays*, edited by Caryl Emerson and Michael Holquist, ix–xxiii. Austin: University of Texas Press, 1986.

Hopkins, Robert. "Moral Luck and Judgment in Jane Austen's *Persuasion*." *Nineteenth-Century Literature* 42, no. 2 (September 1987): 143–58. https://doi.org/10.1525/ncl.1987.42.2.99p0089v.

Horace.*Ars Poetica: Epistle to the Pisos*. In *Horace: Satires, Epistles, and Ars Poetica*. Translated by H. Rushton Fairclough. Cambridge: Harvard University Press, 1929.

Hull, Edward. *A Sermon on the Duty of Obedience to Civil Governors*. Liverpool: G. Cruickshank, 1819.

Jefferson, Thomas. *Two Sermons, on the Reasonableness, and Salutary Effects of Fearing God, as Governor and Judge of the World*. Tunbridge, UK: Maunder and Holmes, 1808.

Jenkyns, Richard. *A Fine Brush on Ivory*. Oxford: Oxford University Press, 2004.

Johnson, Claudia L. *Jane Austen: Women, Politics and the Novel*. Chicago: University of Chicago Press, 1988.

– "A 'Sweet Face White as Death': Jane Austen and the Politics of Female Sensibility." *Novel: A Forum on Fiction* 22, no. 2 (Winter 1989): 159–74. https://doi.org/10.2307/1345801.

Johnson, Samuel. "*Rambler* 148." In *The Rambler*, vol. 5. London: J. Payne, 1752.

Johnston, Freya. "Histories." In *Jane Austen, Early and Late*, 158–99. Princeton, NJ: Princeton University Press, 2021. https://doi.org/10.2307/j.ctv1j66659.11.

Justice, George. "Must and Ought: Moral and Real Conditions in Emma." *Persuasions* 25 (2003): 228–32.

Kaplan, Deborah. "Female Friendship and Epistolary Form: 'Lady Susan' and the Development of Jane Austen's Fiction." *Criticism* 29, no. 2 (Spring 1987): 163–78.

Kaufmann, David. "Closure as Covenant: The Means Justify the End." *Religion & Literature* 20, no. 3 (Autumn 1988): 89–108.

Keim, Debenneville Randolph. *The Handbook of Official and Social Etiquette and Public Ceremonials at Washington*. Washington, DC, 1889.

Kenney, Theresa M. "'And I Am Changed Also': Mr. Knightley's Conversion to Amiability." *Persuasions* 29 (2007): 110–20.

– "Anne De Bourgh Smiles." *Persuasions On-Line* 34, no. 1 (Winter 2013). https://jasna.org/persuasions/on-line/vol34no1/kenney.html.

– "A Tale of Two Captains: Whose Heart Is Worth Having?" *Persuasions On-Line* 39, no. 1 (Winter 2018).

– "Benevolence and Sympathy in *Emma*." *Persuasions* 38 (2018): 66–80.

– "'The Happiest, Wisest, Most Reasonable End': Silence and the Sublime in *Pride and Prejudice*." *Persuasions* 45 (2024): 127–37.

– "*Mansfield Park* and the Conscience Outside the Self." In *Mansfield Park by Jane Austen*, edited by Eleanor P. Donlon, 522–32. San Francisco: Ignatius Press, 2010.

– "'Slyness Seems the Fashion': Dexterous Revelations in *Pride and Prejudice*." *Persuasions* 27 (2006): 263–69.

– "Why Tom Bertram Cannot Die: 'The Plans and Decisions of Mortals'." *Persuasions On-Line* 35, no. 1 (Winter 2014). https://jasna.org/persuasions/on-line/vol35no1/kenney.html.

Kermode, Frank. *The Sense of an Ending: Studies in the Theory of Fiction*. Oxford: Oxford University Press, 2000. First published 1966. https://doi.org/10.1093/oso/9780195136128.001.0001.

Kindred, Sheila Johnson. "The Happy Endings of *Mansfield Park*." Posted on Sarah Emsley's website, 26 December 2014. https://sarahemsley.com/2014/12/26/the-happy-endings-of-mansfield-park/.

Kinney, Cheryl. "Why Tom Bertram Is Right That Dr. Grant Will 'Soon Pop Off.'" Posted on Sarah Emsley's website, 30 May 2014. https://sarahemsley.com/2014/05/30/why-tom-bertram-is-right-that-dr-grant-will-soon-pop-off/.

Kirkham, Margaret. *Jane Austen, Feminism and Fiction*. New York: Methuen, 1983.

Klemann, Heather M. "Ethos in Jane Austen's *Emma*." *Studies in Romanticism* 51, no. 4 (Winter 2012): 503–32. https://doi.org/10.1353/srm.2012.0001.

Knox, Vicesimus. *Elegant Extracts in Prose*. Vol. 1. London: C., 1790. Reprint D. O'Sullivan, 1845.

–. *The Spirit of Despotism*. London: Wilson & Blackwell, 1795.

Knox-Shaw, Peter. *Jane Austen and the Enlightenment*. Cambridge: Cambridge University Press, 2004. https://doi.org/10.1017/CBO9780511484353.

Kubic, Amanda Marie. "Aristotelian Ethical Ideas in the Novels of Jane Austen." *Persuasions On-Line* 36, no. 1 (Winter 2015). https://jasna.org/publications-2/persuasions-online/vol36no1/kubic/.

Kukkonen, Karin, and Sonja Klimek, eds. *Metalepsis in Popular Culture: An Introduction*. Berlin: De Gruyter, 2011. https://doi.org/10.1515/9783110252804.

Larrow, Michele. "'Could He Even Have Seen into Her Heart': Mr. Knightley's Development of Sympathy." *Persuasions On-Line* 37, no. 1 (Winter 2016). https://jasna.org/publications-2/persuasions-online/vol37no1/larrow/.

Lascelles, Mary. *Jane Austen and Her Art*. Oxford: Clarendon Press, 1939.

Le Faye, Deirdre. *Jane Austen: An Family Record*. 2nd ed. Cambridge: Cambridge University Press, 2004.

– *Jane Austen: The World of Her Novels*. London: Frances Lincoln, 2002.

–, ed. *Jane Austen's Letters*. Oxford: Oxford University Press, 1995.

Levine, Jay Arnold. "*Lady Susan*: Jane Austen's Character of the Merry Widow." In "Nineteenth Century." Special issue, *Studies in English*

Literature, 1500–1900 1, no. 4 (Autumn 1961): 23–34. https://doi.org/10.2307/449385.

Lewis, C.S. "A Note on Jane Austen." In *Selected Literary Essays*, edited by Walter Hooper. Cambridge: Cambridge University Press, 2013. First published 1954.

Lewis, Judith S. "When a House Is Not a Home: Elite English Women and the Eighteenth-Century Country House." In "Material Culture." Special issue, *Journal of British Studies* 48, no. 2 (April 2009): 336–63. https://doi.org/10.1086/596124.

Lindstrom, Eric. "*Sense and Sensibility* and Suffering; or, Wittgenstein's Marianne." *EHL* 90, no. 4 (Winter 2013): 1067–91. https://doi.org/10.1353/elh.2013.0044.

Litvak, Joseph. "The Most Charming Young Man in the World." In *Strange Gourmets: Sophistication, Theory, and the Novel*, 46–54. Durham, NC: Duke University Press, 1997. https://doi.org/10.2307/j.ctv11hpqh1.

– "Reading Characters: Self, Society, and Text in *Emma*." In *Emma: A Casebook*, edited by Fiona Stafford, 763–73. Oxford: Oxford University Press, 2007. https://doi.org/10.1632/S0030812900134935.

Litz, A. Walton. *Jane Austen: A Study of Her Artistic Development*. Oxford: Oxford University Press, 1965.

Lodge, David, ed. *Jane Austen: Emma: A Casebook*. Nashville: Aurora, 1970.

Lyons, William. "Conscience: An Essay in Moral Psychology." *Philosophy* 84, no. 4 (October 2009): 477–94. https://doi.org/10.1017/S0031819109990076.

MacIntyre, Alasdair. *After Virtue: A Study in Moral Theory*. South Bend: University of Notre Dame Press, 1984.

Mahoney, John. *The Making of Moral Theology*. Oxford: Clarendon Press, 1987.

McMaster, Juliet. "*Emma*: The Geography of a Mind." *Persuasions* 29 (2009): 26–38.

– "Surface and Subsurface in Jane Austen's Novels." In *Jane Austen the Novelist: Essays, Past and Present*, 5–24. New York: St. Martin's Press, 1996.

Meyer, Rosalind S. "Mr. Knightley's Education: Parallels in *Emma*." *English Studies* 79, no. 3 (1999): 212–23. https://doi.org/10.1080/00138389808599127.

Miller, Christopher R. "Jane Austen's Aesthetics and Ethics of Surprise." *Narrative* 13, no. 3 (October 2005): 238–60. https://doi.org/10.1353/nar.2005.0021.

Miller, D.A. "Good Riddance: Closure in *Mansfield Park*." In *Mansfield Park and Persuasion: Contemporary Critical Essays*, edited by Judy Simon, 178–85. New York: Macmillan, 1995.

– *Narrative and Its Discontents*. Princeton, NJ: Princeton University Press, 2003.

Miller, J. Hillis. *Fiction and Reception: Seven English Novels*. Cambridge, MA: Harvard University Press, 1985.

Moody, Ellen. "A Calendar for Pride and Prejudice." Accessed 21 January 2025. http://www.jimandellen.org/austen/p&p.calendar.html.

Morris, Ivor. *Jane Austen and the Interplay of Character*. London: Athlone Press, 1987.

Morrison, Robert. "Deeper in a Life of Sin: The Regency Romance of *Sense and Sensibility*." Jane Austen Society of North America Annual General Meeting, Victoria, BC, 1 October 2022.

Morton, Anna. "Emma's 'Serious Spirit': How Miss Woodhouse Faces the Issues Raised in *Mansfield Park* and Becomes Jane Austen's Most Complex Heroine." *Persuasions On-Line* 37, no. 1 (Winter 2016). https://jasna.org/publications-2/persuasions-online/vol37no1/morton/.

Mudrick, Marvin. *Jane Austen: Irony as Defense and Discovery*. Princeton, NJ: Princeton University Press, 1952.

Mullan, John. *What Matters in Jane Austen: Twenty Crucial Puzzles Solved*. London: Bloomsbury, 2014.

Nabokov, Vladimir. "Jane Austen: *Mansfield Park*." In *Lectures on Literature*, edited by Fredson Bowers, 9–62. New York: Harcourt, 1980.

Nash, Ralph. "The Time Scheme for Pride and Prejudice." *English Language Notes* 4 (1966–7): 194–8.

Newton, Judith Lowder. "Pride and Prejudice." In *Women, Power, and Subversion: Social Strategies in British Fiction 1776–1860*, 55–85. Athens: University of Georgia Press, 1981.

Nicolson, Nigel. "Jane Austen's Houses in Fact and Fiction." *Persuasions* 19 (1992): 89–93.

Nietzsche, Friedrich. "On Truth and Lies in the Nonmoral Sense." In *The Portable Nietzsche*, edited by Walter Kaufmann, 42–50. New York: Viking Press, 1945. First published 1873.

– "Twilight of the Idols." In *Complete Works of Friedrich Nietzsche*, edited by Oscar Levy, 463–563. Edinburgh: T.N. Foulis, 1888.

– *The Will to Power*. Translated and edited by Walter Kaufman. New York: Vintage Books, 1968. First published 1873.

Norris, Christopher. *Truth and the Ethics of Criticism*. Manchester: Manchester University Press, 1994.

Nye, Eric W. "Pounds Sterling to Dollars: Historical Conversion of Currency." Accessed 14 November 2018. http://www.uwyo.edu/numimage/currency.htm.

O'Connell, Lisa. *The Origins of the English Marriage Plot: Literature, Politics and Religion in the Eighteenth Century*. Cambridge: Cambridge University Press, 2019. https://doi.org/10.1017/9781108757706.

Ong, Yi-Ping. "The Novel and the Unfinished Work of Art." In *The Art of Being: Poetics of the Novel and Existentialists Philosophy*, 194–234. Cambridge, MA: Harvard University Press, 2018. https://doi.org/10.4159/9780674916098-006.

Ovid. *The Metamorphoses of Ovid*. Translated by Allen Mandelbaum. New York: Mariner Books, 1995.

Page, Norman. *The Language of Jane Austen*. Oxford: Basil Blackwell, 1972.

Paris, Bernard J. *Character and Conflict in Jane Austen's Novels*. New Brunswick, NJ: Routledge, 2017. https://doi.org/10.4324/9781315081540.

Pawell, Amy J. "Fanny Price and the Sentimental Genealogy of *Mansfield Park*." *Eighteenth-Century Fiction* 16, no. 2 (January 2004): 287–315. https://doi.org/10.1353/ecf.2004.0040.

Poovey, Mary. *The Proper Lady and the Woman Writer*. Chicago: University of Chicago Press, 1984.

Pope, Alexander. "An Essay on Man, Epistle II." In *The Major Works*, edited by Pat Rogers, 280–9. Oxford: Oxford University Press, 1993. First published 1733.

– "An Essay on Man: Epistle IV." In *The Poems of Alexander Pope: A Reduced Version of the Twickenham Text*, edited by John Butt, 298–309. New Haven, CT: Yale University Press, 1963. First published 1734.

Potkay, Adam. "Joy and Happiness." In *A Companion to the Eighteenth-Century English Novel and Culture*, edited by Paula R. Backscheider and Catherine Ingrassia, 321–40. Hoboken, NJ: Wiley- Blackwell, 2005.

– "Narrative Possibilities of Happiness, Joy, and Unhappiness." *Social Research* 77, no. 2 (Summer 2010): 523–44. https://doi.org/10.1353/sor.2010.0057.

– *The Story of Joy from the Bible to Late Romanticism*. Cambridge: Cambridge University Press, 2007.

Probert, Rebecca. "Control Over Marriage in England and Wales, 1753–1823: The Clandestine Marriage Act of 1753 in Context." *Law and History Review* 27, no. 2 (Summer 2009): 413–50. https://doi.org/10.1017/S0738248000002054.

Radcliffe, Ann. *The Italian*. London: Penguin Books, 2000. First published 1796.

Raia, Anne. "Women's Roles in Plautine Comedy." Fourth Conference on Greek, Roman, and Byzantine Studies. St. Joseph's College, Windham, ME, 1 October 1983.

Ray, Joan Klingel. "Do Elizabeth and Darcy Really Improve 'On Acquaintance'?" *Persuasions* 35 (2013): 34–49.

– "The Professor Is In." Jane Austen Society of North America Annual General Meeting, Kansas City, 29 September 2018.

– *Simply Austen*. New York: Simply Charly, 2017.

Richardson, Samuel. "Coquetry." In *The Beauties of the Rambler, Adventurer, Connoisseur, World, and Idler*. 2 Vols. Vol. 1, 277–84. London: Kearsley, 1787. Reprint of *The Rambler* 97 (19 February 1751).

Rieff, Phillip. *My Life among the Deathworks: Illustrations of the Aesthetics of Authority, Sacred Order, Social Order*. Charlottesville: University of Virginia Press, 2006.

Rosmarin, Adena. "Misreading *Emma*: The Powers and Perfidies of Interpretive History." *ELH* 51, no. 2 (Summer 1984): 315–42. https://doi.org/10.2307/2872948.

Ruderman, Anne Crippen. *The Pleasures of Virtue: Political Thought in the Novels of Jane Austen*. Lanham, MD: Rowman Littlefield, 1995.

Runcie, Charlotte, and Scott Campbell. "Could Mr. Darcy Afford a Stately Home Today?" *Telegraph* (London), 29 August 2014. https://www.telegraph.co.uk/culture/books/11063670/Could-Mr-Darcy-afford-a-stately-home-today.html.

Ryle, Gilbert. "Jane Austen and the Moralists." *Oxford Review* 1 (1966): 5–18.

Sabor, Peter. "Portraiture as Misrepresentation in the Novels and Early Writings of Jane Austen." In *Art and Artifact in Austen*, edited by Anne Battigellli, 24–43. Newark: University of Delaware Press, 2020. https://doi.org/10.2307/j.ctvwvr2z6.7.

Sayre-McCord, Geoff. "Moral Realism." In *The Stanford Encyclopedia of Philosophy*, edited by Edward N. Zalta, Summer 2021. https://plato.stanford.edu/archives/sum2021/entries/moral-realism/.

Schorer, Mark. "The Humiliation of Emma Woodhouse." In *Jane Austen: Emma – A Casebook*, edited by David Lodge, 170–87. Nashville: Aurora, 1970.

Scott, Sir Walter. *Marmion*. Philadelphia: Henry Altemus, 1899.

– "Review of *Emma*." *Quarterly Review*. 1815. Reprint in *Jane Austen: Emma – A Casebook*, edited by David Lodge, 37–44. Nashville: Aurora, 1970.

Shaftesbury, Anthony Ashley Cooper, Earl of. *Letters of the Earl of Shaftesbury, Author of the Characteristicks, Collected into One Volume*, 1716.

Shakespeare, William. *As You Like It*. Edited by Juliet Dusinberre. London: Arden Shakespeare, 2006.

– *A Midsummer Night's Dream*. In *The Riverside Shakespeare*, edited by G. Blakemore Evans and J.J.M. Tobin. Boston: Houghton Mifflin, 1996.

– *Much Ado About Nothing*. Edited by Claire McEachern. London: Bloomsbury Press, 2006.

Shannon Edgar F., Jr. "Emma: Character and Construction." *PMLA* 71, no. 4, pt. 1 (September 1956): 637–50. https://doi.org/10.2307/460635.

Sheehan, Colleen A. "To Govern the Winds: Dangerous Acquaintance in *Mansfield Park*." *Persuasions On-Line* 25, no. 1 (Winter 2004). https://jasna.org/persuasions/on-line/vol25no1/sheehan.html.

Sheridan, Richard Brinsley. *The Rivals*. London: A & C Black, 1995. First published 1775.

Sherlock, Thomas. *The Works of Bishop Sherlock, with Some Account of His Life*. Vol. 1. London: A.J. Valpy, 1830.

Sherry, James. "*Pride and Prejudice*: The Limits of Society." *Studies in English Literature, 1500–1900* 19, no. 4 (Autumn 1979): 609–22. https://doi.org/10.2307/450251.

Sleath, Eleanor. *The Orphan of the Rhine*. Richmond, VA: Valancourt Books, 2014. First published 1798.

Smith, Adam. *The Theory of Moral Sentiments*. London: A. Millar, 1759.

Snow, Malinda. "The Judgment of Evidence in *Tom Jones*." *South Atlantic Review* 48, no. 2 (May 1983): 37–51. https://doi.org/10.2307/3199730.

Southam, Brian. *Northanger Abbey and Persuasion: Casebook*. London: Macmillan, 1976.

Spacks, Patricia Meyer, ed. *Pride and Prejudice: An Annotated Edition*. Cambridge, MA: Harvard University Press, 2010.

Spurr, David. "La frivolité chez Jane Austen." *Poétique* 152, no. 4 (January 2007): 387–401. https://doi.org/10.3917/poeti.152.0387.

Stanford III, Thomas W. "'What Do I Not Owe You!': An Examination of Gratitude in Jane Austen's *Pride and Prejudice*." *Logos: A Journal of Catholic Thought and Culture* 18, no. 1 (Winter 2015): 152–68. https://doi.org/10.1353/log.2015.0003.

Stillman, Whit, dir. *Love and Friendship*. Westerly Films, 2016.

Stovel, Bruce. "'A Nation Improving in Religion': Jane Austen's Prayers and Their Place in Her Life and Art." *Persuasions* 16 (1994): 185–96.

Swift, Jonathan. "The Art of Political Lying." *The Examiner*, no. 15, 2–9 November 1710.

Tarpley, Joyce Kerr. *Constancy and the Ethics of Mansfield Park*. Washington, DC: Catholic University Press, 2010. https://doi.org/10.2307/j.ctt284w6v.

– "Manhood and Happiness in *Emma*: Liberal Learning and Practicing the Language of Marriage." *Renascence* 70, no. 1 (Winter 2018): 23–41. https://doi.org/10.5840/renascence20187013.

Taylor, Jeremy. *Ductor Dubitantium or the Role of Conscience*. 2 vols. London: Royston, 1660.

Tobin, Vera. *The Elements of Surprise: Our Mental Limits and the Satisfactions of Plot*. Cambridge, MA: Harvard University Press, 2018. https://doi.org/10.4159/9780674919570.

Todorov, Tzvetan. "Les catégories du récit littéraire." *Communications* 8 (1966): 125–51. https://doi.org/10.3406/comm.1966.1120.

Tomashevski, Boris. *Theory of Literature: Poetics*, 1925.

Toner, Anne. "Apophatic Austen: Speaking about Silence in Austen's Fiction." *Revue de la Société d'études anglo-américaines des XVII*[e] *et XVIII*[e] *siècles* 73 (2016). https://doi.org/10.4000/1718.739.

– "Free Speech, Jane Austen, Robert Bage, and the Subversive Shape of Dialogue." *English Studies in Italy* 3 (September–December 2017): 167–88. https://doi.org/10.7370/89357.

– *Jane Austen's Style: Narrative Economy and the Novel's Growth*. Cambridge: Cambridge University Press, 2020.

Toran, Katherine. "The Economics of Jane Austen's World." *Persuasions On-Line* 36, no. 1 (Winter 2018). https://www.jasna.org/publications-2/persuasions-online/vol36no1/toran/.

Torgovnick, Marianna. *Closure in the Novel*. Princeton, NJ: Princeton University Press, 1981.

Trilling, Lionel. "*Mansfield Park*." In *The Opposing Self: Nine Essays in Criticism*, 206–30. New York: Viking Press, 1955.

– *Sincerity and Authenticity*. Cambridge, MA: Harvard University Press, 1972. https://doi.org/10.4159/9780674044463.

Tucker, George Holbert. *Jane Austen the Woman: Some Biographical Insights*. New York: St. Martin's, 1994.

Twain Mark. "Jane Austen." Unpublished essay. Richard A. Watson and Chase Manhattan Bank as Trustees of the Mark Twain Foundation, 1999.

– "Letter to Joseph Twitchell, September 13, 1898." In *The Letters of Mark Twain and Joseph Hopkins Twitchell*, edited by Harold K. Bush. Athens: University of Georgia Press, 2017.

Vachris, Michelle Albert, and Cecil E. Bohanon. "Human Nature and Civil Society in Jane Austen." *Independent Review* 25, no. 3 (Winter 2020/21): 357–68.

Valihora, Karen. *Austen's Oughts: Judgment after Locke and Shaftesbury*. Newark: University of Delaware Press, 2010.

Van Ghent, Dorothy. *The English Novel: Form and Function*. New York: Holt, Rinehart, and Winston, 1953.

Vickery, Amanda. "A Man's Place." *At Home with the Georgians*. Season 1, Episode 1, BBC Scotland, 2010.

Vinaver, Eugène. *The Rise of Romance*. Oxford: Oxford University Press, 1971.

von Balthasar, Hans Urs. *Tragedy under Grace: Reinhold Schneider on the Experience of the West*. San Francisco: Ignatius Press, 1997.

Waldron, Mary. "Men of Sense and Silly Wives: The Confusions of Mr. Knightley." *Studies in the Novel* 28, no. 2 (Summer 1996): 141–57.

Wallace, Tara Ghoshal. "*Northanger Abbey* and the Limits of Parody." *Studies in the Novel* 20, no. 3 (Fall 1988): 262–73.

Watt, Ian. "On Sense and Sensibility." In *Jane Austen: A Collection of Critical Essays*, edited by Ian Watt, 41–51. Hoboken, NJ: Prentice Hall, 1963.

– *The Rise of the Novel: Studies in Defoe, Richardson and Fielding*. Berkeley: University of California Press, 1961.

West, Jane. *A Gossip's Story*. Richmond, VA: Valancourt Press, 2015. First published London: T.N. Longman, 1796.

Wiesenfarth, Joseph. "*Persuasion*: History and Myth." *Wordsworth Circle* 2, no. 4 (Autumn 1971): 160–8. https://doi.org/10.1086/TWC24039228.

Wilt, Judith. "The Powers of the Instrument, or Jane, Frank, and the Pianoforte." *Persuasions* 5 (1983): 41–7.

Wiltshire, John. *The Hidden Jane Austen*. Cambridge: Cambridge University Press, 2015. https://doi.org/10.1017/CBO9781107449435.

– *Jane Austen and the Body: "The Picture of Health."* Cambridge: Cambridge University Press, 1992. https://doi.org/10.1017/CBO9780511586248.

Wolff, Miriam Elizabeth Antonia. "Jane Austen and Belles Lettres: The Rhetorical Influence of Hugh Blair in Jane Austen's Fiction." PhD diss., Northern Illinois University, 2015.

Wolfson, Susan J. *Northanger Abbey: An Annotated Edition*. Cambridge, MA: Belknap Press, 2014.

Wood, James. "The Birth of Inwardness: The Heroic Consciousness of Jane Austen." *New Republic*, 17 August 1998, 25–8.

Woolf, Virginia. "Virginia Woolf Wonders What Greatness Austen's Death Prevented." *New Republic*, 30 January 1924, 261.

Yeazel, Ruth Bernard. "The Boundaries of Mansfield Park." *Representations* 7 (Summer 1984): 133–52. https://doi.org/10.2307/2928460.

Yorke, Philip Lord Hardwicke. "An Act for the Better Preventing of Clandestine Marriage." In Danby Pickering, *The Statutes at Large, from the 26th to the 30th Year of King George II*, 127. London: Joseph Bentham, 1766.

Index